Economics
and the Environment

Allen V. Kneese

Penguin Books

Penguin Books Ltd, Harmondsworth,
Middlesex, England
Penguin Books, 625 Madison Avenue,
New York, New York 10022, U.S.A.
Penguin Books Australia Ltd, Ringwood,
Victoria, Australia
Penguin Books Canada Ltd, 41 Steelcase Road West,
Markham, Ontario, Canada
Penguin Books (N.Z.) Ltd, 182-190 Wairau Road,
Auckland 10, New Zealand

First published 1977

ISBN 0 14 08.0902 3

Printed in the United States of America by
Offset Paperback Mfrs., Inc., Dallas, Pennsylvania
Set in Monotype Times

Table of Contents

List of Tables

Economics and the Environment

List of Figures and Maps

Preface

The word *environment* is frequently used with a vagueness matched only by the fervor with which it is invoked. The title of this book is guilty of the vagueness even though it may lack the usual fervor. My excuse is that titles are necessarily, and desirably, brief. Therefore, this preface is intended to tell the reader what the book is really about. The human environment in general can, I think, be fairly regarded as the whole set of surrounding conditions in which a human being lives and over which he has relatively little individual control other than by moving to a different location with other environmental characteristics. There are, to take a few examples, cultural conditions, social conditions, the visual features of man-made objects and the landscape disruptions associated with the extractive industries. This book is about the effects of human production and consumption activities on some of the *natural environmental systems* – watercourses, the atmosphere, and large ecological systems – which are used in one way or another in those activities. Within that category of environmental effects, I have concentrated largely on environmental pollution. The main reason for this limitation is that virtually all of the theoretical and applied work in economics pertaining to environmental problems has been on the range of issues surrounding the discharge of polluting substances to environmental media.

These statements should not be taken as an apology, for environmental pollution presents an exceedingly significant set of economic issues. Nevertheless it is important that

13

economists attempt to apply their insights and analytical models to the broader range of problems which may reasonably be regarded as environmental.

Another limitation of the present book is that the analysis and conclusions contained in it are directly applicable only to economies where private markets are regarded as the main vehicles for the development and allocation of resources. Many of the specific methodologies explored in it, for example mathematical programming of industrial processes, are applicable in socialist-type systems, perhaps even more than to market systems. But the general theoretical framework of the book, the theory of resource allocation in competitive markets, is not. However, although, as this book argues, a major cause of environmental problems in market systems is failure of the incentives generated by those markets to lead toward efficient use of environmental resources, one should not therefore jump to the conclusion that socialist systems are free of environmental problems. This is not so, indeed it has been argued that incentives in such systems, at least as exemplified by the Soviet Union, are at least as detrimental to the environment as they are in market economies.[1] The reasons are the incentives for maximizing output from production facilities, a penchant for giantism in public works, and ideological resistance to any sort of pricing of natural resources. As yet there is only a limited literature, at least outside the Iron Curtain countries, on environmental problems in socialist societies. It is, however, an intriguing topic which deserves further exploration.

Another prefatory comment is in order. In the writing of this book I have tried to be as non-technical as possible without becoming superficial. Since even a small amount of mathematics can sometimes greatly increase the depth with which a topic can be treated or greatly expedite exposition of a concept or methodology, I have not forgone the use of mathematics entirely. Accordingly, some familiarity with the calculus and matrix algebra will be an advantage. The vast bulk of the book can, however, be understood without any mathematical knowledge. Chapter 6 would be the only major exception and it can be passed over without great loss of continuity.

Finally, I apologize to my readers outside the United States for the fact that, while I have tried to maintain an international perspective throughout, most, but not all, of the detailed discussion of applied research projects is of those done in the United States. This is perhaps defensible because I am much more familiar with these and have been involved in many of them, they have fairly general implications, and perhaps a detailed and informed consideration of a few cases is more useful than a second-hand discussion of more. Furthermore the history of environmental economics research is much richer in the United States than in any other country. Should the last statement be regarded as unduly nationalistic I should note that, on the other hand, national environmental legislation in the United States seems to me to be particularly misguided. The one, I hope, is not the cause of the other.

Chapter 1
Environment as an Economic Problem

Introduction

Throughout history most of mankind has been quite content to perform its daily production and consumption activities without much reflection on how they might fit into a larger pattern. Yet, since the time of the Greeks, there have always been a few people who have sought to comprehend how the larger economic system functions. To many of these economic theorists the reason for giving thought to the matter was pure intellectual curiosity – an interest in trying to understand how the totality of an economic system comes to be more than the sum of its individual parts. In addition, except in the simplest of economic systems (those characterized by Marx as involving 'simple reproduction'), there have also always been economic problems which required some sort of action on the part of those in authority. Accordingly, there has been a demand for these speculations about economic systems as a whole, and for the past few hundred years economists have in one way or another been involved in the public policy-making process.

Coincident with the rise of the modern national state there came into being a body of doctrine generally called mercantilism which held that money was a store of wealth and that the overriding object of a state was to earn money abroad by exporting the utmost possible quantity of its products and importing as little as possible. The mercantilists sought to serve the purposes of monarchies which in turn aimed for the political and economic supremacy of their nation.

In the eighteenth, nineteenth and twentieth centuries however, especially in Britain, France, the Scandinavian countries and the United States, a body of economic doctrine arose which called into question the main premises of mercantilism. Moreover, this particular body of thought has displayed an enduring fascination with market processes. The result is an elaborate structure of theory which explains and evaluates the functioning of market processes under highly idealized conditions. Today, therefore, when economists speak of the market, they usually have a particular type of intellectual construct in mind – not the corner grocery store or even the stock exchange. This conceptual, or in more recent decades, mathematical, model is the product of an evolutionary process going back at least as far as Adam Smith's *Wealth of Nations*, which was published at the close of the nineteenth century.

The model grew out of the observation of a curious phenomenon. Economic activities such as farming, mining, industrial production, selling and finance activities were unplanned and, on the surface at least, appeared entirely uncoordinated. Yet, in the end there seemed to be order in the results (the often used modern illustration of this rather amazing situation is that the right number of bottles of milk, cream, etc., wind up on the right step of every household in New York or London every morning, yet the whole process starts with the conception of a calf perhaps in Wisconsin or Jersey). Adam Smith saw clearly that prices, the powerful signalling and incentive forces generated by private exchange in markets, were at the core of a process which, via the decisions of many independent economic units, transformed resources into products and distributed them to consumers. Hence, his famous phrase 'the invisible hand of the market'. Clearly, in spite of the occasional spectacular failure, markets do produce an orderly and directed production process. But economists have also been very interested in trying to discover if this order was just orderly or whether it might have other desirable or normative properties.

Welfare economics, which despite its name has nothing to do with welfare programs in the ordinary sense, is the branch of modern economics which concerns itself with such questions.

It has found that the results of an ideal market process are desirable if a basic value judgement is accepted and if the market-exchange economy has certain structural characteristics.

The value judgement is that the personal wants of the individuals in the society should guide the use of society's resources. This is also the premise which is at the root of Anglo-American political theory.

The three structural characteristics are that:

(1) all markets are competitive; by this is meant that no particular firm or individual can affect any market price significantly by decreasing or increasing the supply of goods and services offered. In this sense, all participants in the market-exchange process must be small units. A good example is an individual grain grower. He can sell or hold his crop as he wishes and yet affect the market price for grain not at all.

(2) all participants in the market are *fully informed* as to the quantitative and qualitative characteristics of goods and services and the terms of exchange. This can, of course, be only approximately true in any market.

(3) and this has usually been implicit – all valuable assets can be *individually owned* and managed without violating the competition assumption. This, plus competitive market exchange, implies that all costs of production and consumption are borne by the producer and consumer.

If these conditions held, it could be concluded that the best social solution of the problem of allocating society's scarce resources to alternative ends is to limit the role of government to deciding questions of income distribution, providing rules of property and exchange, enforcing competition, and letting exchange of privately owned assets in markets take care of the rest.

The Idea of a Pareto Optimum

Market exchange, with each participant pursuing his own private interest, will then lead to a 'Pareto optimum'. The proof that ideal markets can achieve a Pareto optimum may be regarded as the basic theorem of modern welfare economics. Perhaps the simplest way of intuitively grasping the meaning of such an optimum is to regard it as a situation where all possible gains from voluntary exchange have been exhausted. Money is the medium of exchange and prices are the terms of exchange at which real goods and services of all kinds are traded. Under the conditions postulated, an exchange takes place only when both parties feel they benefit by it. When no additional exchanges can be made, the economy has reached a situation where each individual in it cannot improve his own situation without damaging that of another – in other words, unless a redistribution of assets favorable to him takes place. When no one can be better off without someone else being worse off, Pareto optimality has been reached. In economic parlance this situation is called *efficient*. Pareto optimality has been demonstrated to result from exchange in theoretical competitive market models which contain labor markets, markets for intermediate goods, and markets for consumer goods, in other words, for a reasonably complete if highly abstract characterization of the functions performed in an actual economy.[1]

We must be careful to note the exact sense in which a Pareto optimum can be equated with a maximum position of economic welfare in a society. A Pareto optimum is efficient in fulfilling consumer wants. This means, to put it in a slightly different way, that if the use of any productive service were changed, or if any consumer good or service were made available to a different consumer other than the one who had a claim to it, someone would have to be made worse off. This concept of the efficiency of a whole economic system is a rather subtle but vastly important idea. But we must be clear that a Pareto optimum is the highest welfare position for the society only in relation to the particular distribution of rights to assets which exists. It says nothing about the *justice* of the distribution of claims. That is, about the issue of distribution (an ethical problem) as contrasted with efficiency. If the distribution of claims is changed, say, by making transfer payments from rich to poor, a new exchange equilibrium will result. If we have an ideal competitive market, a welfare maximum will once again be achieved with respect to that new distribution of income. But, whether this one is better or worse than the other cannot be decided unless a criterion is available by which the desirability of alternate states of distribution can be evaluated. The Pareto criterion for the functioning of an economy is therefore known as an 'efficiency' criterion in the economic literature. It can only be said that an exchange economy of the type I have been discussing will achieve an *optimum optimorum*, 'the best of all possible (economic) worlds', if the prevailing income distribution is ethically ideal – a judgement which, in western liberal societies, can be made legitimately only through the political process. However, in general we usually regard ourselves as striving for an egalitarian society, the main obstacle being the possible effects on incentives of extreme redistribution measures. Accordingly, movements leading toward greater equality are usually regarded as being better (*ceteris paribus*) than movements leading toward greater inequality.

It should be underlined that the theoretical analysis of market economies implies that an adequate explanation of economic phenomena within, let us say, one of the western countries, must view these phenomena as forming part of a system.

Communication of information by price changes is very rapid in this theoretical system. Factors of production move rapidly and in response to small differences in price and so on. Certain factors are explicitly abstracted from many of the complicating factors that are actually present in order to show precisely what the ultimate effect of certain changes would be if these changes could work themselves out with other variables remaining constant.

Economics and the Environment

How Useful is Market Theory?

The usefulness of this abstract interrelated economic system may not be immediately obvious, but those engaged full time on explaining economic phenomena do, by and large, regard the idea of an interrelated economic system as an indispensable aid to thinking about what really happens. Real economic functions are more or less accurately simulated in market-type systems. The desires of consumers are communicated to producers by their purchases, production is organized and takes into account the scarcity of certain productive services through the medium of the price system and the information conveyed by prices. Rewards for participation and productive activity are determined as part of this system, although the resulting distribution of income may be modified through taxation and through the system of transfer payments.

Nevertheless there has been a wide range of opinion, even within the economics profession, as to how far reality in fact departs from this idealized structure of market theory. Shortly I shall relate this structure to environmental problems and show how reality departs from the idealized system; I shall claim that the discrepancy is much more than trivial. Questions raised by environmental deterioration are as far-reaching for this model as the ones which occurred in other connections during the Great Depression of the 1930s. Until then, it had been an article of faith of market economics that prices would adjust in such a fashion as to secure full employment should there be a change in the total flow of expenditure for goods and services. This clearly did not happen during the Great Depression of the 1930s, and Keynesian or 'macro' economics developed in response to this departure from ideal functioning of the market.

But macroeconomics developed at quite a different level of aggregation than microeconomics. It is associated most prominently with the name of Lord Keynes and concerns itself with total flows of income, expenditure and employment in the system. It never made any real connection with the body of market or 'micro' theory, which had been evolving for such a long time. But the development of macro theory permitted the economics profession to carry along two separate theories which aspire to explain different phenomena – somewhat like the wave and particle theories of light in physics. Macroeconomic theory is concerned with the total level of employment, income, and prices while micro theory concerns itself with how the economy operates in detail when the macro problems are solved. The theory of efficient markets is part of microeconomics. Macroeconomics thus provided a means of 'saving' the body of inherited market theory.

A few economists, voices in the wilderness, argued that while the model provided a highly useful insight into the functioning of market processes, there were other serious departures from the model besides unemployment. They particularly claimed, although they did not quite put it that way in their day, that the third structural assumption indicated above, the holding of all valuable assets in discrete units of private property, was a severe simplification of reality for actual existing economies. At the turn of the present century Alfred Marshall in his *Principles of Economics*[2] had introduced, as well as most of the other major ideas found in contemporary market theory, the notion of external costs and benefits. These terms describe instances in which the activities of one fiscally independent economic unit, let us say a firm, directly affected the position of another fiscally independent unit, say a consumer, without the intervention of the market. Early examples were offered that were environmental in nature. A much used one refers to sparks from the locomotive engine setting fire to the farmer's field, or, on the external benefits side, the beekeeper's bees pollinating the orchard owner's apple trees. In the last three or four decades writers like Pigou, in Britain, and Kapp and Baumol, in the United States, called attention to what they regarded to be the importance of such phenomena in actual economic systems.

While well taken, it is fair to say that their warnings carried very little weight with the profession as a whole. Perhaps it was because the structure of market theory, welfare economics, was so tightly and beautifully developed that there was a great reluctance to modify it in any way, especially if those modifications were to be 'messy'.

During the 1960s and especially toward the end of that decade a large amount of activity developed within the economics profession trying to come to grips with environmental problems. There was a fair amount of theoretical development and also a substantial amount of applied work. Both of these lines of activity have continued to accelerate in the early 1970s and this book may be regarded as an effort to set forth the main methods used and the results attained so far, and to evaluate them.

While the activity of the sixties and early seventies can fairly be said to have created a new field of environmental economics, complete with text-books and journals, the profession still continues to be somewhat schizoid in its approach to the economic system. This is perhaps best illustrated by the fact that the most popular text-book on microeconomics in the United States even now contains no more than a few paragraphs on anything but the classical market model.[3]

Emergence of Pollution as a Center of Major Concern in Economics

The rather frantic tone of discussions of environmental pollution during the late sixties and early seventies served to call attention to a severe and much neglected problem and, as noted, greatly stimulated interest in it among economists. But the nature of these discussions could leave a false impression. The fake impression would be that suddenly we are confronted with a totally new problem. This is not the case. But the nature of the pollution situation has certainly changed over time and in some ways it has become more ominous. It is not difficult to uncover stories about horrible environmental conditions in medieval and even relatively modern times. The deplorable history of pollution in the city of London is especially well documented and illustrates that pollution is certainly not a new problem. In the fourteenth century butchers had been assigned a spot at Sea Coal Lane near Fleet Prison. A royal document about this reads

by the killing of great beasts from whose putrid blood running down the streets and the bowels cast into the Thames the air in the city is very much corrupted and infected. Whence abominable and most filthy stinks proceed sickness and many other evils have happened to such as have abode in said city or restored to it.[4]

Queen Elizabeth I kept out of London because she found herself so annoyed with the smoke of sea coal, and other stinks, and in the nineteenth century the Thames was in such a condition that it presented severe problems which were debated by the Houses of Parliament. Vivid language was used in both Houses. The Thames was described 'as a vast sewer which would surely spread disease and death around'.[5]

Charles Dickens was reported to have been moved to say of London 'he knew of many places unsurpassed in the accumulated horrors of their long neglect by the dirtiest old spots in the dirtiest old towns under the worst old governments of Europe.'[6]

But the situation was not limited to London as an old poem about the Rhine shows:

> The River Rhine it is well-known
> Doth wash the City of Cologne.
> But, pray dear God what power divine
> Will henceforth wash the River Rhine?

By the late nineteenth century, with the development of coal mining, followed by steel and steel finishing, plus chemical industries in the last half of the nineteenth century, conditions in the Ruhr region of Germany, particularly in the Emscher watershed, had become desperately bad. Subsidence in the mining areas soon created depressions that were filled with the waste of industries and municipalities, causing massive aesthetic and health damage in the region. In the United

States large-scale development of the industrial revolution came somewhat later than in Britain and western Europe and, because of the size of the country, the ability of the atmospheric resources, particularly the watercourses and the air mantle, to assimilate waste materials was much larger. Accordingly, severe environmental degradation was largely delayed until the first half of the twentieth century. By this time, however, some of the most serious classic pollution situations in Europe, especially in Britain and Germany, had begun to improve.

Everything taken together, environmental conditions which directly and immediately affect the daily lives of the mass of humanity improved immensely in developed countries at least from the beginning until the middle of the twentieth century, leaving aside some major aberrations like the Great Depression and the World Wars, during which the quality of life dropped sharply in many areas. There was a long period of time, say from the turn of the century until after the Second World War, that environmental problems could be, or at least were, regarded as only a minor perturbation in the smooth functioning of market processes.

What happened then in the late sixties and early seventies to make us rather suddenly so acutely aware of environmental pollution?

Apart from the world population growth problem, which is so overwhelming as to be a major topic by itself – I will discuss it in Chapter 5 – three things which have come upon us slowly, but more or less simultaneously, are chiefly responsible, I think.

First, recent decades have seen immense increases in industrial production and energy conversion. Associated with this are massive flows of materials and energy from concentrated states in nature to degraded and diluted states in the environment. This has begun to alter the physical, chemical, and biological quality of the atmosphere and hydrosphere on a truly massive scale. Furthermore, scientists and technicians now have the means to detect even very small changes in these natural systems so that we are much more aware of what is happening than in the past.

Second, 'exotic' materials are being introduced into the environment. The near-alchemy of modern physics and chemistry has recently subjected the world's biological systems to strange, unnatural inputs to which they cannot adapt (or at least not quickly); or adaptation may occur in some species but not in others and thus the balance of species will be upset.

Third, ordinary folk have come to expect standards of cleanliness, safety and wholesomeness in their surroundings that were the exclusive province of the well-born or rich in earlier times.

What is to be done in the face of these profound new forces in the world? And why do our institutions seem not to be coping with them at all well? First, we must try to understand the basic sources of the pollution problems which affect the economies of most of the non-socialist industrialized world.

Sources of the Problem

As a first step toward gaining insight into why this growing divergence between private ends and social ends has come about, it is useful to invoke one of the most basic physical principles – that of mass balance. When minerals, fuels, gases, and organic materials are extracted and harvested from nature and used by producers and consumers, it is immediately apparent that their mass is not altered in these processes, except in trivial amounts. Material residuals are generated in production and consumption activities, and their mass must be about equal to that initially extracted from nature.

The services which material objects can yield are used, and market exchange works to allocate these services to those who desire them most, but their physical substance remains intact. The important implications this has for the allocation of resources in a market system is that while most extractive harvesting, processing, and distributional activities can be

27

conducted relatively efficiently through the medium of exchange of private ownership rights, the inevitable residual mass returned to the environment goes heavily into what the economist calls common property resources. The same is true of residual energy. Common property resources are those valuable natural assets which cannot, or can only imperfectly, be reduced to private ownership. Examples are the air mantle, watercourses, complex ecological systems, large landscapes, and the electromagnetic spectrum. The nature of all these resources violates the third structural assumption for an efficient market – that all valuable assets can be individually owned and managed without violating the competition assumption.

It is obvious what will happen when open and unpriced access to such resources is permitted. From careful study of particular common property or common pool problems like oil pools and ocean fisheries, it is well known that unhindered access to such resources leads to overuse, misuse, and quality degradation. Market forces, while marvelously efficient in allocating owned resources, work to damage or destroy common property resources.

The laws of conservation of mass and energy have no doubt always held. But at lower levels of population size and economic activity, the return of 'used' materials and energy to the environment has only local effects, most of which can be dealt with by means of ordinances and other local government measures to improve sanitation in the immediate vicinity of cities. Thus butchers can be moved, sewers can be installed, and the streets can be cleared of trash and offal.

But, as economic development proceeds, more and more material and energy tend to be returned to the environment *pari passu* with the increased production of material objects. Indeed, some forces press in the direction of increasing the proportion of residual waste to final usable output – resort to progressively lower-quality ores or the use of shales for the production of oil is a case in point. Larger 'problem sheds' are affected and greater numbers of people more remotely located

28

in both space and time suffer adverse impacts. Common property assets, which cannot enter into market exchange, are progressively degraded because the industries, governments, and individuals use them as dumps at no cost to themselves even though important assets arising from other uses are degraded or destroyed.

In summary, a profound asymmetry has developed in the effectiveness and efficiency of the system of economic incentives inherent in market systems. On the one hand, it works well in stimulating the exploitation of basic resources, and processing and distributing them, but it fails almost completely in the efficient disposal of residuals to common property resources.

Seen from this perspective it is clear that Marshall's external costs are not freakish random events which for some reason sometimes happen. They are a systematic part of the economic development process in economies where common property resources have become, and are getting increasingly scarce.

These market failures are substantially aggravated, at least in the United States, by government policies, such as depletion allowances and other special tax treatment, and by regulations which discriminate against recovered materials in favor of virgin resource exploitation. In addition, the system of taxes and public expenditures in the States has enormous built-in subsidies for large families – especially for the relatively well-to-do – and discriminates severely against single people and childless couples. All of these are hangovers from the time when single-minded development was the order of the day. While differing in detail this description would in general fit most modern tax systems.

The total result of market failures and government policy is that the economic incentive system makes virgin materials too cheap, stimulates too much materials flow through the system, generates inadequate reuse of secondary materials, and produces a vastly excessive discharge of dispersed and degraded materials to environmental media:

In the next chapter I briefly review some of the essential facts about contemporary environmental pollution. We need this as background for the discussion of the application of economic models and analysis to environmental problems which occupies the remainder of the book.

Chapter 2

A Brief Survey of the Substantive Nature of Environmental Problems[1]

Although the term is used universally the concept of environment is infrequently defined. It is used to cover such diverse matters as crime in the streets, the cultural milieu in which life takes place, and air pollution. As the preface points out this book does not treat the more cultural and sociological aspects of human environment but limits itself to those associated with natural systems, the atmosphere, watercourses, large ecological systems, and light and visibility.

For a clear understanding of the following chapters it is necessary to have at least a bare-bones knowledge of the substantive aspects of the environmental problems which will be subjected to economic analysis. By far the largest proportion of economic thought and research given over to environmental questions has been about the residuals associated with the production and consumption activities of human societies. Many classification schemes for these residuals have been suggested or can be conceived. For our purposes we will require only a few major categories of residuals.

One is a broad classification as to type. Whether the residual is a material substance, energy, or radioactivity.

Another useful broad distinction is whether the residual is degradable or not and what degree of degradability it displays. Degradable residuals are, for instance, ordinary organics like domestic sewage which is attacked by bacteria and changed in form over a relatively short period of time once it enters a watercourse. Another example, this time an energy residual, is noise which is quickly dissipated and disappears forever. An illustration of a nondegradable substance is salt which tends to retain its form unaltered when, for example, it is delivered into a watercourse. Many residuals fall between these rather extreme categories and are referred to as being persistent. Chlorinated hydrocarbon pesticides and 'hard' detergents are examples of this class. Certain types of radioactivity also fall into it, although the decay rates of some radio-nuclides are so slow as to make them practically nondegradable. If not taken too literally the degradable/nondegradable/persistent classification scheme has a certain utility for orderly thought about residuals problems.

Finally, it is often useful to distinguish between a residual discharged at a single well-identified point – called a point source – and a residual from a non-point source, whose discharge is diffused and soon dispersed. Industrial outfalls are examples of the former while residuals bearing runoff from agricultural land is an example of the latter.

In the public mind the most dramatic examples of potentially harmful residuals discharge are those which would have a world-wide or 'global' effect. These will be given only the briefest attention here since so much uncertainty surrounds what the actual effects might be, and it is therefore extremely difficult to apply standard forms of economic analysis to the question. Indeed when there is so much uncertainty it is very difficult to decide what constitutes any kind of a rational action except a rather ill-defined effort to be prudent. It is, for example, possible that the continually expanding use of fossil fuels will so increase carbon dioxide content of the atmosphere that the planet will tend to heat up, the ice caps will melt, inundating the coastal cities, and other unforeseen climatic effects will occur.[2] Whether such events are a genuine danger is still a matter of uncertainty and even dispute among scientists. The decisive question is whether the global natural systems are in essentially stable or unstable equilibrium. Sinks for carbon dioxide may respond non-linearly to its increase: a rise in temperature would increase evaporation and, accordingly, the earth's reflectivity (the meteorologists call it albedo). It is thus quite possible the earth could absorb the large increase in carbon dioxide, particulates, and energy residuals with hardly any visible effect. On the other hand it might plausibly be argued that the world is a state of unstable equilibrium so that a relatively small perturbation will stimulate reinforcing factors causing irreversible change. About the best one can do under such extreme conditions of uncertainty is to monitor carefully and try to construct analytical models which will help basic understanding of climatic and other global impacts of human activity. Fortunately both enterprises are being initiated on a substantial scale.[3]

The kinds of environmental impacts which are considered explicitly and in detail in this book are in general those which are more limited geographically. They are regional in the sense that the impact is largely constrained by some fairly definable environmental system that is less than global. Thus, they may be mostly confined to a particular river basin, a lake, an air mass over a city, or a certain landscape. I refer to these problems as being regional rather than national or local or provincial because the pertinent environmental systems in most cases do not conform to defined governmental jurisdictions but rather to the pulses, rhythms, and flows of the particular natural systems involved.

As implied by the mass balance principle there are often strong interdependencies among the various types of environmental problems, for instance those associated with discharge of liquid, gaseous or solid residuals. But, since we cannot discuss them all simultaneously, it will be convenient to consider their substantive aspects primarily on the basis of the environmental media affected. Let us turn first to that life-giving mantle of gases – the atmosphere.

Airborne (Gaseous) Residuals

There is virtually no limit to the number of residuals that may be, and sometimes are, discharged to the atmosphere, but the ones usually regarded as being of central interest and therefore

33

most commonly measured are carbon monoxide, sulfur dioxide, oxides of nitrogen, hydrocarbons and particulates. The direct and observable effects of these residuals on people (and other forms of life) range in severity from the lethal to the merely annoying. Except for extreme air pollution episodes, fatalities are not, as a rule, directly traceable individually to deterioration of air quality. Instead, air pollution is an environmental stress that, in conjunction with a number of other environmental stresses, tends to increase the incidence and seriousness of a variety of diseases, including lung cancer, emphysema, tuberculosis, pneumonia, bronchitis, asthma, and even the common cold. Acute episodes of poor air quality, that is, short periods of high concentrations of residuals, have been correlated with increased death rates and increased rates of hospital admissions. Such occurrences have been observed in Belgium, England, Mexico, the United States, and elsewhere. But the most important health effects appear to be associated with chronic exposure, that is, exposure to relatively low concentrations for long periods of time, conditions that exist in most large cities.[4]

In terms of weight, *carbon monoxide* is the largest gaseous residual in developed countries. Most carbon monoxide comes from the incomplete combustion of gasoline in internal combustion engines, although all actual combustion processes generate it to some extent (as contrasted with ideal ones which produce only water and carbon dioxide). The primary short-term effects of heavy exposure to carbon monoxide are well known – impairment of mental and physical functions and, at higher concentrations, death. The symptoms of dizziness, headache, and lassitude occur at concentrations that are not infrequently recorded at street levels in cities. Little is known about long-term effects of repeated exposure.

Coal and oil burned for space heating, electric energy generation, and industrial heat, contain various amounts of elemental sulfur as an impurity. When the fuel is burned the sulfur also burns, producing *sulfur oxides*.. When discharged into the atmosphere sulfate particles and sulfuric acid result.

For humans, acute high-level/short-duration exposure to these residuals is known to have adverse effects on the functioning of the lungs. Sulfur oxides can also cause damage to vegetation, exterior paints, and other materials. There is now a substantial body of evidence that chronic (low-level/long-term) exposure to sulfur oxides has serious adverse health effects and is associated with an increase in mortality rates.[5]

Several *oxides of nitrogen* are formed in combustion processes in automotive transportation and in electric energy generation. In this case the basic elements which form the compound are not in the fuel itself but in the air which supports the combustion. The oxides of nitrogen are primarily of concern because of their contribution to the formation of photochemical smog. In addition, nitrogen dioxide at high concentrations has been found to have adverse effects on laboratory animals, and has caused leaf damage and reduced growth in plants. It may have adverse health effects on humans also.

Unburned and partially burned *hydrocarbons* are emitted primarily through the exhaust pipes of internal combustion engine vehicles. Miscellaneous sources such as evaporation of gasoline and other volatile hydrocarbons in gasoline stations and fuel storage areas, dry cleaners', gas tanks, carburetors, and even drying paints, also contribute substantial quantities. Hydrocarbons at observed atmosphere concentrations have no known directly harmful effects. However, a number of hydrocarbons at low concentrations react photochemically in the atmosphere with nitrogen oxides to produce smog.

Particulates are airborne residuals consisting of a heterogeneous mixture of suspended solids and liquids. Specific particulate substances may be directly harmful to humans – for example, lead from vehicle exhausts. Others may cause serious animal and vegetable damage, as fluorides can, for example. The most common forms of particulates are ash and unburned or partially burned hydrocarbons resulting from combustion of fossil fuels. In some regions seasonal agricultural operations are responsible for the discharge of substantial quantities of particulates. The same is true of forest fires in certain regions. Chronic exposure to particulates has been associated with increased death rates and other health effects.[6] Particulates also may have synergistic relationships with other gaseous residuals.[7]

Photochemical smog, made famous in Los Angeles but by now a problem in many cities across the world, especially in arid climates, is not itself a residual. Rather, it is a mixture of gases and particulates manufactured by energy from the sun, chiefly out of the nitrogen oxides and unburned hydrocarbons emitted from the combustion of gasoline. The major components of smog are oxidizing by nature, and as a class they are called oxidants. The irritation, although possibly not the most important effect of the oxidants, is the most troublesome and most commonly recognized effect in urban atmospheres. At commonly observed levels oxidants make it more difficult for people to breathe, especially those already suffering from respiratory disease. Also important are the effects of oxidants on plant life. Serious damage has been observed to some species of shrubs, trees, leafy vegetable and forage crops. The effect of smog on visibility is also a major concern.

In addition to the five gaseous residuals just discussed, there is a substantial number of chemicals and metallic compounds that are released in relatively small quantities from various mining, manufacturing, and combustion processes. (For example, in the combustion of coal, about 90 percent of the mercury in the coal is released as a vapor discharged from the stack; about 10 percent is incorporated in the residual ash. Generally these compounds are subsumed in the particulates category. Some of these, for example, fluorides from phosphate fertilizer plants, may have quite severe but localized effects. Another chemical which is causing increasing concern is lead, because of accumulating evidence that the severity of the problem has been greatly underestimated and because it is so widespread in the environment. The automobile is a major source. Several studies have shown that people with high occupational (toll collectors, traffic policemen, parking garage attendants) and residential (those living or working adjacent to freeways) exposures have alarmingly high amounts of lead in their bodies. Children housed in the inner city (inner city slums are unfortunately characteristic of many of the world's major cities) may be in the most dangerous situation because of the combined effects of lead ingested from the atmosphere and from lead paints and dusts in old housing, since young children tend to chew anything they encounter.

Asbestos is a material whose widespread occurrence as an airborne residual – asbestos dust – in urban environments has only recently become recognized. The primary sources are the construction and demolition of buildings. The fine particles of asbestos discharged into the air from spraying insulating materials or in dismantling buildings have been found to produce adverse effects on humans exposed to the material. The wearing down of vehicle brake shoes is an additional source of asbestos in urban environments. Because of the cumulative nature of the effects the problem has only comparatively recently been recognized.

The above listing is clearly not exhaustive. Many other materials are discharged to the atmosphere, such as pesticides and some types of radioactive residuals. (In fact, transport of pesticides in the atmosphere appears to be the major mechanism of their distribution around the globe.)

SOURCES AND QUANTITIES. To provide an idea of the quantities involved, the amounts of the five largest gaseous residuals, by weight, discharged in the United States are listed in Table 1, along with a broad indication of their source. It was estimated that altogether about 200 million tons of these gaseous residuals were discharged into the atmosphere in the States in the calendar year 1971. About half of that total is accounted for by the transportation industry, primarily the automobile. Studies have shown that the automobile accounts for about 50 percent by weight of gaseous residuals discharged into the atmosphere in smaller cities and

Table 1. Estimated Discharges of Gaseous Residuals, nationwide by source, 1971 (million tons)

Source	Carbon monoxide	Parti-culates	Sulfur dioxide	Hydro-carbons	Nitrogen oxides	Total
Transportation	77·5	1·0	1·0	14·7	11·2	105·4
Fuel combustion in stationary sources	1·0	6·5	26·3	0·3	10·2	44·3
Industrial processes	11·4	13·6	5·1	5·6	0·2	35·9
Solid residuals disposal	3·8	0·7	0·1	1·0	0·2	5·8
Miscellaneous	6·5	5·2	0·1	5·0	0·2	17·0
Total	100·2	27·0	32·6	26·6	22·0	208·4

SOURCE: Council on Environmental Quality, *Environmental Quality – 1973*, Washington, D.C., 1973, p. 266.

up to 90 percent in some of the large cities. The internal combustion automobile engine is the largest single source of hydrocarbons and nitrogen oxides, which combine to form smog. Fuel combustion, primarily oil and coal at utility and industrial electric power plants and oil for space heating and process steam, is the major source of sulfur oxides and the other major source of nitrogen oxides; combustion with coal as fuel is a major source of particulates. The proportion of the total mass of airborne residuals coming from automobiles is higher in the United States than elsewhere, but they are an important source in all advanced countries and in the major cities of some developing ones. To give an illustration of the differences in the proportions of residuals discharged the figures reported for the Federal Republic of West Germany may be used. For 1969 the estimates were:

8 million tons of carbon monoxide
4 million tons of particulates
4 million tons of sulfur dioxide
2 million tons of hydrocarbons
2 million tons of nitrogen oxides.[8]

The relatively higher quantities of sulfur oxides and particulates reflect the comparatively lower population of automobiles and the relative greater importance of coal-burning industry. For purposes of comparison discharges of sulfur dioxide in the United Kingdom are estimated to be about six million tons annually and particulates about one million tons.[9]

If all of the gaseous residuals discharged into the atmosphere were spread evenly over a country, the air-quality problem would not be as serious as it is, at least with respect to impact on human health. But even if residuals discharges were uniformly distributed, there would still be major interregional differences in ambient air quality, because of differences in meteorological and topographic conditions. In fact, pronounced geographical concentration of air-quality deterioration has resulted from the concentration of population and economic activities in urban areas with quite different capacities for assimilating airborne residuals. This is illustrated in Table 2, which is based on regression analyses using air-quality information from various sources for the late 1960s in the United States. These data indicate that air-quality deterioration has been most severe in large metropolitan areas but many factors other than size – topography, atmospheric conditions, nature and distribution of sources – affect air quality in any particular region.

Table 2. Relative Air Quality by Size of Population in Metropolitan Areas, U.S.

Population	Relative air pollution levels		
	Particulates	Sulfur dioxide	Nitrogen dioxide
100	1·0	1·0	1·0
2,000	1·4	2·3	1·3
10,000	1·6	3·2	1·5

SOURCE: Irving Hoch, 'Urban Scale and Environmental Quality', in Ronald G. Ridker, ed., *Population, Resources, and the Environment* (Vol. III of Research Reports, Commission on Population Growth and the American Future), Washington, D.C., U.S. Commission on Population Growth and the American Future, 1972.

What has happened to the air quality of the world's major metropolitan regions over time can only be speculation, since our information is incomplete.[10] In general large-scale substitution of petroleum for coal as a heat source seems to have reduced particulate discharge in recent years in many instances and sulfur oxides in some. This was largely a result not of pollution control efforts but of relative fuel costs, and a great deal of back pedaling is going on in view of the 'oil crisis'. Other forms of discharge, for example oxides of nitrogen, hydrocarbons, and many trace substances, seem to have been increasing continuously nearly everywhere. There are now programs to reduce discharges of oxides of nitrogen from internal combustion engines in several countries. How successful this will be remains to be seen. In a later chapter the automobile is singled out for discussion from an economic and policy point of view because of its importance and the peculiar problems of regulation it presents.

Noise

Noise is also an airborne residual. But unlike the gaseous residuals discussed above, noise is an energy, not a material, residual. Major sources are motor vehicles, aircraft, construction and demolition activities, and – more recently and especially in the United States – recreational vehicles.

For simplification, two categories of noise residuals are sometimes identified – *residual noise* (an unfortunate term in view of the somewhat different use of the word residual in this book) and *intrusive noise*. The former refers to a continuous ambient level of noise, characteristic of urban areas, the sources of which cannot be identified; the latter refers to distinct sounds which are superimposed on the residual noise level and which can be associated with specific sources, such as overflights by aircraft. Aircraft noise is a serious problem in most urban areas – the outstanding example perhaps being the London region.

As with the other airborne residuals, noise is generated and discharged unevenly over space and, of course, in time. The quantities involved are largest in urban areas, noise tending to increase with city size and density.

With regard to trends in noise generation and ambient noise levels, the sparse data available suggest little change in residual noise levels for areas in which land use has not changed. Intrusive noise has tended to increase in virtually all areas, as a result of the development and spread in use of equipment generating more noise per unit of product or service. Thus, not only is the growth in commercial aviation reflected in the vast increase in number of flights but in the shift in aircraft motive power from piston engines to jet engines. The latter are about 10 to 20 dB noisier than the former.[11]

Waterborne (Liquid) Residuals

As with airborne residuals: (1) there is almost no limit to the variety of residuals which may be, and sometimes are, discharged into water bodies, including heat and radioactive residuals; and (2) the resulting changes in ambient water quality have varying effects on people and other forms of life, thereby detracting from the services people obtain directly and indirectly from the environment. The degradable/nondegradable/persistent categorization introduced in the opening section of this chapter is a suitable framework for the discussion of waterborne residuals.

The major sources of *organic degradable residuals* are industrial activities, human sewage, agricultural operations, and urban storm water runoff. When organic (degradable) residual is discharged at a point into an otherwise 'clean' stream, stream biota, primarily bacteria, feed on the organic residuals and decompose them into their inorganic constituents – nitrogen, phosphorus, and carbon, which are basic plant nutrients. As part of this process, some of the oxygen that is naturally present in dissolved form is used up by the bacteria. But this depletion tends to be offset by the reoxygenation that occurs through the air–water interface and also as a consequence of photosynthesis by the plants in the water. If the discharge of organic materials at the point is not too large, dissolved oxygen (DO) in the stream will first decrease, to a limited extent, and then increase again (assuming no subsequent discharges downstream).

If the quantity of organic residual discharged exceeds a certain amount, the process of degradation may exhaust the DO. In such cases, degradation is still carried forward but it takes place anaerobically, that is, through the action of bacteria that use organically or inorganically bound oxygen rather than free oxygen. Gaseous by-products result, among them carbon dioxide, methane, and hydrogen sulfide. Water in which organic residuals are being degraded anaerobically emits foul odors (it really stinks), looks black and bubbly, and is altogether offensive aesthetically. Anaerobic conditions occur during the summer in some rivers in nearly all developed countries of the world. But developing countries have the problem too – an entire lake near São Paulo, Brazil is continuously anaerobic.

The quantity of organic (degradable) residual present is measured by the amount of oxygen required for oxidation of the material, either by biological or chemical means. The former is termed the biochemical oxygen demand (BOD), and represents the amount of oxygen used in the oxidation of the residual by bacteria under specified conditions, generally five days at 20°C (hence, BOD_5). The chemical oxygen demand (COD) of a material is determined by the amount of oxygen used in the chemical oxidation of the residual, as with potassium permanganate. Both measures are applied to organic residuals of widely different compositions, and are useful for different purposes; however, the measurement of chemical oxygen demand is more common in Europe than in American practice.

Organic residuals are important because of the essential role of DO in the ecology of surface water bodies. It is one of the most important indicators of the life-sustaining capacity of a water body. High levels of DO, 7 to 8 parts per million (p.p.m.) – 8–10 p.p.m. is saturation in most streams and lakes in northern latitudes in summer – are necessary for several important fish species. For most species of fish, lower levels, say 4–5 p.p.m., are adequate for the life cycle. But at DO levels below 2–3 p.p.m., only carp and other less desired fish are likely to survive.

In addition to reducing DO *per se*, discharges of organic residuals can have other potentially adverse effects on receiving waters. When organic material in a stream is decomposed, the materials-balance principle discussed in the previous chapter still applies. The mass is conserved; only its form is

43

changed. The organic materials are broken down into their inorganic constituents, principally carbon dioxide and water, but also significant amounts of inorganic nitrate and phosphate compounds. These compounds are the nutrients for algae and can stimulate their growth. Up to a certain level, algae growth in a stream is not harmful and may even beneficially increase fish food, but large growths can be toxic to fish, produce odors, reduce the aesthetic appeal, and increase water-supply treatment problems. Large algae blooms themselves create a substantial oxygen demand when they die and decompose.

Problems of this kind can be particularly important in comparatively quiet waters, such as lakes and tidal estuaries and especially so in climates with warm summers. In recent years some lakes, or portions of lakes, have changed radically because of the buildup of plant nutrients. The most widely publicized example in the United States is Lake Erie, although the normal 'eutrophication' or aging process has been accelerated in many other lakes, and gone much farther in some lakes than in Lake Erie. For example, even some small lakes in Maine and Wisconsin, with relatively undeveloped shorelines, are experiencing accelerated eutrophication caused by seepage of nutrient-laden 'treated' effluents from septic tanks. A number of celebrated cases of lake eutrophication can be found in other countries. Lakes Geneva, Constance and (potentially) Baikal are major examples. The possibility of excessive algae growth is one of the more difficult problems in water-quality management – especially in lakes, bays and estuaries.

The largest source of waterborne *heat* discharge (a degradable energy residual) is condenser cooling water from large thermal power plants, both fossil-fueled and nuclear. Manufacturing activities comprise another large source; smaller but significant amounts are generated by various commercial/service-type activities, such as commercial laundries; and even household water heating contributes. The artificial injection of heat into a water body reduces, by a well-known law of gases, the capacity of the water to hold dissolved oxygen, accelerates oxygen-using decomposition, and may have more direct adverse effects on a wide variety of temperature-sensitive organisms. For example trout need both low temperature and high DO to thrive.

Infectious bacteria are included among the degradable residuals because they tend to die off in watercourses. Their principal source is human sewage. Because of the universal treatment of drinking water supplies, the traditional scourges of polluted water – typhoid, paratyphoid, dysentery, gastroenteritis – have become almost unknown in advanced countries but are still much of a problem in others. But infectious bacteria and waterborne viruses, such as hepatitis, still pose a health hazard to swimmers, and contaminate seafoods on a large scale even in developed countries. Also some doubt has recently been expressed about the effectiveness of treatment of water supplies against waterborne viruses.

Nondegradable waterborne residuals are not decomposed by stream biota. For most of these residuals, the only significant changes that occur in surface water bodies are dilution and settling; in groundwater bodies settling, adsorption and absorption. This group includes a variety of inorganic chemicals, soil particles, and various types of colloidal matter. When these substances are present in fairly large quantities, they can result in toxicity to some forms of life, turbidity, unpleasant tastes, hardness and – especially when chlorides are present – in corrosion. They may also cause changes in the stream ecology.

For some of the nondegradable residuals, primarily the salts of some heavy metals, natural processes can work perversely. For example, simple mercury compounds are absorbed by the lower forms of plant life, and then, via the food chain, are concentrated to higher levels and converted to forms potentially poisonous to higher order species. Two particularly vicious instances of poisoning by heavy metals occurred in Japan. These are mercury poisoning through eating contaminated fish (Minimata disease) and cadmium poisoning through eating contaminated rice (Itai Itai disease). Several hundred people were affected and more than a hundred died. There is evidence of large-scale and persistent poisoning of land and water by heavy metals in Japan. The Canadian government has forbidden the consumption of fish from both Lake Erie and Lake St Clair because of fear of mercury poisoning; similar situations prevail in several other countries, and mercury has been discovered in tuna and swordfish in quantities declared unsafe by the U.S. government, although in these particular cases the metal appears to be of natural origin.

The so-called *persistent* liquid residuals are considered separately, because they do not fit unambiguously into either the degradable or nondegradable categories. The persistent liquid residuals are best exemplified by the synthetic organic chemicals produced in profusion by our modern chemical industry. They are discharged into water bodies from industrial operations and from many household, commercial, municipal (i.e. park), and agricultural uses. These materials are termed 'persistent' because stream biota cannot effectively attack their complex molecular chains. Some degradation does take place, but usually so slowly that the persistent residuals may travel long distances in water bodies and in ground water, in virtually unchanged form. Pesticides (for instance, DDT) and phenols (resulting from the distillation of petroleum and coal products) are among the most common of these residuals.

Some of the persistent synthetic organics, such as phenols, present primarily aesthetic problems. The phenols can cause an unpleasant taste in drinking water, especially when the water has been treated with chlorine to kill bacteria. Other compounds are suspected of causing public health problems and have been associated with fish kills in streams.

Concentrations of the persistent organic substances have seldom if ever risen to high enough levels in public water supplies to present an *acute* danger to public health. Whatever public health problem may exist centers on the possible chronic effects of prolonged exposure to very low concentrations. However, the existence of chronic effects is extremely difficult to establish conclusively. Similarly, even in concentrations too low to be acutely poisonous to fish, these residuals may have profound effects on stream ecology, especially through biological magnification in the food chain. Higher creatures of other kinds, particularly some birds of prey, hawks and eagles, apparently have been, and continue to be, seriously affected because persistent pesticides have entered their food chain.

The long-lived radioactive materials are included in the category of persistent residuals, because, although they degrade, they do so very slowly. Nuclear power plants are likely to be an increasingly important source of such residuals. Generation of power by nuclear fission produces radioactive residuals that are contained in the fuel rods of reactors. Periodically, these fuels are separated by chemical processes to recover plutonium or to prevent residuals from 'poisoning' the reactor and reducing its efficiency. This reprocessing results in high-level radioactive residuals which must be contained virtually forever: while they do degrade the process is more on a geological than a human time-scale – the half-life of plutonium is 22,000 years! The questions surrounding storage of such material relate not only to technical feasibility but also to the capability of human institutions to monitor the situation and perform maintenance continuously for thousands of years.

In addition, a large volume of low-level radioactive residuals is generated in the day-to-day operation of reactors. Currently these residuals can be diluted and discharged into water bodies, although the permissible standards for such discharge have recently been severely questioned in several countries.

In the opening section a pertinent distinction was also made between 'point' and 'non-point' sources. As the reader will recall, a point source is the distinct location at which a residual is discharged to a water body; a non-point source has no such distinct location. This is an important distinction, because of the possibly different technological and policy

Table 3. Estimated Discharges of Liquid Residuals in the U.S., by source, 1968 (million tons)

Source	BOD$_5$	Suspended solids	Total dissolved solids	Oil and grease	Phosphorus	Heat 10^{15} B.t.u.
Agriculture	26·9	1,791·2	108·8	neg.	0·959	n.i.a.
Forestry	5·3	356·1	20·4	neg.	0·191	,,
Mining	0·9	84·5	5·5	neg.	0·042	,,
Construction	1·3	89·6	5·1	n.i.a.	0·048	,,
Food products	0·5	0·5	2·1	0·032	0·005	,,
Pulp and paper industry	1·5	1·0	9·0	0·032	0·006	,,
Chemical industry	4·4	3·7	26·8	0·512	0·255	,,
Petroleum refining	0·1	0·2	5·2	0·040	neg.	2·5
Primary metals	0·1	0·4	0·5	0·061	neg.	4·5§
Power plants	1·3	1·7	3·0	neg.	0·001	6
Sewage treatment plants	2·5	11·0	27·9	0·296	0·356	n.i.a.
Oil runoff from roads	0·3	neg.	neg.	0·525	neg.	,,
Storm water runoff	0·2	16·5	1·6	neg.	0·013	,,
Other	1·6	4·5	26·8*	0·901†	0·325‡	,,
Natural	16·1	1,074·7	68·1	neg.	0·579	—
Not yet classified	3·1	224·4	20·4	0·001	0·113	—
Total	66·1	3,660·0	331·2	2·400	2·893	n.i.a.

measures for managing residuals of these types. The same material, pesticides, or organic matter, may be discharged from a point source, such as the outlet from a pesticide manufacturing plant, or from a dispersed source, such as from a field of maize.

Agricultural operations – including forestry – natural resource exploitation, construction in urban areas, and urban storm water runoff are the major non-point sources of residuals. Surface and near-surface runoff from cropland and pastures are major sources of organic matter, plant nutrients, persistent pesticides, and sediment. Percolation to ground water from agricultural areas, both irrigated and non-irrigated, is a major source of increased nitrogen, phosphorus, and other dissolved solids in ground water. Timber harvesting, especially clear-cutting, can contribute substantial organic and inorganic residuals to streams within the watershed. Animal feedlots may be point sources, non-point sources, or both – depending on the particular situation. Where all runoff from the feedlot is channeled into a single discharge facility, the feedlot is essentially a point source. Where there is no such channelization, residuals generation is dispersed. Mining frequently exposes sulfur-containing coal and slag to weathering, surface runoff, and groundwater seepage, with the result that surface waters become acid, often with devastating effects on the stream ecology. Because land development usually means the destruction of natural cover, heavy rains

---

neg. – negligible; n.i.a. – no information available.

* Primarily oil and gas drilling.

† Primarily boats and gasoline stations.

‡ Primarily feedlots and laundromats.

§ Iron and steel only, heat residuals discharge for all industry totaled about 20×10^{15} B.t.u.

SOURCES: *For heat* – R. T. Jaske *et al.*, 'A National Estimate of Public and Industrial Heat Rejection Requirements by Decades through the Year 2000 A.D.', AIChE Paper No. 37A, 67th National Meeting of American Institute of Chemical Engineers, Atlanta, Georgia, 17 February 1970, pp. 9–10.

All others – L. P. Gianessi, estimates made in connection with the National Bureau of Economic Research National Accounting and the Environment Project, Preliminary, 1974.

move more quickly and directly into the rivers, carrying primarily sediment with them.

SOURCES AND QUANTITIES. Again to provide a feel for the amounts involved, rough estimates of the mass of liquid residuals discharged into water bodies of the United States in 1968 are shown in Table 3. In terms of total tons, agricultural and forestry activities predominate for all of these residuals except 'oil and grease', and heat. Excluding the natural and 'not yet classified' categories, the approximate percentages of biochemical oxygen demand, suspended solids, total dissolved solids, and phosphorus contributed by agriculture plus forestry are 70, 90, 50, and 50, respectively. Of the remaining 30 percent of BOD discharges, about half is in direct discharges from manufacturing plants and about one sixth from municipal sewage-treatment plant discharges. With respect to suspended solids, the remaining 10 percent comes primarily from construction and mining. The other half of the total dissolved solids residuals discharged are derived about two fifths from manufacturing plants, about a quarter from sewage treatment plants, and about three twentieths from oil and gas drilling. Of the remaining phosphorus discharges, about a quarter is from manufacturing, about a third from sewage treatment plants, and most of the remainder from feedlots and laundromats. There are of course major differences in types of discharges among regions, even in the U.S., reflecting different mixes of economic activities. Other than for agriculture, forestry, and mining, generation of liquid residuals is concentrated in urban areas and the point leading from industrial plants and municipalities frequently presents particularly severe problems because they are so concentrated. Such concentrations may be illustrated by data from Britain, which has recently completed a particularly careful and detailed survey of its watercourses. This discloses that 75 percent of the mileage of grossly polluted streams exist in five regions and that these five regions contain only about one third of the total stream miles and of the population.[12]

The reader can roughly adjust this for the mix of total discharges which may be characteristic of countries other than the U.S. As a large generalization, the United States is a proportionately larger producer of agricultural, forestry, and mining products than other developed countries. The level of sewage treatment and industrial discharge control is probably roughly comparable to that found in Britain, Germany, Scandinavia, and Canada. Both are higher in the U.S. than in the other developed countries, Japan and the Soviet Union for example.

There are even fewer data to judge long-term trends in liquid residuals discharge than in gaseous discharges. General knowledge of the situation suggests, however, that there has been a long-term general upward tendency for nearly all discharges except, in some cases, domestic sewage. There are some notable successes in tackling pollution problems in particular regions, the Ruhr region and the Thames estuary, for example. But it is doubtful that there is any country which has not been experiencing a long-term and more or less continuous increase in the mass of residuals discharged to its water bodies. For example, it is estimated that the streams of the Federal Republic of West Germany are now receiving a quantity of BOD about half as much again as they could assimilate without serious damage.[13]

Solid Residuals

Solid residuals are generated directly in virtually all activities, just as are gaseous and liquid residuals. Furthermore, they comprise one of what might be called the 'ultimate' residuals discharged into the environment, along with carbon dioxide, water (including water vapor), and heat. That is, by the use of sufficient energy and materials it is technologically possible to remove virtually all materials from gaseous and liquid residuals streams, thereby generating secondary solid residuals. Thus, so-called fly ash from a power plant represents the secondary solid residual generated in removing particulates from the stack gas.

Solid residuals are characterized both by type of material and by source, but it is unlikely that an unambiguous classification could be achieved. Table 4 illustrates the various materials involved, and the overlapping of type and source. 'Mixed solid residuals' is a term used to denote virtually any combination of the materials listed in the table – what might be expected in a waste container from a house or a factory.

Although in a few cases there are direct health hazards to man, as with pathological residuals, most impacts of solid residuals are indirect, resulting from the methods used for handling and disposing of the solid residuals. For example, breeding places may be provided for rodents and insects, surface and/or ground water quality may be adversely affected by percolating through landfills, the landscape may be spoilt by the disposal of solid residuals and by burning culm banks.[14]

Table 4. Types of Solid Residuals

Garbage, i.e. from preparation, cooking, serving of food; from storage, handling, sale of produce and meat	
Combustibles	Paper products Wood, boxes, etc. Plastics Rags, cloth Leather, rubber
Noncombustibles	Metals and inert mineral solids Dirt Stones, bricks, ceramics Bottles
Garden debris, i.e., leaves, grass clippings, trimmings, dirt	
Ashes, i.e., from fuel combustion for energy generation, process steam, space heating, cooking	

Bulky items	Large auto parts, tires
	Stoves, refrigerators, other large appliances
	Furniture, large crates
	Trees, branches, palm fronds, stumps

Obsolete vehicles – automobiles, trucks, buses

Street sweepings, catch basin materials

Dead animals	Small animals: cats, dogs, poultry, etc.
	Large animals: horses, cows, etc.

Construction and demolition residuals	Lumber, roofing, and sheathing scraps
	Rubble, broken concrete, plaster, etc.
	Conduit, pipe, wire, insulation, etc.

Special	Hazardous materials, pathological residuals, explosives, radioactive materials, pesticide containers
	Security residuals, confidential documents, negotiable papers, obsolete stamps, etc.

Animal residues, i.e. manure

Crop residues

Slush and logging residues

Tailings and overburden from mining

Sewage treatment residuals, i.e. coarse screenings, grit, septic tank sludge, sludge

SOURCES AND QUANTITIES. Data on the quantities of solid residuals generated and discharged are even more difficult to obtain than for gaseous and liquid residuals. In part this is because the extent to which some types of solid residuals are disposed of on site, such as tailings from mining operations, logging residues, crop residues, is not known. Strictly speaking as I use the term here, only those quantities which pass beyond the boundary of the activity into the environment are 'residuals'. However, unlike gaseous and liquid residuals, solid residuals on the site are often visually very apparent to individuals off the site. Consequently, the data in Table 5 reflect this somewhat broader definition.

Note that the first two categories, which combined comprise essentially 'municipal' solid residuals, represent less than 10 percent of the total in the United States. They are, however, the solid residuals which we are most aware of and to which most attention has been given. In part this reflects the huge handling costs associated with them as well as their propensity to generate external effects.

Table 5. Estimated Quantities of Solid Residuals Generated in the U.S. in 1971, by source

	10^9 tons
Residential, commercial, institutional mixed solid residuals	0·25
Industrial process mixed solid residuals	0·11
Animal residues (mostly manure) >500 Agricultural crop residues (excluding forestry) >1500	2·3
Mining (*excluding* overburden) and minerals processing	1·7
Total	4·0–4·5

SOURCE: C. J. Lyons and D. L. Morrison, 'Solid Waste 1: Where Does It Come From?', *Battelle Research Outlook*, Vol. 3, No. 3, 1971, p. 4.

About 80 percent of the solid residuals from mining and minerals processing are accounted for by eight mineral industries: in order, copper, iron and steel, bituminous coal, phosphate rock, lead, zinc, aluminium, and anthracite coal. If overburden from stripping operations were included, the total tonnage of solid residuals from this sector would be much larger, with bituminous coal being by far the most important contributor in those countries where it is produced in major amounts.

Obsolete vehicles are a special problem particularly characteristic of the United States but becoming worse in other countries. Of the ten to twenty million obsolete vehicles in existence at any one time in the United States, about three quarters are in the hands of wreckers and most of the rest are abandoned and littering the countryside. Most automobile hulks are eventually recycled but in the slow process they impose major external costs upon the society.

There is substantial seasonal variation in the generation of certain types of solid residuals, such as garden rubbish. In spring and fall, garden rubbish can account for as much as 25 to 30 percent of the mixed solid residuals collected from houses; whereas it represents a negligible quantity in winter. Agricultural crop residues are of course very seasonal; in some regions the same is true for logging residues. Some industrial operations likewise have seasonal distributions of solid residuals generation, food processing being the prime example.

The information available indicates that the generation of virtually all types of solid residuals has been increasing for several decades in the United States. The same is probably true of other developed countries since similar forces are at work. The proliferation of packaging, particularly 'throw-away' packaging, is but the most obvious indication. The steady increase in *per capita* use of paper products is also symptomatic. Equally, or perhaps even more significant, is the inevitable increase in the quantities of solid residuals generated per ton of metal, as lower and lower grade ores must be used. In addition, as restrictions on the discharge of gaseous and liquid residuals to the environment are enforced, substantial additional quantities of sludge[15] and other secondary solid residuals will be generated.

Chapter 3
Impacts of Environmental Deterioration and Environmental Controls on Entire National Economics[1]

Introduction

The previous chapter has served to illustrate the many different types of residuals which are generated by modern society and their possible effects on environmental media. Chapter 1 was devoted to a brief consideration of how market forces (externality) contribute to excessive generation and discharge of all sorts of residuals. One line of economic reasoning and research has been focused, over the last decade or so, on how policy changes might influence behavior of individual firms, industries, municipalities and consumers so as to reduce these discharges to a level which could be deemed more nearly 'optimal'. All economic analysis such as this, which concerns itself with the behavior of individual economic entities, is called microeconomics.

Welfare economics is a special branch of microeconomics which concerns itself with the performance of whole inter-dependent economic systems composed of such entities. It gives special attention to the characteristics of the *equilibrium* of such systems, the state they could reach if all exogenous variables (overall income, consumer demand patterns, technological possibilities in production) remained unchanged. When these conditions, stated in terms of the derivatives of the functions involved, or what the economist calls *marginal* conditions, correspond to those of Pareto optimality, the situation is, as we saw in Chapter 1, termed efficient or a welfare optimum. Most of the material in this book from Chapter 5 on is concerned with this mode of analysis as it applies to environmental problems.

In this chapter, however, we will be occupied with an analysis which proceeds at a less detailed level. To start with we must note why the *general* form of economic equilibrium analysis is not applicable to all situations one might wish to analyze.

Limitations of General Equilibrium Analysis

The general equilibrium model of resources allocation which underlies formal welfare economics represents, as I have said, a general analysis of the interrelationships of markets throughout the economy. Because in principle it requires knowledge of the structure of preferences of all consumers and the technologies available to all producers, there is no realistic hope of ever being able to state the whole system empirically. Furthermore, the functions with which it deals are exceedingly general and could give rise to a very large system of simultaneous non-linear equations which would defy quantitative solutions. Accordingly, in actual application small parts of the general system are extracted for detailed analysis. This is known as partial equilibrium analysis. Most of the later parts of this book use such partial equilibrium analysis.

But in the last two decades a drastically simplified general interdependency system known as the *open Leontief input-output model* has found empirical application. In contrast to the general multi-market equilibrium analysis, consumer demands are taken as given exogenously in this model. Also, the industry rather than the firm is taken to be the unit of production, and the production function (the function relating inputs to outputs) of each industry is a constant-coefficient type so that it presents no optimization problem. In other words there is *one way*, and one way only, to produce every industry output; industries rather than firms are taken to be the basic units of production. The return for these radical simplifications is a model which can be empirically implemented in connection with certain planning problems.

Economics and the Environment

Input-Output Analysis

I will give a brief overview of the general Leontief I-O model here to introduce this mode of analysis. In the next section, where an application is discussed, a more detailed exposition of its structure is presented.

Input-output analysis for an entire economy is based on an accounting of the flow of goods and services in dollar terms at a particular time. Part of this flow is an inter-industry flow, goods transferred from an industry to be used in production processes in other industries, and the remainder flows to an exogenously defined 'final demand' sector. This sector generally includes households, government, and foreign trade – often lumped together. For an n-industry economy the inter-industry input coefficients are arranged as a matrix $A = [a_{ij}]$. Such an arrangement is shown below.

$$
\begin{array}{cc}
\text{Input} & \text{Output of industry} \\
\text{from industry} & 1 \quad 2 \ldots n \\
\begin{matrix} 1 \\ 2 \\ \cdot \\ \cdot \\ \cdot \\ n \end{matrix} &
\begin{bmatrix}
a_{11} & a_{12} & \ldots & a_{1n} \\
a_{21} & a_{22} & \ldots & a_{2n} \\
\cdot & \cdot & & \cdot \\
\cdot & \cdot & & \cdot \\
\cdot & \cdot & & \cdot \\
a_{n1} & a_{n2} & \ldots & a_{nn}
\end{bmatrix}
\end{array}
$$

The first column of this matrix says that to produce a dollar's worth of commodity 1, inputs of a_{11} units of commodity 1, a_{21} units of commodity 2, etc., are needed. Frequently the matrix is set up in such a way that no industry uses its own output. In that case, all the elements along the principal diagonal (those from the upper left hand to the lower right hand corner) are zero.

If industry 1 is to produce an output just sufficient to meet the input requirements of the n industries as well as final demand of the open exogeneous sector, its total output, designated x_1, must satisfy the following equation

$$x_1 = a_{11}x_1 + a_{12}x_2 + \ldots + a_{1n}x_n + d_1$$

where d_1 is the final demand for the output of that industry. The equation can be rewritten as follows:

$$(*) \; (1 - a_{11})x_1 - a_{12}x_2 - \ldots - a_{1n}x_n = d_1$$

Except for the first coefficient $(1 - a_{11})$, the others are the same as those in the first row of the A matrix on page 61, except they now have negative signs. Similarly, if we wrote the same type of equation for industry 2, it would have the same coefficients as in the second row of A (but with minus signs), except in position a_{22} where the coefficient would be $(1 - a_{22})$. We can produce this same result in the whole matrix A if we subtract it from the identity matrix 1.

Thus we can write

$$(I - A)x = d$$

where I is an $n \times n$ identity matrix, A is the $n \times n$ coefficients matrix, and x and d are both $n \times 1$ vectors; x is the variable vector and d is the final demand vector. If $(I - A)$ has the rank n (i.e. is non-singular – meaning that the system of equations it represents has a unique solution), its inverse can be found and the system of n simultaneous equations represented by the above matrix equation will have the solution.

$$x = (I - A)^{-1}d$$

Aside from providing a solution for the n simultaneous equations of which equation (*) is an example, representing commodity and service flows from industries to industries and to final demands, the inverse matrix $(I - A)^{-1}$ has great utility. Once it is available d can be premultiplied by this inverse and a new solution vector produced for the industry outputs x, always on the assumption that the coefficients of the A matrix have not changed. Since multiplying a matrix by a vector is a simple operation compared with getting entirely new solutions to simultaneous equations, this is a great advantage. Should one have reason to think that the composition or magnitude of final demand could shift, the consequences of this can easily be played through in terms of inter-industry demands.

Despite its various restrictive assumptions, input-output analysis has come to be regarded as a basic tool for the analysis of national and regional economic systems.

The input-output model is clearly more aggregative than the general systems model of the economy. But still it does deal in terms of specific industries and final demand patterns. Therefore, it can be regarded as intermediate between the general microeconomic model of the economic system and the still more aggregative *macroeconomic* models.

Macroeconomic Models

Macro models deal entirely at the level of national economic aggregates, national income, overall money supply, levels of employment and unemployment at the national level, and price indices. Environmental degradation and environmental controls raise issues even at this highly general level and some of them will be discussed later in this chapter. But first let us turn to an application of the input-output model to environmental problems.

Applying the Input-Output Model to Environmental Problems

A few years ago, Leontief proposed an extension of the basic national open I-O model which would permit forecasting of residuals emissions and at least gross effects of certain types of policy measures with respect to them.[2] Although interpretation of the mathematics is rather straightforward (quite like that reviewed above), I shall describe the system in a little detail because residuals are handled somewhat differently from ordinary commodities and because doing so permits a somewhat deeper penetration into the structure of I-O models which not only contributes to understanding but also helps to reveal both their strengths and weaknesses.

The input-output balance (which may be interpreted either in physical or monetary terms) with pollutants included in the system is shown by the matrix equation in Figure 1. We have

Figure 1. Input-Output Balance

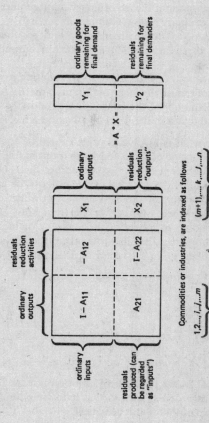

ordinary inputs

residuals produced (can be regarded as "inputs")

ordinary outputs | residuals reduction activities

| I − A11 | − A12 |
| A21 | I − A22 |

ordinary outputs | residuals reduction "outputs"

| X1 |
| X2 |

= "A · X" =

ordinary goods remaining for final demand

residuals remaining for final demanders

| Y1 |
| Y2 |

Commodities or industries, are indexed as follows

$1, 2, \ldots, i, \ldots, j, \ldots, m$ — ordinary goods

$(m+1), \ldots, k, \ldots, l, \ldots, n$ — residuals

m ordinary goods and $n - m$ pollutants, making a total of *n* inputs and outputs.

Each of the A matrices is a matrix of input-output coefficients. For example:

a_{ij} is the amount of the *i*th ordinary input required per unit of the *j*th ordinary output (sub-matrix A_{11}).

a_{ik} is the amount of the *i*th ordinary input required to produce a unit of the *k*th residuals reduction output (sub-matrix A_{12}).

a_{ji} is the amount of the *j*th residual resulting from producing a unit of the *i*th ordinary output (sub-matrix A_{21}).

a_{ki} is the amount of the *k*th residual produced as a result of a unit reduction in the *i*th residual (sub-matrix A_{22}).

To see what is involved in this system of equations, let us separate out one of them and write it out in full. Assume that we have three ordinary commodities and two pollutant reduction activities,[3] a total of five outputs, or 'inputs', in all. Take, for example, the first equation, which is formed by multiplying each member of the first row of A* by the corresponding members of the *x* vector of industry outputs and adding these products together, thereby obtaining the first member, y_1, of the vector of final outputs, Y:

$$[1 \quad -a_{12} \quad -a_{13} \quad -a_{14} \quad -a_{15}] \begin{bmatrix} x_1 \\ x_2 \\ x_3 \\ x_4 \\ x_5 \end{bmatrix} = y_1$$

or,

$$x_1 - a_{12}x_2 - a_{13}x_3 - a_{14}x_4 - a_{15}x_5 = y_1$$

Note that in the matrices of input-output coefficients a_{ii} and a_{kk} are regarded as zero so that industry output is always net of its own output that it uses itself.

This equation simply says that the total output of the first commodity minus the amount used in the production of x_2, x_3, x_4, and x_5 is equal to the amount of the first commodity, y_1, going to final demanders. The last four terms account for all of the x_1 used in production, whether for ordinary goods or residuals reduction.

Now consider an equation in the bottom part of the square matrix, A*, say the last one for the nth commodity, which is a residual. Note that since the output of the residuals processing industry is here measured as residuals reduction, the signs of the elements of the two lower quadrants are reversed from those of the two upper:

$$[a_{51} \quad a_{52} \quad a_{53} \quad a_{54} \quad -1] \begin{bmatrix} x_1 \\ x_2 \\ x_3 \\ x_4 \\ x_5 \end{bmatrix} = y_5$$

or,

$$a_{51}x_1 + a_{52}x_2 + a_{53}x_3 + a_{54}x_4 - x_5 = y_5$$

This says that the residual which is commodity number five that is generated in the production of x_1, x_2, x_3, and x_4 *minus* the amount by which this residual is reduced equals the amount which goes to final demanders.

Thus in abbreviated matrix form, the input-output balance is A*X = Y, where X and Y are vectors of industry outputs and deliveries of final goods, respectively. Industry outputs include residuals reduction, and final goods include residuals received.[4]

The system of equations, A*X = Y, can be solved for the vector X, industry outputs, by pre-multiplying each side by the inverse of the matrix, A^{*-1}, obtaining $X = A^{*-1}Y$. Thus if A^{*-1} has been calculated for a given industrial structure, the industry outputs, X, that would be associated with any specified bill of final goods, Y, can, as I indicated in the general discussion of input-output analysis, be calculated very easily, given, of course, the peculiar assumptions of the input-output scheme as commonly formulated. The main one is that the input coefficients, the a's, are fixed no matter what the size of an industry's output. That is, as also pointed out previously, there is only one way to produce an output, a way that is completely described by one column of *a* coefficients. It is this assumption that facilitates calculation of economy-wide effects of certain policy changes or changes in final demands.

An Actual Application

The input-output approach is designed to be implemented empirically and applications have been made to environmental problems. The first and still the most complete was made at Resources for the Future, Inc., a Washington, D.C. based research firm under contract with a Presidential Commission concerning itself with the impacts of population growth on the future of the United States. I will outline the procedure and results as a concrete illustration of how the analysis can be used. The model incorporated into the analysis is an adaptation of the one just described.[5] The study endeavored to assess the relative significance of various variables thought to be important in determining the magnitude of residuals management problems – economic growth, technological changes, population increase, and intensity of residuals control effort.

Outline of the Model

A schematic of the model is presented in Figure 2. As the illustration reveals, the forces that 'drive' the model are population size and characteristics and overall levels of demand for the goods included in the final demand sector. Final demand projections are used to develop estimates of required production levels by economic sector and year by year into the future. These drive the central element in the projection system in an input-output model of 185 economic sectors, generally similar to the one described abstractly earlier, but with some further modifications. In addition to the sets of residuals generation and treatment coefficients in the

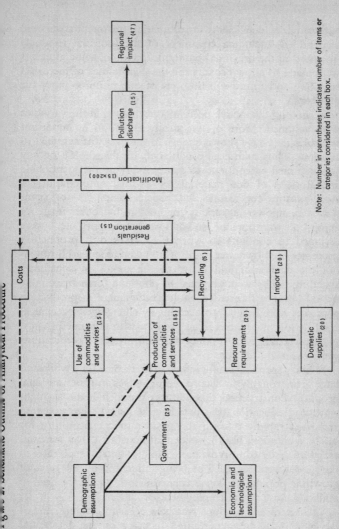

Figure 2. Schematic Outline of Analytical Procedure

Regional impact (47)

Pollution discharge (15)

Modification (15×200)

Residuals generation (15)

Recycling (5)

Imports (20)

Costs

Use of commodities and services (15)

Production of commodities and services (185)

Resource requirements (20)

Domestic supplies (20)

Government (25)

Demographic assumptions

Economic and technological assumptions

Note: Number in parentheses indicates number of items or categories considered in each box.

SOURCE: U.S. Commission on Population Growth and the American Future, *Population, Resources, and the Environment* (Volume III of Commission research reports), edited by Ronald G. Ridker, Washington, D.C., Government Printing Office, 1972, p. 38.

NOTE: Some of the box titles differ from those in the original Population Commission Report.

earlier model, coefficients for estimating treatment costs were also added, including treatment of most of the residuals discussed in the previous chapter. In addition, some attempts were made to allow broadly for the possibilities of increased recycling and future substitutions of one resource input for another.

In running the model, no dramatic changes in the variables were assumed. More or less steady evolution in important variables that have shown change in the past was assumed to continue. Thus, man-hour productivity for the whole economy was assumed to continue to grow; many of the identifiable substitutions of one material for another – aluminium for steel, plastics for metals and paper, computers for semi-skilled manpower, electricity for human and other forms of energy, air transport for land and water transport, etc. – were assumed to continue to work themselves out; production processes used by newer plants were taken to spread throughout the economy; and many of the trends in consumer-spending habits were assumed to continue for a reasonable period into the future. Technological changes in production processes were taken into account by changing the technical coefficient in the matrix in accordance with presumed trends. No basic changes in product mix and product specifications were assumed to occur.

Military spending was assumed to mark time for a while and later grow roughly in accord with changes in gross national product. Construction expenditures on such items as highways and education (the two biggest items) were taken to grow less rapidly than in the past; public expenditure for safety, sanitation, health, residential housing, urban renewal, etc. were assumed to grow more rapidly; and all such rates in the model were regarded as being influenced by the rates of growth in population, in *per capita* income, and in the need to maintain close to full employment.

This set of assumptions was held constant for all runs of the model. Doing so permitted focusing on the differential impact of a smaller set of variables of principal interest;

population growth rates (and associated demographic characteristics such as age, labor force, and size of household), economic growth rates (insofar as they are determined independently of population growth rates), and some policy alternatives with reference to conservation and environmental quality.

The alternative population assumptions used in the model require a word of explanation. They center on U.S. Bureau of Census Series B and E, the former involving an average of 3·1 and the latter 2·1 children per woman. The latter would lead gradually to stability in the population while the former implies continued growth.

Alternative economic growth assumptions were reflected in the model through changes in labor productivity or output per worker, which are in turn a result of differences in number of hours worked. Total output per man-hour is assumed to continue to grow at 2·5 percent per year (about the industrial trend). Two working-hours alternatives were specified: first, that work hours continue to decline as they have in the past, by about 0·25 percent per year; and second, that this rate of decline increases to one percent per year. The former means a decline in the work week from approximately 40 hours to 37 hours by 2000; in the second case, 29 hours per week would be the figure for the year 2000. While this second case represents quite a substantial and perhaps unrealistically rapid increase in leisure time, it is still quite a distance from assuming an end to economic growth.

The population and economic growth assumptions lead to four basic scenarios: a high population and high economic growth case (labeled B-High or B-H), a low population and economic growth alternative (E-Low or E-L), and the two intermediate situations (B-L and E-H).

With respect to residuals, two policy versions are considered. In the first, policy trends with respect to the environment are assumed to continue as one would have expected as of 1967 (the base period for most of the data used). This involves no pressure to search for and introduce technologies which significantly reduce residuals, no increased pressure to recycle, no change in product specifications and product mix, no taxes on the consumption of commodities that are heavy users of common property resources, and so on. But this scenario does not mean that residuals emissions per unit of output will not change over time. It merely means that such changes will arise as a consequence of the businessman's general interest in substituting cheaper for more expensive resources and reducing materials and energy flows to minimize his market-type costs per unit of output. In the second instance, this policy regime is changed, the model is asked to play out the implications of alternative rates of population and economic growth given more active policies aimed at reducing residuals discharge: more recycling, additional process change to reduce residuals generated per unit of output, more trans-formation of residuals to reduce emissions of the most harm-ful substances per unit of residuals generated, alterations in the compositions of demand and output and in product specifi-cations, and so on. At this highly aggregated level of analysis, it is possible to specify such policies only crudely – but well enough to provide some rough order of magnitude estimates of discharges and costs. Much of the latter parts of the book are about the question of the cost-effectiveness of various residuals management strategies. We will see that different implementation strategies can have vastly different costs associated with them.

Table 6 presents residuals discharges for the United States as a whole for 1970 and projections for 2000, assuming no change in abatement policy. Three principal conclusions emerge from these data. First, if residuals modification is not intensified, even a substantial slowdown in the growth rates of both population and economic activities will not be enough to keep the levels of residual discharges in the year 2000 below current levels.

But second, future rates of growth in these residuals will be lower than they appear to have been in recent years. They are lower than assumed rates of growth in gross national product; and for some residuals, they are even lower than growth rates for GNP *per capita* and for population. These results arise principally from two factors. First, the composition of the output for the year 2000 is slightly less residuals-generating than that of 1970, mainly (but not entirely) because of a small, but definite, shift away from goods toward services. Second, while a few individual residual generation and discharge coefficients are expected to increase over time more are expected to decrease as today's best practice becomes more widespread. This is mostly due to a shift toward processes which use materials more efficiently.

While one may have some confidence in these results for the residuals listed in Table 6, an important qualification must be entered for residuals not listed in this table. A number, such as heavy metals, synthetic organics, pesticides, agricultural runoff, and mining residuals, are not considered in the calculations.[6] Furthermore, it may be that more advanced industries will generate new kinds of residuals in the future at a rate that invalidates these results. Unfortunately, from this analysis we have no way of knowing.

Third, residuals discharges seem to be related somewhat more to growth in the economy than to growth in the population, although there are marked differences among different kinds. For example, solid residuals of the types included, and also carbon monoxide, appear to be more closely related to population levels, whereas sulfur oxides, suspended solids, and phosphorus are more closely associated with the level of economic activity. The principal explanation is that a slow-down in population growth induces some offsetting increase in economic growth, whereas an independent slowdown in economic growth involves no comparable offset.

Active Abatement Policy

By an active abatement policy is meant, in the present context, a policy that induces reductions in residuals generation or discharge coefficients, but as we will see later, this by no

Table 6. Residuals Discharged under Various Scenarios, No Change in Policy

	1970	Amount (billion* pounds) 2000				Ratio 2000/1970				Percentage reduction from B-H in 2000		
		B-H	E-H	B-L	E-L	B-H	E-H	B-L	E-L	E-H	B-L	E-L
Air												
Particulates	41	49	45	41	38	1·20	1·10	1·00	0·93	8·2	16·3	22·4
Hydrocarbons	89	207	196	181	171	2·33	2·20	2·03	1·92	5·3	12·6	17·4
Oxides of sulfur	85	132	122	108	100	1·55	1·44	1·27	1·18	7·6	18·2	24·2
Carbon monoxide	231	493	470	489	466	2·13	2·03	2·12	2·02	4·7	0·8	5·5
Oxides of nitrogen	30	58	55	54	51	1·93	1·83	1·80	1·70	5·2	6·9	12·1
Water												
Waste water†	188	323	307	296	283	1·72	1·63	1·57	1·51	4·9	8·4	12·4
COD‡	202	462	416	398	359	2·29	2·06	1·97	1·78	10·0	13·8	22·3
BOD§	68	134	121	115	103	1·97	1·78	1·69	1·51	9·7	14·2	23·1
Refractory organics‖	6	10	8	10	8	1·67	1·33	1·67	1·33	20·0	0·0	20·0
Suspended solids	804	1,591	1,441	1,352	1,229	1·98	1·79	1·68	1·53	9·4	15·0	22·0
Dissolved solids	137	294	265	251	225	2·15	1·93	1·83	1·64	9·9	14·6	23·3
Nitrogen	23	43	38	37	33	1·87	1·65	1·61	1·43	11·6	13·9	23·8
Phosphorus	8	16	15	14	12	2·00	1·88	1·75	1·50	6·2	12·5	25·5

Thermal to water**	5·6	3·55	3·30	2·65	0·63	0·59	0·52	0·39	7·0	18·3	25·4
Solid											
Solid waste††	321	863	718	860	715	2·69	2·24	2·68	2·23	16·8	3·5	17·1

* U.K.: thousand million. † 10^{12} gallons. ‡ COD – chemical oxygen demand. § BOD – biochemical oxygen demand (5 day).
‖ The results for refractory organics are an artifact of the method of calculation: there are no data on this pollutant except for the household sector. ** 10^{15} B.t.u. †† 10^{12} pounds

SOURCE: U.S. Commission on Population Growth and the American Future, *Population, Resources, and the Environment* (Volume III of Commission research reports) edited by Ronald G. Ridker, Washington, D.C., Government Printing Office, 1972, p. 46.
NOTE: The figures in this table differ from those in the original Population Commission Report in that they contain estimates of the costs of controlling thermal discharges. These were not contained in the original figures. The estimates for thermal discharges were made by Chris Sandberg of Resources for the Future, Inc., Washington, D.C.

means exhausts the list of policy options – nor is it necessarily always the most attractive. Even discharge reduction can be done in a number of ways, and much of the rest of the book is devoted to discussing and assessing these alternatives. Here, in order to apply the input-output framework, it is simply assumed that discharges are limited to certain specified levels, controlled by residuals modification (treatment) processes; the effect that this has on aggregate discharge levels and costs of production is observed.

The effluent standards used for this demonstration are roughly the 1973 water and 1975 air discharge standards recommended by the Environmental Protection Agency (EPA). These effluent standards were accepted for this exercise only after it was ascertained that it is technologically feasible (or soon will be) to meet them without assuming any dramatic technical breakthroughs. For a number of sectors and residuals, methods of reducing generation and discharge coefficients to meet the standards are already used on a scale sufficiently large for one to have reasonable confidence in the cost estimates. An important case in point is waste water treatment where the EPA standards call for 'secondary treatment'. This is a well-established procedure (at least for municipal waste modification plants) that removes 90 to 95 percent of the biological oxygen demand and suspended solids from waste water. In other cases – for example, nitrogen oxide reduction and sulfur removed from fuel – where abatement strategies that would meet the standards are not used commercially at the present time, it was ascertained that at least one strategy was available; the most feasible one was accepted and cost estimates were developed accordingly. It is quite possible that between now and the year 2000 considerably more stringent effluent standards will be achieved and costs will be accordingly higher – perhaps much higher. But the standards used here are sufficient to reduce discharges considerably below present levels, even at year 2000 levels of population, production, and consumption. For purposes of the projections, the assumption is made that measures needed to reach the standard will be introduced gradually between now and the year 2000.

Before proceeding to a discussion of the results, it should be noted that the projections procedure was not able to account separately for the reactions of one residuals stream on others. As the reader will infer from my earlier discussion, this is a significant omission. Because of this and a number of other inadequacies and uncertainties, in the final interpretation of results the quantitative outcomes must be regarded as merely order-of-magnitude estimates.

Table 7 presents the results of the active abatement exercise for a representative set of residuals. The rows labeled A, provided for background, are the levels of residuals that would be generated using 1970 technology so far as residuals generation coefficients are concerned. The rows labeled B indicate actual discharges for 1970, and estimated discharges for the year 2000, assuming no change in abatement policy from the base period. A comparison of rows A and B indicates the extent to which changes in generation and discharge coefficients which will reduce emissions are likely to come along anyway. Rows C indicate the level of discharges likely in 2000, assuming the active abatement policy outlined above. It can be seen that such a policy would bring all included residuals levels down significantly below current ones (except for dissolved solids where standards are not very stringent, partly because available modification technologies are very expensive).

Table 8 indicates the annualized costs associated with residuals modification of such an active policy. While it does not include a number of cost items that a broad clean environment policy would entail – for example, additional water storage facilities, separation of storm and sanitary sewers in those cities where this might prove necessary, correction of damages caused by strip mining, and control of non-point sources of residuals (and these would no doubt be large sums) – it does contain those items which have been conventionally included in official cost estimates. In 1970, such

Table 7. Pollution Generated and Discharged under Alternative Assumptions*

	1970	2000			
		B-H	E-H	B-L	E-L
Particulates					
A	54·2	175·2	160·0	153·8	133·7
B	41·4	49·0	45·3	41·4	38·3
C		5·6	5·2	4·7	4·4
Hydrocarbons					
A	96·5	270·1	254·0	233·2	218·8
B	89·4	207·4	196·2	180·9	170·9
C		31·4	29·4	27·4	25·6
Oxides of nitrogen					
A	29·9	80·5	76·0	72·7	68·5
B	29·9	57·6	55·0	54·0	51·3
C		17·8	16·6	16·7	15·8
Biological oxygen demand					
A	71·9	186·3	167·2	160·3	143·8
B	67·6	134·4	120·8	114·8	103·1
C		16·9	15·2	14·4	12·6
Suspended solids					
A	846·3	1,998·4	1,808·5	1,698·2	1,534·8
B	804·0	1,591·2	1,440·6	1,352·3	1,229·2
C		98·9	89·5	84·0	76·4
Dissolved solids					
A	137·2	363·1	328·9	305·2	275·6
B	137·2	294·5	264·8	250·9	224·7
C		284·7	256·1	242·5	217·3
Thermal (to water)†					
A	5·6	3·55	3·30	2·90	2·65
B	5·6	2·95	2·75	2·40	2·20
C	–	0	0	0	0

* A = Residuals generated assuming 1970 technology, that is, no changes in residuals generation coefficients (technological changes resulting in substitutions amongst inputs – e.g., plastics for metals – are included, however). B = Residuals

costs amounted to about $9 thousand million (1967 dollars); by 2000, the figure could amount to more than $50 thousand million, growing at a faster rate than GNP.

The most rapid period of rise appears to be the next decade. Thereafter, because the United States may have caught up somewhat with the past neglect and because sufficient time would have elapsed to find less costly ways to reduce discharges – such as substitute materials, products, processes with less residuals generation – the increase in costs could be much less rapid. The same need to catch up in order to achieve the assumed standards suggests that in 1980, if the lower rather than the higher population projections were to occur, the savings involved would be negligible. By the year 2000, however, these savings would amount to around ten percent.

Thus, while not huge over the time period being considered, the difference between rapid continued population growth and a tendency toward stabilization would nevertheless be significant. If one were to consider the problems associated with the congestion in cities, roadways, and recreation areas, the differences might be considerably greater. In any case, a tendency toward population stabilization would be helpful in coping with environmental problems. Various changes – attitudes about and availability of birth control devices – seem,

---

discharges in 1970 and in 2000 assuming changes in residuals generation coefficients and efficiency of modification likely to come along even without an active abatement policy. C = Residuals discharges in 2000 assuming use of production and modification processes induced by an active abatement policy. Figures for B–L and E–L in row C are approximations, interpolated from the B–H and E–H estimates calculated in detail.

† 10^{15} B.t.u.

SOURCE: U.S. Commission on Population Growth and the American Future, *Population, Resources, and the Environment* (Volume III of Commission research reports), edited by Ronald G. Ridker, Washington, D.C., Government Printing Office, 1972, p. 48.

NOTE: The figures in this table differ from those in the original Population Commission Report in that they contain estimates of the costs of controlling thermal discharges. These were not contained in the original figures. The estimates for thermal discharges were made by Chris Sandberg of Resources for the Future, Inc., Washington, D.C.

Table 8. Annualized Cost of an Active Pollution Abatement Policy under Two Population Assumptions

Pollutant medium	1970	1980 (billions of 1967 dollars)		2000 (billions of 1967 dollars)		2000 compared to 1970				
						Ratio		Annual growth rates		Percentage savings from B-H
		B-H	E-H	B-H	E-H	B-H	E-H	B-H	E-H	
Air	0·45	11·68	11·67	14·87	14·05	32·00	31·20	12·3	12·1	5·52
Water	3·26	9·71	9·55	18·22	16·84	5·58	5·17	5·7	5·4	7·57
Solid	5·18	10·61	10·50	18·77	16·85	3·62	3·25	4·4	4·0	10·23
Total	8·89	32·00	31·72	51·86	47·74	5·83	5·37	5·9	5·6	7·94
Percentage of GNP	1·10	2·60	2·64	1·99	1·97	—	—	—	—	—

SOURCE: U.S. Commission on Population Growth and the American Future, *Population, Resources, and the Environment* (Volume III of Commission research reports), edited by Ronald G. Ridker, Washington, D.C., Government Printing Office, 1972, p. 49.

NOTE: The figures in this table differ from those in the original Population Commission Report in that they contain estimates of the costs of controlling thermal discharges. These were not contained in the original figure. The estimates for thermal discharges were made by Chris Sandberg of Resources for the Future, Inc., Washington, D.C.

in fact, to be carrying the United States rather rapidly in that direction in any case. The nation is now at or slightly below a net reproduction rate of one. If this persists, U.S. population will stabilize at a level about one third higher than at present. Population growth does not seem to be a dominant factor in environmental deterioration in developed countries, although it is by no means irrelevant, especially where population distribution is taken into account. It is, as we will have occasion to see later, the dominant factor in most developing countries.

The costs of environmental improvement will be large and perhaps considerably larger than those shown. Because of the various omissions from the projections, a truly *comprehensive* program of residuals control through national effluent standards might easily cost twice what has been estimated.

Even so, growth of GNP during the time period would keep these costs from being overwhelming. In 1970, actual costs amounted to something like one percent of GNP. Under the higher cost estimates, by 1980 they might be 3 percent and by the year 2000 might have dropped back to around 2 percent. In view of the great number of demands placed upon our national production, these figures are by no means negligible – even given the huge economic capacity of the United States.

They do suggest, however, that if the United States approaches its environmental pollution problems with reasonably efficient programs and permits some time for adjustments to be made, it will be possible to reduce residuals discharge very substantially below current levels while at the same time enjoying the growth of marketable output at only a moderately diminished rate. This would be true whether high or low population growth occurs. Low population growth does yield a considerable saving in pollution control costs and appears to be highly desirable on a number of other grounds.

To this point no similar study has been made in any country other than the United States. However, with due caution concerning such matters as continuing energy shortage – which are difficult to foresee – the conclusions just stated should be broadly applicable to most developed countries. In my view the situation in the developing world may be quite different and I take the matter up in a little detail in the following chapter.

Even for developed countries the conclusions do assume that abatement policy is successful. As we will see in later chapters, environmental policy in many countries has not been notable for either its effectiveness or its efficiency.

As a concluding note I should point out that the United Nations has undertaken a study, Impact of Prospective Environmental Issues and Policies on the International Development, under the leadership of Professor Leontief. Its methodology is very similar to that reported here but it is intended to provide a worldwide perspective. It divides the world into fifteen regions and it contains forty-five economic sectors and twenty-two pollutants (air – 7; water – 12; solids – 3). The results are awaited with great interest.[7]

An Assessment of the Input-Output Approach

As the discussion on pp. 64–77 shows, the input-output approach is of considerable value in environmental analysis. But it also has some substantial shortcomings. Briefly put:

1. The system as discussed up to this point is on a national scale whereas pollution 'problem sheds' tend, as we saw in the last chapter, to be on a regional scale, and sometimes the region is quite small. The regions defined for the United Nations study are aggregations of nations.

2. It has not accounted in a logically complete manner for the residuals generated in production and consumption in the initial attempts at application. In other words the requirements of mass conservation are not met and some residuals may not be accounted for. In principle, however, the pollutant categories could be expanded to include *all* residuals. If the classification were rather detailed, there would be many pollution 'control' industries with zero output.

3. It is usually not correct to think of residuals control as

taking place in a separate residual control sector or even in separate residual control activities – especially in the case of industrial activities. In most industries, process changes resulting in residual control and greater production of usable products are important alternatives to separate residual control activities either outside or within the industry. The only way such changes resulting either from new application of existing technology or development of new technology can be inserted into the input-output approach is by changing coefficients relating residuals generation to output. There is no internal optimizing method for selecting industrial processes in view of their residual generation characteristics and other economic attributes – unless I-O analysis is abandoned for its close relative, activity analysis, which we will call on in later chapters.

4. The model focuses on residuals generation and discharge. It does not analyze what happens to residuals once they enter into the environment nor does it incorporate any consideration of damages. The processes of transportation and transformation in the environment, as affected by hydrological, meteorological, biological, and other natural system conditions have, again as we saw in the last chapter, a significant bearing on the damaging effects of a given amount of residuals discharge.

5. The model focuses on residuals control costs but gives no attention to the value of the loss in function of common property resources when their quality deteriorates due to the effects of residuals discharge.

Some of the deficiencies of the input-output approach as just described can be remedied within its framework, but only at the cost of considerable complication. For example, the limitation associated with the national scale of the model immediately suggests regional input-output models. A number of such models are now being built at various locations in the world. However, even this extension would leave two important limitations: the linearity of the system, which limits the extent of the changes with which it can deal and the one relationship between process and product. Furthermore, the regional model still will not permit identification of specific sources of discharge, their influence on the environment, and their cost of control – considerations which are important in many policy and management situations. In later chapters we will review some microeconomic models which do not have these limitations – but which do, alas, have some of their own.

Supplementing Monetary National Accounts with Material Flow Accounts

Since input-output models are organized by industrial sectors and the national income accounts of many nations are also arranged in the same manner, a full-scale materials balance for input-output analysis will also yield a set of materials accounts coordinate with the national monetary accounts. Indeed such materials accounts might prove quite useful in their own right quite aside from their embodiment in an input-output or activity analysis format.

A strategy to produce materials accounts (an analogous set could be produced for energy) if successfully developed and followed, should, for example, greatly increase the usefulness of the national accounting system as a component of an environmental information system for policy makers and analysts. Specifically, the modification in the accounts would help illuminate the important relation between the size and composition of industrial, agricultural, mining, and forestry, activities and residual generation as well as the relationship between alternative industrial, agricultural, mining and forestry processes and overall residuals generation.

National accounting systems describe the flows of goods and services among 'sectors', defined by a variety of criteria such as geography (e.g., foreign v. domestic account), type of ownership (e.g., public v. private enterprises), type of product produced (e.g., manufacturing v. agriculture), etc. Generally, the goods and service flows are measured in market-determined value units; and, indeed, the existence of a defined market has been an important criterion for inclusion.

The basic strategy for expanding the accounts to include materials flows would be: (1) to expand the list of commodity and service flows to include all physical non-market inputs and outputs (regardless of whether they are conventionally considered as pollutants), and (2) to emphasize process distinctions as the basic criterion of sector definition.

An illustrative application, using such expanded accounts, has been done for the Norwegian economy. Norway was chosen for this exercise[8] because it combines a relatively simple economy with comparatively good data. In this brief discussion it is not appropriate to go into the strategy developed in detail – there is a monograph reporting this[9] – but a summary of the application to the Norwegian pulp and paper industry will give a good flavor of the nature of the analysis and results.

The sectors selected were the Norwegian sulfite pulp industry and the sulfate or kraft pulp industry. These industries were chosen for two reasons. In the first place a comparison of these two accounts after they have been expanded to include the flows of non-market inputs and outputs served well to illustrate the gain in information resulting from defining sectors according to 'process' rather than by 'product'. In the Norwegian accounts, a full accounting of even the market-transacted inputs and outputs is made only for the aggregation of these two sectors: chemical pulp. While sulfite pulp and kraft pulp are similar and, depending on the amount of bleaching, can in fact be close substitutes for certain uses, they differ substantially in their use and generation of 'non-market' inputs and outputs.

The second reason for illustrating the accounting concepts with data for the chemical pulp industry is that available information permitted detailed estimation of the use and generation of 'non-market' outputs without new data.

The latter was possible because previous studies of the pulp and paper industry had yielded flow charts which could be used to identify non-market physical outputs associated with the processes. These flow charts were used in the following manner. For the base year (1969), each of the establishment survey questionnaires of the Norwegian Central Statistical Office for the sulfite industry and the questionnaires for the sulfate industry were examined first to determine: (1) what process was employed (by scanning the list of reported inputs), (2) how much pulp was produced, (3) what proportion of the pulp was bleached, and (4) what proportion was dried. With some modification which need not concern us here, the appropriate flow charts were then applied to each establishment in order to estimate total use of air and water and total generation of a long list of residuals. As many as three flow charts would have to be applied if the establishment in question produced pulp of which some or all was bleached or dried (one chart for pulping, one for bleaching, and one for drying).

Table 9 shows the 'expanded' accounts for the two industrial sectors after the appropriate aggregations were made. It reveals substantial differences between the sulfite and sulfate sectors with respect to their relative use and generation of non-market inputs and outputs. Also, the composition of these non-market items differs substantially from the composition implied for the aggregate of these two sectors.

For example, the large generation of dissolved solids for the chemical pulp industry (776 kg per ton pulp) is dominated by the dissolved solids generated by sulfite processing where more than a ton of these dissolved solids per ton of pulp is produced (the amount of course depends on the extent of recovery of pulping liquor). On the other hand, the sulfate sector generates per ton of pulp far more dissolved chlorine (negligible for the sulfite sector) reflecting the fact that sulfate pulps require relatively more bleaching to achieve the same brightness. The information provided by these detailed 'expanded' accounts shows, among other things, that the amounts and composition of residuals generated in a nation's economic activities can differ greatly depending on the processes selected, even without the installation of pollution control equipment.[10]

Table 9. Comparison of Selected Estimates of 'Non-Market' Inputs and Outputs, Norwegian Pulp Industry (2721 and 2722), 1969

	Sulfite* (2721)		Sulfate (2722)		Total (2721 + 2722)	
	Total (metric tons)	Per ton bleached pulp	Total (metric tons)	Per ton bleached pulp	Total (metric tons)	Per ton bleached pulp
INPUT						
Water	116,849,890	190·730 t	20,026,820	100·802 t	136,576,710	168·341 t
Air	900,682	1·470 t	1,320,210	6·645 t	2,220,892	2·737 t
OUTPUT†						
Liquid						
Water	110,936,073	181·080 t	17,920,271	90·199 t	128,856,344	158·825 t
Total dissolved solids	626,939	1,023·348 kg	3,041	15·307 kg	629,980	776·498 kg
Organic	624,185	1,018·852 kg	514	2·587 kg	624,699	769·985 kg
Inorganic	2,754	4·496 kg	2,527	12·719 kg	5,281	6·509 kg
Fiber	1,804	2·945 kg	112	0·564 kg	1,916	2·362 kg
Carbohydrates plus chlorine combined	0	0	2,621	13·193 kg	2,621	3·231 kg
Gas						
Cl2	238	0·388 kg	23	0·116 kg	261	0·322 kg
Residual sulfides	5	0·008 kg	1,940	9·764 kg	1,945	2·397 kg
SO2 total	40,281	65·760 kg	1,482	7·460 kg	41,763	51·476 kg
From processing‡	32,249	52·640 kg	352	1·772 kg	32,601	40·183 kg
From fuel oil	8,032	13·111 kg	1,130	5·688 kg	9,162	11·293 kg
Solids§	660,000	1,081·198 kg	24,729	124·470 kg	687,109	846·914 kg

TOTAL PULP PRODUCTION, 1969:
Sulfite pulp 198,674 metric tons estimated dry weight   Sulfate pulp 612,635 metric tons estimated dry weight

* These figures reflect the distribution of Norwegian establishments among the various sulfite processes. † Assumes no pollution control equipment or other residuals processing. ‡ Assumes S content 2%. § Includes substantial water content. Dry value for sulfite is approximately 30,600 metric tons and for sulfate approximately 3,000 metric tons.

Economics and the Environment

Materials accounts could be valuable tools for understanding the sources of residuals generation for national or regional economies – how the sources are related to industrial structure, and what tendencies they may exhibit in the future, under alternative assumptions. They would also provide a firmer and more internally consistent data base for projection models, like that discussed earlier in this chapter, than is now available. Work directed toward development of such expanded accounting systems is proceeding at several institutions in the U.S. and elsewhere.

What about Gross National Product and Environment?

The large-scale emergence of environmental concern raises other questions about how nations measure their overall natural economic performance. The chief means up to this point has been the national monetary accounts – gross national product (GNP), net national product (NNP) and related measures.

GNP is designed to measure the production of 'final' goods and services in the economy as a whole. The final 'consumers' of these goods and services are taken to be individuals and households (consumers in the usual sense), government, and nonprofit institutions. The assumption is made that these particular economic agents do not usually use inputs to provide intermediate services (such as, for example, a transportation company would), but rather that they 'use up' the utility embodied in the goods and services which the economy produces. This is a working assumption to which there are numerous exceptions.

At any given time there exists a list of goods and services which is officially defined to be 'final'. These goods and services are exchanged in markets,[11] and therefore there is a corresponding set of market-exchange-determined prices attached to them in some base year as well as in the current period. As time passes, new types of goods and services are often 'wedged in' to help keep the list more nearly complete.

To calculate price-corrected or 'real' GNP, the changing numbers of physical units of the final goods and services produced are multiplied by the unchanged base-period prices – in the U.S. currently those of 1958. The system of national accounts is of the double entry type. In *current* prices the total GNP calculated from the product side must balance GNP calculated as the sum of values added of all activities contributing to GNP (value added is the value of sales minus purchased inputs). This is not true of price-corrected, or *real*, GNP, however, because no deflator has been devised with which the value-added side could be price-corrected.[12] Accordingly, since this discussion deals with real GNP, reference here will be to the product side calculations.

If all salient goods and services were exchanged in markets; if the degree of competition in these markets did not change; if the programs of government and nonprofit institutions did not change in ways that alter substantially the welfare they produce relative to the final goods and services that they absorb; if population stayed constant; and if the distribution of income did not change; then alterations in real NNP (GNP minus capital consumption allowances) could be taken to be a good indicator of changes in the economic welfare of the population.

This is an imposing string of assumptions, however, none of which correspond exactly to reality. To the extent that they are violated, NNP diminishes in usefulness as a welfare measure. In fact, the gap between reality and this set of assumptions is large and significant in some cases (to take a pertinent instance, the existence of common property resources is neglected). Accordingly, the usefulness of NNP as a welfare measure is severely limited.

Of course the system of national accounts, which include much more than total production – for example, the large set of industrial sector breakdowns – has been designed to serve a number of purposes. Even the aggregates serve multiple purposes. They are intended to provide information useful for short-run economic stabilization policies and programs, and they are intended to furnish an estimate of the total production of goods and services which the society has available to meet alternative ends. To be fair, one must recognize that the designers of the accounts thought that at best they would serve to provide only a rough indicator of one dimension of welfare of the society.

But to segregate discussion of the accounts entirely from broader questions of welfare, as some students and practitioners of accounting would do, is a serious mistake. Whether it was the original intent or not, total NNP or GNP is now explicitly or implicitly viewed as an index of welfare change. Furthermore, to understand what the accounts do measure, it is important to recognize explicitly that there are enormous flows of services and disservices, valued by people, which do not enter into market exchange and which therefore are not in the list of final goods and services. Unless care is taken to recognize and observe these flows, NNP may become grossly misleading as to what is happening even to production of potentially marketable goods and services in the economy. For instance, should there be a large-scale transfer from purchases of services (e.g., house painting, grass cutting, construction, household services) to self-provision of these services by households, the NNP would tend to fall whereas it need not be true that production would have declined. The reason that NNP would tend to fall is that the labor going into these self-provided services is not among the defined final products, so that working time shifted toward them 'disappears' from the account. The reason that such services provided to themselves by households are not in the official list is that the accountants have found them too difficult and costly to identify and evaluate – although there could be reason to reconsider this position in view of current data collection and handling techniques and in view of the many attempts to define 'value of time' – in commuting, leisure activities, etc.

It is illuminating to regard objections of the 'environmentalist' to the accounts as revolving around the question of what is or is not in the list of final products. When he argues that GNP overstates growth, the environmentalist implicitly incorporates in his list of final products many entirely real service flows which, however, do not enter into market exchange and accordingly are not in the official list of outputs. Moreover, he implicitly believes that the net effect of bringing omitted service flows into the accounts would be to reduce real product. His implicit list would probably include, for example, the life-support, aesthetic qualities, and convenience of high-quality air, high-quality water, and spacious surroundings – all of which, as we have already seen, are in some of their aspects common property resources not entering into private exchange. At present, the only way in which a change in these service flows could influence the aggregate measures of national output is if their changed quality or quantity made the production of items which are in fact included in the list easier or more difficult. In reality, at least until now, such feedbacks on the national accounts from altered quality of the common property resources are probably trivial compared with the direct effects on the consumer of any deterioration of these resources, i.e., lower-quality air, water, or land. These are nowhere reflected as such in the list of final products, although they may affect some items that are. It is the deterioration of the environmental services not included in the official list that mainly concerns the environmentalist.

That burdens on the common property assets tend to rise with increasing production, unless effective, collectively imposed controls are undertaken, is obvious from observation and from considering the implications of mass balance. There are also some reasons to believe that this rise will tend to be more than proportional to production growth in developed economies. As I have observed several times, conservation of mass implies that all material resources used as inputs to the extractive, productive, and consumptive activities of the economy must appear as residuals. These have in some manner to be returned to the environment – except, of course, for changes in the inventory of mass. If the use of materials should rise faster than production of final goods and services, residuals generation must too. There are counteracting trends affecting materials use in the economy. But the fact that as lower-quality ores are used, greater quantities of unwanted material must be processed to get a given quantity of wanted material, implies a tendency for residuals to rise faster than final production of goods and services 'embodying' materials. Also, energy usage recently has been rising more rapidly than real NNP, and so long as it is obtained primarily from conversion of fossil fuels, this implies a rapidly rising flow of residual materials and gases as well as energy itself. In fact, it appears that net energy output per unit of energy input is decreasing (i.e., deeper wells to extract crude petroleum, where effects of depth are greater than effects of improved technology). Other sources of nonlinearities can be readily identified. Indeed, discontinuities or thresholds are sometimes encountered, as when a water body becomes anaerobic and its ecological functioning changes dramatically for the worse insofar as services such as recreation and fishing are concerned.

Most national accountants would probably agree that if it were practical to extend the list of final goods and services to include service flows from the natural environment this should be done. But the difficulties of doing it are truly imposing.[13] Consequently, it is often concluded that the best we can do is to supplement the real NNP with physical, chemical or biological indicators of the state of the environment. This has been advocated, and seems to be a very good idea – but the methodology is still in a rather primitive state of development. I discuss one such possible extension in the following section.

But are there any less ambitious adjustments that should be made to the monetary accounts themselves? One possibility would be to deduct consumer 'defensive' expenditures from the NNP. If environmental service flows remained constant, then 'defensive' expenditures made voluntarily by consumers would be on the same footing as any other consumer expenditures, being carried to the point where utility gained is equated with alternative cost in utility lost. It would make no difference if environmental service flows are included in the list of final products so far as indication of welfare changes over time is concerned.

If environmental service flows change, however, then it is clear that a list of final products that omits either these flows or the defensive consumer expenditures may give incorrect indication of welfare change over time. If defensive expenditures were simply deducted from the present GNP, the necessary implicit assumption would be – if welfare change is to be correctly indicated – that these defensive expenditures exactly offset the decline in value of the environmental services that 'ought' to but does not now affect the GNP. Even if this strict assumption is not accepted, it probably would still be of general interest to try to estimate consumer defensive expenditures.

Defensive expenditures by industry are already appropriately treated from the exclusion point of view since they never appear in real NNP. There is no need to develop the explanation of this behavior of the accounts here since it is quite similar to that developed in some detail for residuals control expenditures below.

Costs of Meeting Environmental Standards

Up to this point we have been discussing common property environmental resources, *vis-à-vis* the national accounts, as though their use were completely unrestricted. In the United States, this would have been a pretty good approximation of reality until recently but public policy is now proceeding rapidly to the regulation of the use of these resources for residuals disposal. It is intended to lead to the development of ambient environmental standards and is already leading toward the development of discharge standards on both regional and national bases. If these standards become effective they will, as our discussion of the projection model has shown, give rise to large expenditures for the control of residuals generation and discharge. The time pattern these expenditures will follow is uncertain, but the projections suggest that they will 'hump' in the next five to ten years during the cleanup phase. Thereafter, they may decline slightly for a time, following which they may tend to rise nonlinearly with increasing input. The question is, how should these expenditures be treated in the NNP?

Before trying to answer, it is necessary to understand how such expenditures are treated under present practice. The, perhaps surprising, fact is that they are handled differently depending on whether they are incurred by consumers and government on the one hand or by industry on the other. In the following discussion I will neglect expenditures for pollution control directly by consumers, because I think they will be small (with one major exception which I discuss later), and in any case no different principles are involved for them.

The differential effect on the accounts of industry and government expenditures for residuals control can be illustrated by a simple example, shown in Table 10. Assume an economy in which only two commodities, haircuts and bread, are produced in the base period (the citizens will be nude but well clipped). The list of final products will, therefore, consist of haircuts and bread. Assume further that the production of haircuts generates no significant amount of residuals but that the production of bread does do so. Suppose also that barbers can be diverted to control residuals if that is desired (the bread can be produced with less residuals if more labor is used).

In the base period there is a standard for the discharge of residuals but the production of bread is just low enough to avoid violating it. In period 1, a change in family composition causes a shift in demand from haircuts to bread together with an increase in residuals. If there had been no standard for discharge of residuals, the situation would be that labeled 1a. That is, $500 of productive services would have been diverted from the production of haircuts to bread and residuals discharge would have increased.

We have assumed, however, that there is a standard for residuals discharge, however, and it is not, of course, being met in situation 1a. If it is met by a diversion *within the industry* of barbers to residuals control, NNP will register a decline as compared with period 0. This is shown by 1b. In contrast, if the government hires these same men to limit the discharge of residuals to the standard level, NNP will show no decline, as

Table 10. Example Showing Effects of Industry and Government Expenditures on National Accounts

		Q	P_0	NNP
			$	$
Period 0	Haircuts	100	10	1,000
	Bread	100	10	1,000
				2,000
Period 1a	H	50	10	500
(as it would be without residuals control)	B	150	10	1,500
				2,000
Period 1b	H	25	10	250
(as it would be if industry had to control residuals by diverting 25 extra barbers)	B	150	10	1,500
				1,750
Period 1c	H	25	10	250
(as it would be if government hired the extra bakers and set them to controlling residuals)	B	150	10	1,500
	G	25	10	250
				2,000

in 1c. The reason for these results is that there is nothing in the list of final products corresponding to residual controls, and so the activities directed toward that end cannot be reflected in NNP evaluated at base year prices. However, since government is in effect regarded as a final consumer, its expenditure for the barbers (converted into residuals controllers) is included in NNP.

Economics and the Environment

Observations on Treating the Costs of Environmental Standards

If we visualize a situation in which governments establish effective environmental standards which must be continuously met, NNP treatment of industry outlays would seem to indicate the direction of welfare change more appropriately than the present treatment of similar government outlays. The reason is that the net outlays made for residuals control can be viewed as simply being necessary to maintain the service flow naturally provided by the common property assets. In that sense they could be regarded as expenditures necessary to maintain the unproduced capital stock. Failure to treat them in this way could result in an anomalous situation in which a progressively larger share of production would have to be devoted simply to environmental-quality maintenance with NNP all the time continuing to rise. It would be hard to claim that this rise could in any way be regarded as indicating increased welfare even in the limited sense of increased availability of marketable goods and services contributing to consumer satisfaction. If this view were accepted, the appropriate procedure would be to continue to treat industry outlays for control as at present but to change the procedures in such a way that government outlays for control could be treated similarly to business outlays. This would require identification of government expenditures for residuals control, which should not be very difficult, and their subtraction from the present NNP for presentation as an auxiliary series.

The one major exception to the view that consumer expenditures to control residuals will be small is the cost of controlling emissions from automobiles. The approach which has recently been adopted in the United States is essentially to add items called control devices to the list of final products in the official series. If this were not done, the price deflator would tend in the direction of reduced real production of automobiles.

This approach is inconsistent with the view concerning appropriate industrial outlays expressed above. To treat the consumer symmetrically, he would be regarded as producing a service for himself, the production of which generates residuals. In the interest of maintaining the service flow from common property assets he is required to incur a cost. To add such costs to NNP over time would have the same anomalous results as those already described in the case of industry. In this case, as with industry, the accounts should be permitted to function as they normally would.

As I have already indicated, my view on these matters appears to be contrary to the views of some experts in national income accounting.[14] Their position apparently rests on two major considerations. The first reflects the special problem of dealing with a catch-up phase such as we are now experiencing in connection with the control of residuals discharge. When new standards for a higher environmental quality first become effective, some of the expenditure will result in actual improvements in environmental quality over its current state and the benefits of the improvement would presumably exceed its costs. Thus, if control expenditures are not included in the accounts, the anomalous situation would arise that the population actually experiences an improvement in welfare while the associated influence of NNP is downward. Some have proposed that the list of final products be expanded to include industrial outlays for residuals control to avoid this situation. For reasons already explained, this approach appears to be in conflict with that appropriate from the longer-term welfare indicator point of view. It would seem preferable not to add the outlays but to prorate them over a longer period of time, especially to earlier periods when NNP tended to be overstated as an indicator of welfare.

The argument is also made that to exclude production directed toward residuals control would distort labor productivity series which, at the aggregative level, are obtained by dividing NNP by man-hours worked. The proper point of view on this is highly contingent on what is regarded as being measured by labor productivity. If it is taken to be the output per man-hour net of the output needed to maintain the service flows of all assets – private and common – then it is wholly appropriate that productivity should tend to fall if a larger proportion of total effort has to be expended in order to meet environmental standards.

Conclusions on National Accounts

The national product and income accounts are not directed very closely to the single objective of measuring changes in social welfare. Furthermore, considerable uncertainty surrounds some of the possible changes that have been discussed – both as to implications and practicality. Accordingly, it would appear to be unwise to change the official definitions at this time. However, expenditure series should be prepared that reflect, at least in part, the growth of activities and expenditures that seem to be needed simply to maintain environmental quality and which would permit various types of adjustment to be made by individual players of the accounting game as they deem appropriate.

To this end, I would suggest the regular preparation and publication of the following series:

1. Industrial expenditures for residuals control.
2. Government expenditures for residuals control.
3. Consumer expenditures for residuals control.
4. Consumer, industry, and government defensive expenditures.

None of these is prepared currently, and the preparation of each offers considerable difficulty, but these can probably be overcome. It would probably be desirable to publish auxiliary series supplementing the current official series. The following are some of the possibilities, with all series assumed to be price corrected:

1. GNP – including all residuals control in the list of final products.
2. NNP_1 – GNP minus net depreciation of private assets.
3. NNP_2 – GNP minus net depreciation of private assets and minus the non-industry cost of residuals control and defensive expenditures (and in principle all other costs which

may be induced by the growth process itself, for example, congestion costs).

It would be a mistake, however, to think that any such adjustments can come close to indicating changes in 'true' welfare so far as flows of environmental services are concerned. This is because an essential ingredient is lacking – a valuation for the environmental services themselves and, on capital account, an expression for decreases or increases in the value of the corresponding natural assets. Fortunately research is actively proceeding on the possibilities of remedying these deficiencies.

Chapter 4
World Perspectives

Environment and the Developing World

Environmental problems are often thought of as being uniquely characteristic of highly developed industrialized societies and it is certainly true, as the discussion so far has already indicated, that they exist there in high degree. But, it may well be that within the next few decades, the environment in developing countries will become at least as large an issue as it is in the developed world today. This may seem paradoxical in view of the dominant position of developed countries in the use of resource materials and the associated discharge of waste materials and energy to environmental media. But there are two main reasons that may call for a significant shift of attention to developing countries in the near future.

The first is that the economically advanced countries may have turned the corner in their ability to cope with pollution-related environmental problems. If they are reasonably successful in the further development of policy, institutions, and technology, their environment, in a pollution sense, should, as the input-output study reported in the previous chapter suggests, improve considerably in the coming few decades. If it does not they will have only themselves to blame.[1]

The second reason is the situation existing in many developing countries, where there are complex developing environmental pressures, the result of rapid population growth, unprecedented rates of urbanization, and the urgent need to pursue economic development 'at whatever cost'.

The most appalling aspect of mankind's future is the tremendous rate of population growth in those parts of the world which are already desperately poor. To go from this situation to one in which there is a low birth rate/low death rate equilibrium will be very difficult indeed. Furthermore, if the world does finally manage to arrive at such an equilibrium through non-catastrophic means it will be at a much higher level of population – probably around fifteen thousand million persons – than the optimum for the human condition. One feels a sense of helplessness in the face of this because there really does not seem to be anything that can be done about it, at least not for a very long time to come.

To understand why there is this tremendous inertia in the face of the recent rapid population growth in developing countries it is necessary to look at the reasons for it. It appears, although this is controversial, to be caused primarily by the introduction of a very specialized technology, that of disease control, to the developing countries, mostly after the Second World War.[2] Because of this technology, death rates quickly dropped, particularly among infants and children. Unfortunately birth rates have remained generally at a high level and even increased – although there are a few cases of decreases as well. Today the world's seven largest nations have about three fifths of the world's population. These are China, India, the U.S.S.R., the United States, Pakistan, and Indonesia. Only two of these have reached advanced stages of economic development and the population of the poor countries is growing much faster than that of the richer ones.

One result, which some would view as a curse, of a reduction in infant mortality is that we now have an extremely youthful population in the developing countries. On the average about 40 percent of the population in these countries is below fifteen years of age. There are about seventy-five dependents for every hundred persons of working age (fifteen to sixty-four years). This foreshadows a long period of continuing population increase as these massive numbers move through the child-bearing ages, even if net birth rates for those in these age brackets should fall. By contrast, in the economically developed world, because both mortality and the birth rate have been declining for a long time, only about 30 percent of the population is under fifteen. While this is a much better situation than that in the developing world, nevertheless in some countries like the United States youthful populations will drive population growth upward for a long time. For example, in the United States the net reproduction rate has recently approached unity and even fallen slightly below it. Should this situation persist the nation's population will still increase by about one third before equilibrium is reached some time in the next century. This is because the young people move into child-bearing age brackets and will be represented there in disproportionate numbers for many years.

But, to return to the situation in the developing countries. The projections displayed in Table 11 show population growth in the developing countries to be about five times as great as in the more developed countries during the second half of this century. Probably more than three quarters of the world's population will live in poor countries by the end of this century as contrasted with about two thirds at the present time. Furthermore, as population continues to increase after the turn of the century the balance will weigh even more heavily in the direction of low-income countries.

Accompanying these large increases in population are unprecedented rates of urbanization in the developing world. Many of the world's largest cities are already found there and they are growing at rates far in excess of any in the developed world. From what has already happened in a number of cases with which we are all familiar it is clear that the combined forces of population growth and urbanization will put tremendous strains on ecological systems. Environmental conditions have deteriorated drastically, and, I think, dangerously, even in relatively advanced cities like São Paulo, Mexico City, and Seoul just to mention a few. One sees the results in terms of turbid and acrid-smelling atmospheres and severely polluted water, but what is not so easily seen may be just as significant. Immense numbers of different kinds of persistent chemical substances which can be highly toxic at low concentrations are being continuously discharged to the environment. I will return to this point shortly.

The basic sanitation problem presented by the great masses of people are immense, and the sheer congestion with its

Table 11. Population Estimates According to the U.N. 'Medium' Variant, 1960–2000, for Major Areas and Regions of the World

Major areas and regions	Population (in thousands)			
	1960	1970	1985	2000
World total	2,998,180	3,591,773	4,746,409	6,129,734
More developed regions*	976,414	1,082,150	1,256,179	1,441,402
Less developed regions†	2,021,766	2,509,623	3,490,230	4,688,332
A. East Asia	794,144	910,524	1,104,903	1,287,270
B. South Asia	865,247	1,106,905	1,596,329	2,170,648
C. Europe	424,657	453,918	491,891	526,968
D. U.S.S.R.	214,400	245,700	296,804	353,085
E. Africa	272,924	345,949	513,026	767,779
F. Northern America	198,664	226,803	283,105	354,007
G. Latin America	212,431	283,263	435,558	638,111
H. Oceania	15,713	18,711	24,793	31,866

* Including Europe, the U.S.S.R., Northern America, Japan, temperate South America, Australia and New Zealand.

† Including East Asia less Japan, South Asia, Africa, Latin America less temperate South America, and Oceania less Australia and New Zealand.

SOURCE: World Population Prospects as assessed in 1963 *United Nations Population Studies*, No. 41.

associated noise, inconvenience, and high propensity for disease transmission are clearly great and rapidly increasing difficulties. Indeed one of the very striking aspects of environmental problems in developing countries is the fearsome rate at which they are getting worse.

But it may prove to be the indirect effects of such extreme rates of population growth and urbanization which will put the most severe strains on the environment. In many instances these strains will be more than locally or even nationally significant.

The cold fact is that most developing countries must strive as hard as they can to achieve economic development if they are to make any progress at all in improving the material circumstances of their people. Indeed if they do not the result would quickly be massive starvation. One of the most worrying things about this situation is that developing countries may be disposed to take very dangerous risks and sometimes they will be aided and abetted in this by interests in developed countries, both private and governmental, because the latter see opportunities for operating in developing countries in ways in which would not be permissible at home.

Some of the potential types of dice game with nature can already be identified. Especially in view of the energy crisis which beset the world toward the middle seventies, and the associated high costs of fuels, many of the major developing countries are disposed to push hard for the development of nuclear energy – with much encouragement from the atomic energy agencies of the nuclear powers. Despite reassurances from the world's atomic energy establishments, nuclear energy must be regarded as very dangerous. Reactor failures, problems of storing nuclear wastes, the diversion of nuclear materials weaponry, and the presence of terrorists groups willing to take advantage of any situation are real and tough problems. As we know so well from experience, the environmental problem posed by nuclear radiation cannot readily be limited to any sort of confined area like a nation state. I will return to these matters and the problems they present for economic analysis later in this chapter.

Another kind of technology that may be mentioned in this connection is the use of persistent pesticides in agriculture. They are cheap, they are effective, and many of them stay around to reach higher concentrations higher up the food chain for many, many years. When the pressures for growing food are as severe as they are at present in many developing countries the temptation to use a cheap technology even though it may have long-term and indirect adverse effects will be immense.

A closely related matter ˮconcerns trace materials of industrial origin. Japan is an excellent case in point. In its single-minded push for development Japan has poisoned land and water surrounding major cities and industrial establishments at a rate not heretofore seen in the world. Mercury, cadmium, polychlorinated biphenyls (PCBs) and probably many other substances not yet identified persist in the land and in the water, and make their way through food chains. As a result, over a hundred people have died from eating contaminated food (pp. 45–6). Some of the more subtle effects on human beings are only now starting to come to light.

Another effect of this pressure for development may well be the massive destruction of certain types of 'renewable' resources. As well as the large-scale destruction of tropical forests, cultivation of less fertile, sub-marginal lands is clearly likely, with associated adverse effects on soils, species extinction and, speculatively at least, adverse effects on the world's atmosphere and climate. There is, for example, by now considerable evidence that economic development efforts financed by well-intentioned Western aid have contributed greatly to development of desert conditions in the Sahelian zone of West Africa.[3] In this connection it may also be noted that 80 percent of the households in the developing world use wood for fuel and its use is decreasing much more slowly than it did in the developed world. Widespread destruction of the remaining trees in the more arid parts of the developing world can, therefore, be expected.

Clearly, this type of environmental insult could be of more than national significance. The world community will therefore take an interest in them whether the nations that perpetrate them like it or not.

Recognition of this last point has lead some developing countries to adopt a quite understandably defensive and nationalistic attitude on environmental questions. In capsule form the argument is as follows: You (the developed countries) have done your species extinction, taken your risks, and used your resources promiscuously to achieve development, and now you are rich and sensitive about your health and your surroundings and want to stay at the top of the heap. You do not want to give us (the developing countries) the opportunity to use our resources in such a way as to improve our material wealth if it involves any risks or destruction of things that you regard as valuable. Once we have developed as you did then we will begin to give some consideration to environmental questions. Then we, too, may have resources such as you now have which make this possible without much sacrifice of our material welfare.[4]

There is undeniably a lot of truth in this argument but major qualifications which cannot be ignored must be registered.

First, there are clearly some important international concerns. I listed only a few of them. But, it is the responsibility of the whole world community to give them attention and try to deal with them. One hopes that the new Environmental Program of the United Nations will provide at least a beginning of an institutional arrangement for doing this.

Second, population control is extremely urgent for *both* environmental *and* economic development reasons. The drain on the economic system of having such a high dependency ratio is immense; under such circumstances it is difficult, probably impossible, to improve substantially the quality of human beings via improved health care and education. From the broader view point of the world society the idea of a world population of fifteen or twenty thousand million people, the vast majority having to devote all of its talents and energies to getting enough food to stay alive, is simply appalling. I will return shortly to the question of whether this will even be possible.

Thirdly, the attitude characterized, or perhaps almost parodied, above may cause opportunities for beneficial and practical environmental protection to be overlooked. It has been amply demonstrated by many economic studies that prevention of environmental problems is often much cheaper than cure. We know, for example, from a number of detailed studies of industry that it is much cheaper to design processes which are low in destructive discharges than to try to modify those waste streams once they have been generated.[5]

It appears then, that it is becoming very important for developing countries explicitly to include environmental considerations in development planning and to develop a much higher level of environmental expertise than now exists. The latter is needed not only for planning purposes but also in the development of intelligent policy making and to provide an independent view of both developmental and environmental investments. Most if not all developing countries are excessively dependent on foreign consultants and on multi-national corporations. There should be some machinery for the independent assessment of technological processes and the opportunity to develop technologies more suited to the circumstances of developing countries than are those now being directly transplanted from the developed world. Environmental problems are not limited to the developed world. The developing countries will find them crowding in from all directions in the next few decades.

Will Malthusian Checks Prevent Development?

But, one may ask, will population growth in the developing countries in fact continue for long, or will resource scarcity bring it to a halt in the near future? The well-known *Limits to Growth*[6] study concluded that Malthusian checks are imminent. That may be so, but many – and I am among them – do not believe that the analysis presented in the study actually sheds much light on the question. A short appendix to this chapter gives some arguments for this point of view.

The question is nevertheless real and will not go away. Unfortunately, at this stage of our knowledge treatment of it is necessarily partial and inevitably somewhat anecdotal. But there are some things that can be said about it.

Economics and the Environment

The Minimum Imperatives – Energy and Food

Let us assume that the world economy is capable of operating
on much reduced quantities of non-renewable natural
resource commodities, and that the rich–poor gap, which
seems inevitable, can be maintained without catastrophe.
Even so, the world, if it is to have any hope of achieving a
sustainable economy at a population level of fifteen thousand
million persons, must be able to produce energy and food in
huge amounts – even if much less wasteful ways of using the
former are found.

It does not appear that energy as such will prove to be an
ultimate constraining factor. While available reserves of
petroleum and natural gas must inevitably begin to run out –
probably by the end of the century – there are very large
reserves of low-quality coal, lignite, and oil shale, which could,
if society is willing to tolerate what is sure to be a substantial
amount of unavoidable environmental degradation, supply
large amounts of energy for a number of decades, probably at
something like present (high, 1974) prices.

The developed countries have put their long-term hopes
primarily in nuclear power, and this may become a major
source for developing countries too. High-quality uranium
sources are limited, also, but plutonium breeder reactors
could make it possible to extend vastly the availability of
nuclear fuel. Thorium, also, is a potential source of nuclear
power, and vast quantities exist in recoverable quantities in
granite. Fusion power may be limited by the availability of
lithium-6 (to produce tritium), rather than deuterium, but
lithium is not a rare element on the earth's surface. Both solar
and geothermal power can also be tapped in large quantities –
though their cost is uncertain. Technologically speaking, it is
probably feasible to capture solar power outside the earth's
atmosphere and ship it back to earth either in the form of a
high-intensity coherent electromagnetic beam or as synthetic
chemical fuels. (It must be remembered that we are speaking

of a scenario of the distant future in which space technology is highly developed and by no means exotic.)

Also, it does not appear that food availability as such will necessarily be limiting in the very long run if population stabilizes – leaving aside the question of whether the necessary technology can be developed rapidly enough. Food is, basically, biologically available energy – in the form of carbohydrate, protein, or fat – plus some needed chemical building blocks which the human organism cannot synthesize from basic elements. These essential components of food include some twenty amino acids. Food must also include a number of minerals such as sodium, potassium, calcium, phosphorus, and iron, of course.

Much remains to be learned about the chemical synthesis of amino acids and vitamins, but most of the basic steps have already been duplicated in the laboratory. There is absolutely no reason to doubt that, in the far-off future, food could be manufactured in a chemical plant, given the availability of sufficient energy, capital equipment, and knowledge. This is not to imply that synthetic food would necessarily replace food derived from biological origins. Certainly as far ahead as one can foresee, the latter is likely to be both more palatable and more economical to produce. Ultimately, however, chemical synthesis of food may have to be introduced too.

Food production, whether based on photosynthesis or chemical synthesis, is evidently energy-limited. We are confronted with an apparent paradox here. World food production based on photosynthesis is apparently quite limited. Some experts have predicted world-wide famine within a decade or two. Others, citing the 'green revolution', are much more optimistic.[7] But it is painfully clear that conventional agriculture is beginning to approach its limits, and that while the present world population could probably be fed adequately (though two out of three people on the globe are now receiving inadequate diets), and conceivably even the population of year 2000 and beyond could be supported if new strains of grain and the use of fertilizers spread rapidly enough through

Asia and Latin America, it is almost impossible to see how conventional agriculture could support fifteen thousand million people at the present U.S. or European dietary standard, with 40 percent (or more) of dietary calories derived from animal sources. But unconventional agriculture perhaps could.

By unconventional agriculture, I mean a system based mainly on harvested or recycled cellulose – rather than carbohydrates – which is converted by bacterial action into feed for cattle, hogs, poultry, or fish. All solid organic wastes, whether cornstalks and cobs, brush, grass clippings and leaves, food processing wastes, waste paper, animal manure, and even sewage, can be converted into animal feed and thus recycled without benefit of additional photosynthesis. The overall efficiency of conversion of solar energy to food can thus be increased manyfold – probably by an order of magnitude – without increasing the intensity of cultivation or altering the primary ecology. Whatever agricultural processes might be found compatible with maintaining at a high level a population of fifteen thousand million indefinitely, one thing is clear – they must be arranged so that much less pesticide and plant nutrient is lost to the environment relative to output than with 'developed' agriculture at the present. The results of failing to achieve this would be profoundly destructive to ecological systems.

Some More Big Questions

I will not comment further about how mankind got itself into an idiotic race between population growth and technological development. But if technical progress can be sustained or accelerated, despite the incentives which seem inherent in stationary societies to slow it down, it is not on the face of it ridiculous to suppose that an ultimate world population of fifteen thousand million people could be maintained at at least a minimal standard of living. This would necessarily use very large amounts of energy, but not so large as to damage greatly the habitability of the planet, while at the same time having drastically lower material throughout per unit product than the developed countries of today.

But one cannot conclude on even this vaguely optimistic note without calling attention to two more truly major reservations about the ability of mankind to achieve this relatively favorable outcome.[8] The first is that it is questionable whether the potential for technological progress is truly limitless for practical purposes. The second is that coping with the increased human interdependence and the risks of some of the more promising new technologies may be beyond the capacity of human institutions.

Is Technological Progress Limitless?

One may suspect that scientific research and development is ultimately subject to diminishing returns. The classical economists of the eighteenth and nineteenth centuries felt that economic growth would be brought to an end as an increasing amount of labor was applied to a fixed resource stock so that, eventually, further increments of labor would not yield any additional output. Actually, this dismal result was avoided – or at least put off for a long time – mainly due to technology. Labor productivity has been rising fast and almost steadily since the beginning of the industrial revolution. In fact, as we have seen, increased productivity has been the main element in economic growth. To get this result, the developed economies have been increasing technology as a production factor faster than the other inputs for a long period of time. Most projections of economic activity and resources utilization implicitly assume that we will continue to achieve at least constant returns from scientific and technological input. In other words, labor productivity will continue to rise as it has in the past few decades. In the United States this means at about 3 percent per year. This may be quite justifiable if one is looking relatively few decades into the future. But on the longer time scale doubts may well arise, even if institutional arrangements can successfully sustain a higher level of sceintific enterprise and innovative behavior.

The noted classical economists, Malthus and Ricardo, were products of the Enlightenment, which restored western man's confidence in his ability to understand the workings of the world through reason. And their works are strong testimonials to the power of this confidence. But the scientific method, the Enlightenment's systematic, analytic engine, was just beginning to evolve. A method of discovery was being discovered. It is not hard to understand why the classical economists could not grasp fully the implications of this other product of the Enlightenment. The industrial revolution at first produced enormous productivity gains through the application of reason and ingenuity to mechanical devices without the benefit of systematic science. For example, Cartwright, who made the first power loom and other important textile equipment, was a clergyman who wrote verses, and Benjamin Huntsman, who first made cast steel, was a clockmaker. It was only gradually that industrial innovation moved beyond the basically mechanical and began to incorporate more esoteric accomplishments of formal science, such as chemistry.[9] But once it took hold, science continued to propel productivity forward despite the fact that some of the more obvious improvements permitted by the spirit of the Enlightenment had been made. As Sir John Hicks, the eminent British economist, has stated in his recent commentary on economic history:

There might have been no Crompton and Arkwright, and still there could have been an industrial revolution; in its later stages it would have been much the same. The impact of science, stimulating the technicians, developing new sources of power, using power to create more than human accuracy, reducing the cost of machines until they were available for a multitude of purposes; this surely is the essential novelty . . .[10]

The application of science to industry has continued to increase the productivity of labor and more or less steadily push back resources scarcity, despite huge increases in labor and capital inputs. Perhaps it will continue to do so for a long time to come. But it would seem strange if the application of effort to science and technology were entirely immune from diminishing returns. One may speculate that the return from the applications of resources to scientific discovery and technological development in certain important instances has already begun to diminish. For example, most of the basic mathematical concepts which are used in today's applied science were well known by the beginning of this century.

While there are always new discoveries to be made, although not necessarily at an undiminished pace, there are some basic reasons why quantitative technological improvements may require greater efforts to bring about and why the percentage rate of improvement in many fields, as measured in terms of functional indices, will inevitably begin to decline. The efficiency of energy conversion is a good illustration of the point. Power plants have increased in efficiency from 1 to 2 percent to more than 40 percent in the most advanced power plants today. Thus we have already experienced a forty-fold improvement in two centuries. The next thirty years may conceivably see a further increase to 60 percent overall efficiency, but this only represents a 50 percent improvement over the present level. Obviously the rate of advance thereafter must slow down markedly if only because 100 percent efficiency is the absolute upper limit, and it can never actually be reached. In many other areas, also, this same phenomenology holds true.[11]

Should we encounter strongly diminishing returns to scientific technological development, it may well prove to be impossible to converge to a stable, sustainable economy of fifteen thousand million persons in which labor productivity is relatively high. Indeed it may not be possible to sustain indefinitely that level of population at any worthwhile level of living. Thus, science and technology is not the villain but the potential hero of the piece, if it can be properly developed and directed and if it continues to be highly productive of improved ways of doing things. But unfortunately we cannot have high confidence that it will do so indefinitely.

Economics and the Environment

Can Human Institutions Cope with New Technology?

A second nagging doubt stems from the imperfections of social organization and social institutions. I have already hinted at this but it seems useful to spell it out a little. It is a commonplace that industrialization has increased interdependence. So while it can produce high levels of material welfare, it can do so only if a high degree of social order is maintained. The system becomes not only vulnerable to breakdowns in the technological chain, but also to human error and malevolence. Some of the technologies which can be foreseen for simultaneously increasing productivity over the long-term future and reducing dependence on non-renewable resources seem to carry with them huge extensions of interdependence in both space and time. Even without an all-out catastrophic war, which we cannot rule out, such interdependence may come to be viewed as intolerable and may severely limit the application of certain technologies.

Another possibility, which I raised earlier in this chapter, is that certain potentially harmful technologies may be presumed to be necessary and will be applied anyway – with possibly disastrous results. As noted, this may be particularly a possibility in the less developed countries (see pp. 100–102).

That these problems are not remote and hypothetical is amply demonstrated by the debate going on even now over whether the world should become dependent upon a large-scale nuclear fission energy economy. Some regard this technology as the only one which could possibly sustain the enormous energy demands which future conditions will entail. Others are alarmed by the prospect.

The Atomic Energy Commission in the United States has suggested that the problem of whether or not to develop such a large-scale fission economy can be solved by benefit-cost analysis.[12] Benefit-cost is a mode of microeconomic analysis which was originally developed in the United States for the economic evaluation of water-resources projects. There have now been several decades of experience with its application. It proceeds by simulating a market where none exists, for the output of the public project, and comparing streams of benefits, measured by consumers' 'willingness to pay',[13] with costs. These two streams are annualized so that they become comparable. The use of benefit-cost analysis has now expanded beyond the water resources area and beyond the United States and is used in the evaluation of different sorts of public works in several countries. I will show some applications to environmental quality problems in later chapters.

But this frequently very valuable mode of analysis cannot answer the most important policy questions surrounding the issue of whether to develop a large-scale world-wide nuclear energy economy. This is so because these questions are of a deep ethical character. Benefit-cost analysis certainly cannot solve such questions and may well obscure them.

Since most of this book is about how economics can help improve understanding of environmental problems and policies, a discussion of this issue provides a useful opportunity to look at some of its limitations.

The ethical questions have to do with whether society should strike the Faustian Bargain – the evocative description of Alvin Weinberg, former director of an Atomic Energy Agency laboratory – with the atomic scientists and engineers.[14] If a technology as unforgiving as large-scale nuclear fission energy production is adopted, it will impose a burden of continuous monitoring and sophisticated management of a dangerous material, essentially for ever. The penalty of not bearing this burden may be unparalleled disaster. This irreversible burden would be imposed even if nuclear fission were to be used only for a few decades, a mere instant in the pertinent time scales.

Clearly, there are some major advantages from using nuclear fission technology, otherwise it would not have so many well-intentioned and intelligent advocates. Residual heat is produced to a greater extent by current nuclear-generating plants than fossil-fuel-fired ones. But otherwise the environmental impact of routine operation of the nuclear fuel cycle, including the burning of the fuel in the reactor, can very likely be brought to a lower level than will be possible with fossil-fuel-fired plants. In general, the cost of nuclear and fossil fuel energy, with the latter having a fuel cycle in which residuals generation is controlled to a high degree, do not seem to be so greatly different. These advantages, plus the bureaucratic interests of atomic energy agencies, have given rise to a strong push to develop nuclear energy although this has not proceeded as rapidly as many experts predicted. However, the western European commitment is even stronger than that of the United States and, if things go according to plan, few new non-nuclear power stations will be built there in the future. A number of developing countries have come to lay their hopes for future energy abundance almost entirely on nuclear power.

Unfortunately, the advantages of fission are much more readily quantified in the format of a benefit-cost analysis than are the associated hazards. Therefore there exists the danger that the benefits may seem more real. Furthermore, it is a basic assumption of benefit-cost analysis that the redistributional effects of the project are, for one or another reason, inconsequential. Here we are speaking of hazards which may afflict humanity many generations hence, and of national and international distributional questions which can neither be neglected as inconsequential nor evaluated and weighted on any known theoretical or empirical basis. This means that technical people, be they physicists or economists, cannot legitimately base the decision to generate such hazards on technical analysis. Society confronts a moral problem of great profundity.

In his excellent article referred to above, Weinberg emphasized that part of the Faustian Bargain is that to use fission technology safely, society must exercise great vigilance and the highest levels of quality control, continuously and indefinitely. In part this is because of the great hazards involved in imperfect operation of reactors and the nuclear fuel cycle. In particular the breeder reactor involves large quantities of plutonium, which is one of the most toxic substances known to man and which could be used to fabricate nuclear weapons. As the fission energy economy grows, many plants will be built and operated in countries with comparatively low levels of technological competence, a greater propensity to take risks, and a strong desire to reduce their dependence on foreign oil which proved so disastrous in the middle seventies. Transportation of hazardous materials will increase greatly, and safety will become the province of the sea captain as well as the scientist. Moreover, even in countries with higher levels of technological competence, continued success can lead to reduced vigilance. We should recall that the United States space program managed to incinerate astronauts due to a very straightforward accident in a highly technological operation, where the utmost precautions were allegedly being taken.

But even deeper moral questions surround the storage of high-level radioactive wastes. Estimates of how long these waste materials must be isolated from the biosphere apparently contain major elements of uncertainty, but current ones seem to agree on 'at least two hundred thousand years'.

In the United States, great importance was laid on storing these wastes in salt formations, and a site for experimental storage was selected at Lyons, Kansas. This particular site proved to be defective. Oil companies had drilled the area full of holes, and there had also been solution mining in the area which left behind a hitherto unknown residue of water. But comments of the Kansas Geological Survey raised far deeper and more general questions about the behavior of the pertinent formations under stress and the operation of geological forces on them. The ability of solid earth geophysics to predict for the time scales required proves very limited. Furthermore, there is the political factor. An increasingly informed and environmentally aware public is likely to resist the location of a permanent storage facility anywhere.

Because the site selected proved defective, and possibly in anticipation of political problems, emphasis is now being placed in the United States upon design of surface storage facilities intended to last a hundred years or so, while the search for a permanent site continues. These surface storage sites would require continuous monitoring and management of a most sophisticated kind. A complete cooling system breakdown would soon prove disastrous; even greater tragedies can be imagined.

Just to get an idea of the scale of disaster that could be envisaged, consider the following scenario for the United States. Political factors force the federal government to rely on a single above-ground storage site for all high-level radioactive waste accumulated until the year 2000. Some of the more obvious possibilities would be existing storage sites like Hanford or Savannah. A tactical nuclear weapon hits the site and vaporizes a large fraction of the contents of this storage area. The weapon could come from one of the principal nuclear powers, a lesser developed country with one or more nuclear power plants, or it might be crudely fabricated from black-market plutonium by a terrorist organization. The radiation fallout from such an event would exceed that from all past nuclear testing by a factor of 500 or so, with radiation doses exceeding annual dose from natural background radiation by an order of magnitude. This would be a drastically unfavorable, and long-lasting, change in the environment of the majority of mankind. That massive numbers of deaths might result seems clear, but the exact magnitude of the disaster is apparently quite uncertain.

Furthermore, by the year 2000 high-level wastes would have just begun to accumulate in the United States. Estimates for 2020 put them at about three times the 2000 figure.

The problem appears to be no closer to solution in Europe than it is in the United States. For example a major international processing plant located in Belgium generated 850 cubic meters of high-level waste during its period of operation. Now that it has shut down it is very unclear who is responsible for the wastes or what will be done with them.[15]

Sometimes, analogies are used to suggest that the burden placed upon future generations by the 'immortal' wastes is really nothing so very unusual. The Pyramids are cited as an instance where a very long-term commitment was made to the future and the dikes of Holland as one where continuous monitoring and maintenance is required indefinitely. These examples do not seem at all apt. They do not have the same quality of irreversibility as the problem we are considering, and no major portions of humanity are dependent on them for their very existence. With sufficient effort, the Pyramids could have been dismantled and the Pharaohs cremated if a changed doctrine so demanded – also it is worth recalling that most of the tombs were looted already in ancient times. After the Second World War the Dutch dikes were in fact opened. Tragic property losses, but no destruction of human life, ensued. Perhaps a more apt example of the scale of the Faustian Bargain would be the irrigation system of ancient Persia. When Tamerlane destroyed it in the fourteenth century an economy collapsed and a civilization ended.

But none of these historical examples tell us much about the time scales pertinent here – one speaks of two hundred thousand years. Only a little more than one hundredth of that time span has passed since the Parthenon was built. No government has ever existed whose life was more than an instant by comparison with the half-life of plutonium. There also seems to be a noticeable upward trend not only in the capacity for, but in the frequency of, large-scale violence. Much of this has happened in our lifetime and several notable 'incidents' have happened quite recently or are still in progress.

It seems clear that there are many factors here which a benefit-cost analysis can never capture in quantitative, commensurable terms. It also seems hard to believe that the nuclear fuel cycle will not sometime, somewhere, experience major unscheduled events. These could range in magnitude from local events to an extreme disaster affecting most of mankind if a large part of the high-level wastes in storage were released. Whether these hazards are worth incurring in view of the benefits achieved is not a question natural scientists or economists can answer. As specialists, they can try to provide pertinent information, but they cannot legitimately make the decision, and it should not be left in their hands. It is a value choice of great dimensions which in a democracy can be made only through the instrumentality of representative government.

Concluding Comment

Can mankind converge monotonically toward an economic and environmental state in which human life is both pleasant and more or less indefinitely viable? This is a very open question, it seems to me. It is one on which, despite my congenital optimism, I am rather pessimistic. But the uncertainties are so great that it is difficult to see how present policies could be rationally influenced to take account of possibilities on the pertinent time scale. The only clear signal seems to be that if we fail to bring world population under control soon – very soon – humanity's future problems may be totally insoluble. If we do succeed, there is a chance.

The dangers that perhaps impress me most are subtle ones. The probability is that, as human society makes greater and greater demands on available resources, margin for error decreases. As it decreases, a more and more interdependent, elaborate, and fail-safe organization is required simply to prevent the system from collapsing at the first perturbation. Recent unhappy experiences with massive breakdowns or congestion of essential public services – electric power, telephones, sanitation, transportation, and especially international distribution of petroleum – suggest very clearly the magnitude of potential instabilities inherent in a system which depends, for example, on maintaining regular communications in space or beneath the ocean or the eternal 'fail-safe' monitoring and management of certain materials. The elemental need to prevent catastrophic breakdowns or hold-ups may conceivably result in the development of a rigidly structured, rather inhuman *1984* type of social system which subordinates individual talents, needs, or desires to the survival of the social organism as a whole. Or else, the world may 'solve' its otherwise insoluble problems by war, famine, or anarchy.

What does seem clear is that humanity faces a future full of stresses and strains and that life will not be comfortable for any persistent periods for a long, long time to come – if ever. Analyses, of which there have been many, that describe the question of the long-term viability of a very numerous humanity solely in terms of potential technological, or even economic, capabilities miss some of the central questions. I wish I could answer them.

From the lofty peaks and great, if indistinct, vistas of this chapter we must now return to the fertile plain of solid economic research on less grand but immediately important environmental management problems relevant primarily to developed market systems. This research is based on the concepts of microeconomic theory which we sampled in Chapter 1 and which must now be developed a little further.

Appendix to Chapter 4

If the reader comes away from this chapter in a spirit of uncertainty and pessimism this reflects the author's mood also. But the highly popular book *Limits to Growth*,[1] sponsored by the Club of Rome, is even more pessimistic, or at least tries to bring more precision to its pessimism. The vehicle is a computer simulation in which a number of variables, including natural resources, capital investment, pollution, population, and the quality of life, are linked by assumed relationships. Figure 3 shows a basic scenario generated by the model. It is characterized by drastic declines in population, the economy and the quality of life. Indeed the study claims to demonstrate that the only way to avoid cataclysmic increases in world death rates within the next 100 years is to stop all population and material economic growth during the next two decades or so.

The study certainly called world attention to some profound potential problems but economists generally have been very critical of the model and the way it was used to draw apparently precise conclusions. Perhaps the most concise criticism of the model was presented by Ronald Ridker in an article in *Science*

Figure 3. Basic Behavior of the World Model drawn up by the Club of Rome, showing how industrialization and population are suppressed by falling natural resources

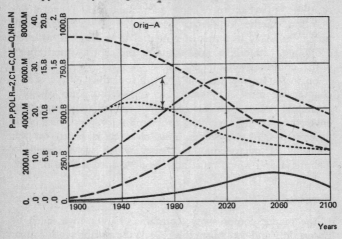

SOURCE: D. H. Meadows, P. L. Meadows, J. Randers and W. W. Behrens, III, *The Limits to Growth*, New York, Universe, 1972.

magazine[2] and I quote several paragraphs from that article to give the reader a flavor of the criticism.

First, the model used in *Limits* contains few of the important adjustment mechanisms that have helped the world avoid similar catastrophes to date. There is no price mechanism to signal pending shortages, to make it profitable to invest more in exploration and research, or to induce consumers to reduce their consumption and shift to substitutes. There is no government to monitor the situation and to supplement the price mechanism where it does not provide adequate signals. Nor does anyone learn from the experience of others and change his behavior accordingly.

Closely related are the problems arising because of the extreme degree of aggregation incorporated in the model. There is only one composite industrial output, one non-renewable resource, one 'pollutant', and one geographic unit – the world as a whole. Not only does such a formulation greatly reduce the confidence one can have in the postulated relationships between the aggregates, it seriously compounds the problems arising from inadequate adjustment mechanisms. Consumers cannot substitute one output for another; producers cannot substitute one resource for another; society cannot alter the composition of output – for example, deciding to spend less on military and more on research, development, and exploration. Since the model does not allow for these possibilities, there is really no alternative to reductions in population and economic growth.

Third, the study incorporates highly pessimistic assumptions about technological progress, future reserves of non-renewable resources, the ability to control and absorb pollution, and the extent of population growth that is likely in the next two centuries. In addition to leaving out the possibilities of technological break-throughs such as fusion and solar energy – the omission of which may make sense in a fifty-year projection, but not beyond that – the use of shale oil, tar sands, and geothermal sources of energy were ignored. The authors allow for the possibility that reserves of their aggregate resource could increase five times over the next 100 years, a seemingly generous allowance until one recalls that estimates of iron ore reserves increased about five times just between 1954 and 1965, and estimates for copper reserves by 3·5 times since 1935, according to the U.S. Bureau of Mines. Moreover, promising underwater sources of minerals are ignored: in reviewing the possibility of such sources, the World Bank finds that within the next twenty years it should be possible to recover on a commercial basis 100 million tons of nodular materials from the seabed each year and that such recovery could be increased and sustained 'indefinitely' at the level of 400 million tons. The smaller of these figures 'would add to the annual production of copper, nickel, manganese, and cobalt to the extent of roughly one fourth, two times, six times, and thirteen times, respectively, compared to the current free-world production levels. One need not concur entirely with this judgement in order to assert that this possibility should not be ignored.

As far as pollution is concerned, there is no scientific evidence for the functional relationships assumed in the model: for the amount of pollution that can be safely absorbed by the earth's environments, for the effect of pollution on birth and death rates, or for the degree to which treatment and changes in processes can reduce emissions of pollutants per unit of output. And as far as population growth is concerned, the historical relationships between birth and death rates and the level of development cannot blithely be projected into the future. Public health and family planning programs, the availability of modern contraceptives and the spread of knowledge about them, plus changing attitudes toward marriage and sex are all operating to weaken the historic linkages. Indeed, recent census data (not available at the time *Limits* was written) suggest that a slowdown in population growth may have already started in more than half of the seventy or so countries for which data are available.

Contrary to what *Limits* says, all these factors can make a significant difference in our estimate of when and how growth must stop. First, a correction of the overly pessimistic assumptions could result in a postponement, by several centuries, of the date at which growth must stop, even without introducing additional adjustment mechanisms. Second, as that limit is approached, all kinds of adjustment mechanisms will come into play to slow down and elongate the decline. Indeed, the whole idea of talking about a specific 'date' is wrong. The adjustments are continuous and occur without benefit of any social knowledge that some limit is being approached. Assuming we avoid nuclear war, the world will surely end 'not with a bang, but with a whimper'.

Ridker's criticisms are all valid even though his relative optimism may not be well based. The point is that world modelling of the type found in *Limits* is, to put it mildly, highly premature and the false precisions it represents can be very dangerous. The authors of *Limits to Growth* advocate stopping economic growth right away; should this be followed disaster would occur immediately, as I hope this chapter has helped to show. Population growth could not be stopped world-wide right away, short of the most draconian measures. Unfortunately our view of mankind's long-term future must be based on partial information and understanding. To some extent it will also be a function of our particular glandular system.

Chapter 5
Back to Microeconomics and the Environment

In the last few chapters we have reviewed the substantive nature of residuals-related environmental problems and tried to gain a broad perspective on their nature and tendencies, and on the possibilities, costs, and limits, for coping with them. We must now return to the concepts briefly introduced in the first chapter – the competitive market model and common property resources – and develop them further. This is necessary because the studies of particular cases and much of the policy analysis which follows derive their conceptual foundations from the microeconomic analysis of market processes and especially from welfare economics.

As was noted in Chapter 1, conservation of mass, taken together with the peculiar characteristics of environmental resources, has important implications for the allocation of resources in a market system. Most extractive, harvesting; processing, and distributional activities can be conducted relatively efficiently through the medium of exchange of private ownership rights as the market model envisages, however, the residual mass returned to the environment mostly affects common property resources, and so has no place in the market model.

To review briefly, the term common property resources refers to those valuable natural assets which cannot, or can only imperfectly, be reduced to private ownership and therefore cannot be effectively exchanged in markets. Examples are the air mantle, watercourses, large ecological systems, landscapes, and the auditory and electromagnetic spectrums.

When open and unpriced access to such resources is permitted, it is apparent what happens. From detailed study of particular common property problems like oil pools and ocean fisheries, it is well known that unhindered access to such resources leads to overuse, misuse, and quality degradation. It is, of course, apparent that a market system containing scarce common property resources cannot achieve Pareto optimality (as defined in Chapter 1, pp. 19–20).

But if we could stretch our minds and envisage a situation where these common property resources could be reduced to private ownership in pieces small enough to be exchanged in competitive markets, then the market could function just as efficiently to allocate them as any other resource. Prices would be generated, for example, for the use of air and water for waste disposal. The prices would be checks, an incentive to cut down the effluent discharged, and would affect the whole complex of decisions about the use of common property resources: the design of industrial processes, the kinds of raw materials inputs, the nature of the final products, and the modification – not elimination, conservation of mass and energy prevents this – of residuals streams. Conservation would then become good business. Instead, in many countries throughout history these resources have mostly remained as *open access* common property.

It is not only that common property resources like air and water get overused and misused because of their open access status, but opportunities to improve their quality (increase the yield of their services) are not grasped by the market either. The ability of streams to receive waste waters without damage to other uses can often be enhanced by raising low flows through reservoir storage and release and by mechanically introducing air into them. A substantial body of research in water-quality management makes this clear and I will review some of it in the next chapter.[1] Also, degraded ecosystems can sometimes be improved – through introduction of exotic species, such as the successful introduction of the Coho salmon into Lake Michigan in the United States. Different land-use patterns and transportation systems can affect environmental quality. Market exchange does not provide the incentive for improvements of this kind; if they occur, it must be through collective investment and management. This suggests that an optimal public policy would have to include prices for resources at present unpriced, and collective action implementing *regional-scale* measures to improve the environment where appropriate. Several of the case studies in the succeeding chapter deal with the measures of the latter type. But let us return to the matter of putting a price on waste discharges.

Pricing the Environment

If bringing the environment into the market system could, in principle, yield such desirable results – lead toward Pareto optimality – why not get on with it and define property rights to environmental media and let the market take over? There would be two conceivable ways of approaching this possibility. One would be to distribute the rights to persons who might be disadvantaged by environmental deterioration and then require those wishing to engage in an environment degrading activity to purchase the right to do so. But how are the appropriate owners to be identified, and what share of rights are they to be given? Is the New Mexican who comes to New York City or the New Yorker who goes to London occasionally to be accorded a piece of the visited city's air? How could the purchaser who wishes to use the environment find and pay each of the thousands, if not millions, of people involved? The administrative costs of creating a market in this way would be enormous. The economist refers to such costs as *transactions costs*.

Since residuals dischargers are often small in number relative to affected parties, it has sometimes been suggested that ownership rights be vested in them. But this is no way out either, because it would be very difficult for affected parties to organize and pay them for reducing discharges (purchase all or part of the right). Once again, we come up against transactions costs. The importance of such costs may be gauged by considering the many instances in which governments have failed to protect common property resources in the interest of the public, thereby, by default, granting *de facto* ownership rights to entities which put them to destructive use. There are virtually no actual cases of damaged parties paying residuals dischargers to stop or reduce their discharge. Another reason for this is that if one damaged party did this, he would simultaneously benefit many others also damaged by the discharger. This is because environmental improvement is, in the economist's language, a *public good*. We will define and use this term again shortly. Here we merely wish to point out that because of this characteristic the benefit from improving the environment, say by reducing residuals discharge to it, is the *sum* of damages done to many *different* individuals by the same discharge. Accordingly, the overall damage might be very large relative to the costs of reduction, but no individual would find it in his interest to pay for its reduction.

For these reasons, if the use of the environment in residuals discharge is to be priced it cannot be done by any usual type of market exchange. The government must do it, acting as an agent for the public. But on what activities is the government to levy a price? A general answer is on destructive uses of the common property resource.

Not all uses of common property resources are destructive. Animals, including ourselves, breathing the air, and even combustion processes, do not normally deplete oxygen to an extent that measurably affects the breathing of others or other combustion process. People viewing a landscape do not diminish its beauty (unless the viewers themselves become an unwanted part of the landscape). A manufacturing firm which pumps water, uses it in a nondegrading way, and puts it back into the stream does not impose costs on other users of this environmental asset.

There are two main sets of circumstances under which the use of a common property resource may not be destructive.

First, for certain purposes its service flow may be so copious that the effect of the use is negligible. Oxygen for breathing is an example. The economist refers to assets yielding such practically limitless service flows as *free goods*. The other set of circumstances occurs when the service stream being provided has the characteristic of a public good, that is, a good which can be used by one person without diminishing its availability to another – an uncrowded scenic view is an example. In the economics literature this phenomenon is called *jointness in supply*. Thus, for example, if an emitter of airborne residuals reduces his discharge and improves the air and thereby visibility, he provides a public good because the improvement is available to a large number of landscape viewers simultaneously. If someone then increases his viewing of the landscape now that it can be seen better, he does not reduce its beauty by his actions. In our terminology, the discharge of residuals is a destructive use of the resource, which imposes external costs and must be priced if the resource is to be allocated efficiently. Viewing is the enjoyment of a public good which does not impose any external cost and therefore should not be priced.[2]

How High a Price?

On the assumption that destructive users have been properly identified, how high a price should they be charged? In principle, they should be charged on the basis of the amount of external cost that their activities create and I examine this idea a little further below. In practice this will not be possible, and further on in the chapter I discuss a modification of this principle which carries us further toward applicability but still retains many of the desirable efficiency features of a price system as opposed to systems of direct regulation. The latter are products of legalistic, rather than economic, approaches to problems of market failure and I will have a good deal to say about the relative merits of the two ways of approaching these problems throughout the remainder of the book.

To state the pure theory of the matter quite generally and abstractly at first, it has been proven, using a mathematical model of a market economy of the idealized type discussed in the first chapter, that there exists in such a model a set of prices on the destructive use of common property resources which, in conjunction with voluntary exchange of private goods, will yield a Pareto optimum.[3] At these prices the marginal *external costs* (increase in total external costs due to an additional unit of discharge) are equated with the *marginal costs of controlling the external effect* (increase in total control costs associated with an additional unit of control). If a management agency were able to determine these prices with precision and impose them on destructive users, and if it were able to cancel any redistributive effects on income through a system of taxes and subsidies, we could be sure that the result (in the model economy) would be a Pareto optimum at a higher level of economic welfare than before intervention.

It is useful to know that such a set of prices exists but achieving them in actual practice would be a virtual impossibility. Nevertheless, a short discussion comparing an ideal pricing technique with what is usually thought of as its major possible alternative, and the one which has been written into legislation in numerous countries,[4] effluent standards, will reveal some interesting contrasts. Some of these ideal pricing techniques can be applied in pricing systems which are potentially practicable. While the principles apply to any destructive use of a common property resource, I will develop the illustrative example in terms of residuals discharges.

For ideal application of the pricing technique, each individual discharger would have to be confronted with a schedule of prices reflecting the marginal external cost of every possible alternative level of his discharge. In those cases where such a schedule can be determined independently for each discharger, this is all the management agency would have to do (leaving aside for the moment income distributional aspects). The incentive to minimize internal costs would mean that discharge was reduced to the point where to reduce it by one more unit would cost as much as the additional damages incurred. It would not be worthwhile to control the effluent any further, since the cost of control would be *more* than the cost of the damages. On the other hand, setting of effluent standards to achieve that same level of discharge from each source would mean that the management agency would have to take into account both the external costs (the damages) *and* the costs of control. Thus, in this particular situation the pricing approach requires less information to achieve optimal discharge control.

A simple chart can help clarify these statements. In Figure 4 below, the costs incurred by the discharger in controlling

Figure 4. Reduction in Discharge

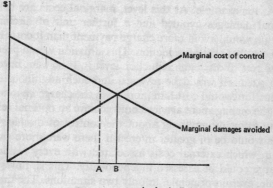

reduction in discharge

residuals discharge and the externally imposed damages avoided when residuals discharge is reduced are shown on the vertical axis. The amount of control or reduction of discharge achieved is measured on the horizontal axis. The curves shown display *marginal* costs of control and *marginal* damages avoided. In economists' usage, marginal cost and marginal benefit refer to the increment or decrement which occurs in

127

total cost or total damages avoided when an additional unit of control is exercised. For instance, if the first unit costs $1,000 and the total cost of two units is $1,100, the marginal cost of the second unit is $100. As we will see in the next chapter in more exact work using the differential calculus the marginal quantity becomes the same as the derivative of a function; economists spent several generations reinventing a crude form of the differential calculus.

The marginal control costs function is known to, or can be estimated by, the discharger. If the management agency informs the discharger of the marginal damages function and requires him to pay a charge equal to marginal damages at whatever level he chooses to discharge, the discharger will choose the level at which marginal costs and marginal damages are equated. Assume he is thinking about reducing discharge to level A, for example. At this level, marginal costs are below marginal damages avoided and a further unit of discharge reduction would avoid more charge payment than it costs him to achieve that unit of reduction. This situation would prevail until he gets to discharge reduction level B. If he went beyond B, the situation would be reversed and each additional unit of reduction would cost him more than the charge he avoids. Thus, the management agency could achieve an optimal result without knowing anything about the control of dischargers.

This would be of greater interest if there were more situations in which external costs associated with every residuals discharge could be assessed independently. This is, however, possible, even in principle, in only two situations. The first is where each discharger has a set of damaged parties who are damaged exclusively by him. The other is where there are multiple damages, but each unit of discharge, no matter what the source, always causes the same increment in damage.[5] When neither of these conditions holds, the marginal damage associated with an *increment* of discharge of a given discharger depends upon the *level* of discharges of all other dischargers affecting the damaged party. In other words it depends on the total discharge of all dischargers affecting the common damaged party. For example, if the overall damage function increases non-linearly with total discharge, the marginal cost of a specific discharge will be higher if the total discharge from all sources is larger. In these cases the management authority must know the cost of control as well as the damage functions of all relevant parties. To optimize, it must know the full general equilibrium solution for the economy (or the relevant subset of it) just as in the case of standards.

There is one interesting difference between the effluent standards approach and the pricing approach, however: the effect on the profitability of engaging in residuals discharging activities would differ as between the two approaches. The reason may be put as follows: a standard which allows some discharge which is unpriced grants a partial subsidy to the destructive users of the common property resource in that they do not have to make any payment for the remaining external costs they will cause. Furthermore, that subsidy is made contingent upon actual participation in that destructive use. Consequently, entry (to the industry and/or region) must be directly restricted to make the solution equivalent to that which would occur if *all* valuable resources in the system were appropriately priced. Thus the standards approach requires discharge controls *and* entry control to achieve optimality.[6]

An Approach Based on Setting Limits to the Use of Common Property Resources

In practice, external costs will seldom be measurable with any degree of precision as a basis for either charges or standards, although sometimes it may be possible to make usable approximations (some proposals for air pollution charges have been based on such approximations – see Chapter 8, for example). This estimation difficulty occurs both because of the complexities just reviewed and because of the very great empirical problems in evaluating a public good for which the market generates no price information. Consequently, microeconomic theory must also concern itself with ways of approximating the theoretically pure result. Economists have therefore explored an approach based, to begin with, on the establishment of ambient standards.[7] *Ambient* standards must be carefully distinguished from *effluent* standards. The latter relate to what comes out of a stack or pipe and are usually in units of weight (pounds or kilograms). The former relate to the condition of the environmental medium itself and are usually in *concentrations*, for example, so many parts per million of sulfur oxides in the atmosphere. Such standards can be set for an appropriate region, by a combination of analytical procedures (cost-benefit or cost-effectiveness analysis) and a political process. An excellent example of the implementation of such a process is found in the establishment of water-quality standards in the Delaware estuary area which I will discuss in Chapter 7. There are many other instances in many countries where ambient standards have been established by more or less rational economic–political processes for both water and air. Once an ambient limit is set, the problem becomes one of *allocating* the now specifically *limited* waste disposal service provided by the environment to its various potential users. For symmetry with our earlier discussion, we may regard an ambient standard as being a particular kind of external cost function, that is one that is vertical at the specified ambient concentration, or one that, in economists' terminology, is perfectly inelastic. Another way of saying this is that the ambient standard implies that no damages occur until the specified level of environmental quality is reached and that damages are infinitely, or at least very, high if that level is reached. This gross assumption is often found acceptable in the interest of practicality.

Ambient concentrations are a result of the amount and pattern of waste discharges and of natural phenomena related to the dispersion and transformation of materials in the environment. For example, the level of dissolved oxygen in a stream is, as we have seen, a complex function of discharges and such things as stream flow, turbulence, and temperature – the last affecting both the rate of biological activity bearing upon dissolved oxygen and the capability of the water to dissolve gases. The mathematical formulations relating *multiple sources of discharge to ambient conditions* are known as *transfer functions*.

Availability of transfer functions, and embodying them in quantitative economic models, permits the building of mathematical computer models for experimenting with different strategies for attaining ambient standards. A substantial amount of such experimentation has been done, especially with respect to water, but also to some extent in regard to air. I review this research and planning experience in Chapters 6 and 7, including a fairly detailed discussion of the methodologies used. Here I just quickly indicate some of the types of experiments conducted and their main results to give context to the remaining theoretical discussion.

One strategy that has been experimented with in the mathematical model framework, and might be called the conventional administrative approach, is to cause each discharger to cut back in proportion to the discharge being made when the standard takes effect (for example, all sources have to cut back 80 percent). While this approach appears to be administratively simple (its simplicity is more apparent than real as we will see in the final chapter) and conveys a certain sense of equity, the studies found, in accordance with theoretical expectations, that it implies much higher costs for achieving the ambient standard than do some alternative strategies. There are two reasons for this: first, the conventional approach neglects the, often large, cost difference among dischargers for cutting back (which also, it might be noted, casts doubt upon the equity of the approach), and second, it ignores the location of the discharger. The latter may be important because dischargers located at varying distances from the point (or points) for which the ambient standard is set generally have different impacts upon ambient quality at that point. This is because some residuals degrade naturally in the environment.

The research studies using transfer functions and mathematical techniques for optimizing discharges, taking into account both differential cost and locations, have in fact shown that the same result can be achieved at much lower costs than are associated with uniform cutbacks.[8] The least cost pattern for achieving a given ambient standard may cost considerably less than half as much. But implementing the least cost solution presents major problems. One possible way to do this is via a 'programmed effluent standards approach'. This would set a particular, individually tailored, effluent standard on each source reflecting the specific costs of control there. It therefore requires large amounts of information, administration, and enforcement. Furthermore, the cost impact is very uneven – some dischargers will have to incur large costs for cutting back and others little, if any.

But instead, a relatively simple pricing scheme can be used. This takes the form of a charge per unit of discharge on all sources at such a level that the incentive to minimize costs will lead to an overall cutback just sufficient to meet the ambient standard. The pricing system has two main advantages over effluent standards approaches.

First, it will tend to have the effect, solely through the economic incentive it provides, to concentrate discharge reductions where they are least costly to achieve. Each discharger will exercise control until the marginal cost of an additional unit is equated to the price (in accordance with the discussion of this process above). Thus, if the price is the same for all waste dischargers, the marginal costs of control will be the same for each source. This is a necessary condition for cost minimization in meeting the ambient standard if the location of discharge does not matter (where location does matter the situation is somewhat more complex as we will see in the next chapter). So long as marginal costs differ from source to source, a unit of control could be moved from a higher cost source to a lower cost source and overall system costs lowered. The charge, by equalizing marginal costs, thus produces a least cost system simply through its incentive effect. The limited amount of environmental capacity available under the ambient standard is allocated efficiently.

Second, less information is required to implement the system than to program a set of effluent standards. If costs of dynamic adjustment could be neglected, it would be possible just to set a charge, observe its effect, and then move it up or down as indicated until the right level is found. In practice it would be desirable to come pretty close to the right charge the first time. The reason is that a trial charge may induce certain decisions (say, size of treatment plant to be built) which, because of the high costs in.olved, could not easily be reversed and would therefore foreclose ever getting to a true least cost system. But even so, there is an information advantage because to implement the charge strategy, only an estimate of the average cost of achieving discharge reduction across all pertinent points of discharge is needed. Knowledge of costs at each point is not needed. Iteration in the neighborhood of the right charge would probably not entail high costs of dynamic adjustment.

In one of the research studies already noted and explored more fully in Chapter 7, a quantitative comparison was possible between a programmed effluent standards approach and a flat-rate charge approach for water-quality management in the Delaware estuary area. The charge approach did indeed produce overall system costs close to, but not quite as low, as the programmed effluent standards approach, and much lower than the uniform cutback approach (about half as high).[9] Similar results have been obtained in air-quality studies; these are viewed in Chapter 8.

The equity aspects of the types of alternatives just discussed is not a subject much illuminated by economic theory. But, it could reasonably be argued that the charges approach is the most equitable of the three. It requires from each discharger the same rate of payment for the use of the resource and would probably produce the most nearly equal distribution of payment (control costs plus effluent charge) of any of the strategies.

Concluding Comment

In the next chapter, I will proceed by first presenting a mathematical restatement of the main theoretical results stated verbally in this chapter. Then I will discuss some methods and models which permit quantitative applications of these ideas for actual cases. Thereafter several case studies are reviewed in a little detail. These plus the presentation of an advanced residuals management model which is on the research frontier, in the following chapter, and some discussion of the actual procedures adopted in various countries set the stage for the policy conclusions presented in the concluding chapter.

Chapter 6
Some Useful Models

In the last chapter I reviewed in very general terms some of the main constructs of economic theory pertinent to environmental problems. Now, as a prelude to a discussion of applied empirical work based on microeconomic models in the following two chapters, it will be useful to set out these ideas a bit more rigorously. Another purpose of this chapter is to introduce the reader to some quantitative economic models which have proven highly useful in the analysis of environmental problems. This chapter is more technical than any of the others in the book and an understanding of it is not strictly essential to grasping the main points of the empirical studies which follow.

One type of model which has been found useful in representing the environmental management problem in abstract terms is actually an adaptation of a model first devised to analyze certain aspects of transportation problems. It may be helpful to start with a brief exposition of a simple version of this transportation analysis.

A Simple Mathematical Model, The Transportation Version[1]

Define total highway cost of providing N trips per unit time as

(a) $$TC = N \cdot C(N, K) + f(K)$$

The first term on the right-hand side represents the variable cost borne directly by drivers, C being the cost of one trip to a driver; the second term is the cost per time period of providing

135

K units of highway capacity. The short-run marginal cost of a trip is:

(b) $$\frac{\partial (TC)}{\partial N} = C(N, K) + N \cdot \frac{\partial C}{\partial N}$$

As I remarked in the previous chapter, when using the calculus a marginal quantity is the same as the first derivative of a function.

Assume that each driver values travel time equally and incurs the same operating costs for his vehicle. Then, when the Nth driver adds his vehicle to $N - 1$ vehicles already on a given highway, he incurs a cost and, in addition, causes the remaining drivers to incur additional costs. In the continuous case, $C(N, K)$ is the variable cost borne by the Nth driver and $N \cdot (\partial C / \partial N)$ is the marginal congestion cost imposed on the remaining drivers. The fixed 'common property' resource is the man-made, augmentable highway in this case, and it is common property because of its conditions of open access.

Proper management would require that each driver pay a marginal cost price made up of two components: $C(N, K)$, the costs he bears directly, plus a toll equal to the costs he imposes on other drivers by adding to congestion equal to $[N \cdot (\partial C / \partial N)]$. The toll revenue can be interpreted as a reward to the authority for providing the services of the (temporarily) fixed factor.

Toll collections would exactly equal the capital costs of an optimum capacity expansion if services of the common property asset can be produced at constant long-run cost. That is, as more units are added to the highway capacity each successive unit costs just the same as each preceding one. This result is now derived.

To find the cost-minimizing level of highway capacity, (a) must be differentiated with respect to K and then the resulting expression set equal to zero.

(c) $$\frac{\partial (TC)}{\partial K} = N \cdot \frac{\partial C}{\partial K} + f'(K) = 0$$

But if constant returns to scale prevail in the provision of trips (i.e., if a λ percent increase in K and N results in a λ percent increase in TC), C will be a function of N/K and equation (a) can be rewritten as:

$$(d) \qquad TC = N \cdot C\frac{N}{K} + P_K \cdot K$$

where P_K is the constant unit price per time period of capacity. Differentiating this expression with respect to K then yields:

$$(e) \quad \frac{\partial(TC)}{\partial K} = -N^2 \cdot \frac{C'}{K^2} + P_K = 0 \quad \text{where } C' \equiv \frac{dC(N/K)}{d(N/K)}$$

or

$$P_K K = N^2 \cdot \frac{C'}{K}$$

the amount to be spent on highway capacity. This is equal to the toll (derived earlier) required to achieve a welfare maximum when collected from all trips[2]:

$$N \text{ (toll from each trip)} = N\left(N \cdot \frac{\partial C}{\partial N}\right) = \left(N^2 \cdot \frac{C'}{K}\right)$$

The Environmental Variant

This development of the economics of highway tolls and highway capacity can now be adapted to an environmental situation. I will refer to water pollution but the analysis could be applied to air pollution without major changes. The main practical difference between the two situations is that no known technical means exist for augmenting the waste assimilative capacity of the air whereas in the case of water this is an important alternative to effluent control in some instances.

First, let us assume n business firms are located around a lake which provides both water supply and residual absorption services. This common property resource yields no other services. The discharge of wastes reduces the utility of the lake for water supply.

Industrial firm $i(i = 1, \ldots, n)$ manufactures Y^i units of a product sold in a competitive market at a price P_i. The firm also uses X_i units of an input (labor) purchased competitively at rate W. Output of Y^i is also a function of the amount of waste material (Z_i) which the firm puts in the lake and the quality of water obtained from the lake (q). Each firm produces the same type of waste. Here adaptations other than output effects are neglected to simplify the exposition. Other adaptations might, for example, include process changes, waste water treatment, and water supply treatment.

Quality of the lake water depends on the amount of waste discharge of each of the n firms and certain natural attributes of the lake (L) which may be altered by the application of resources (say, by inducing mixing). These natural attributes are not affected by waste discharges.

The objective is taken to be maximizing the difference between the value of output $\Sigma P_i Y^i$ and the sum of the cost of X inputs $\Sigma W X_i$ and the cost of securing the desired lake characteristics, L, for the n firms subject to constraints resulting from the interrelationships among water supply and waste disposal. This maximization is performed by using standard Lagrangian analysis.

$$(f) \quad \max U = \Sigma P_i Y^i(X_i, Z_i, q) - \Sigma W X_i - C(L) - \lambda[q - Q(Z_1, \ldots, Z_i, L)]$$

The constraint says the quality of water available for input depends on waste discharges to the lake and lake assimilative capacity.

When this expression is differentiated with respect to X_i, Z_i, q, and L [q being determined by $q = Q(Z_1, \ldots, Z_n, L)$], the following first order conditions are obtained for the maximization problem:

$$(g) \quad \frac{\partial U}{\partial X_i} = P_i Y^i_{x_i} - W = 0 \quad (i = 1, \ldots, n)$$

This equation says the value of the marginal product of inputs (labor) should equal the price of these inputs.

(h) $\dfrac{\partial U}{\partial Z_i} = P_i Y_{Z_i}^i + \lambda Q_{Z_i} = 0 \quad (i = 1, \ldots, n)$

(i) $\dfrac{\partial U}{\partial q} = \Sigma P_j Y_q^j - \lambda = 0 \quad (j = 1, \ldots, n)$

(j) $\dfrac{\partial U}{\partial L} = \lambda Q_L - C' = 0$

As the reader will recall, in a constrained optimimization analysis such as this the value of the Lagrange multiplier λ is the increase in the objective function if the constraint is released slightly. Thus λ is the implicit value of a unit of water quality (measured at the optimum position for the system), and is equal to the value of the sum of the marginal products of a unit change in quality q.

Equation (j) says the marginal value of a unit change in lake characteristics, L, is to be equated to the marginal cost of L.

If (i) is substituted into (h), the result is:

(k) $P_i Y_{Z_i}^i + Q_{Z_i} \Sigma P_j Y_q^j = 0 \quad (i, j = 1, \ldots, n)$

The ith private firm acting in its own interest will ignore the effect on the productivity of all firms via water quality, q, resulting from an increase in its Z_i. Even the effect on Y_q^i of an increase in Z_i is negligible in comparison with $Y_{Z_i}^i$ if there are enough dischargers. Thus to attain the socially optimum Z_is, a tax should be imposed on each unit of Z_i emitted equal to the second term of (k). The Z_is and the X_is will be reduced. That is, the partial derivatives of the Y^i differ according to whether these taxes are imposed or not.

Some possible users of the lake however, might themselves be subject to congestion, say, recreational users, and therefore would have to be priced by the authority.

The effluent charge collected by the lake authority would, by analogy with the highway toll case, in certain instances exceed, equal, or fall short of the long-run cost of improving lake characteristics. If the lake is naturally present and investments

139

only augment its capacity, part of the effluent charge will represent an inframarginal rent (or net yield) on the existing asset. The revenue from the charge can only fall short of long-run cost under conditions of decreasing cost above a certain degree.[3]

The analysis presented above can now be extended to a situation in which the firms are located along a stream rather than a lake. Of the n firms located along a stream, firm 1 is furthest upsteam (i.e., no waste discharge above it), firm 2 is next, and firm n is furthest downstream (i.e., an infinite sink is downstream from it). The quality of water available to a particular firm i is then a function of a river characteristic R and waste discharge by only the firms $1, \ldots, i-1$ above it on the river. The maximization problem for the entire river basin now becomes:

(j) $$\max V = \Sigma P_i Y^i(X_i, Z_i, q_i) - \Sigma W X_i - C(R) + \Sigma \lambda_i [q_i - Q^i(Z_1, \ldots, Z_{i-1}, R)]$$

The first order conditions are:

(k) $$P_i Y^i_{X_i} - W = 0$$

(l) $$P_i Y^i_{Z_i} + \sum_{j=i+1}^{n} P_j Y^j_{Q_j} Q^j_{Z_i} = 0$$

(m) $$\left(\sum_{j=1}^{n} P_j Y^j_{Q_j} \right) Q^j_R - C' = 0$$

Equation (k) will again be obtained by profit maximization and (l) by levying a charge on firm i equal to the value of the second term if sites of all activities are given and fixed.

But suppose an entrepreneur (or a river authority) wishes to place a new activity in the existing array of sites. Take as an example a bathing beach which generates no wastes but has a high marginal product for high water quality. Say the choice is between site O (upstream) and site $n+1$ (between n and the infinite sink).

At the upstream location, the beach would involve adding

$P_o Y_Q^o Q_R^o$ to the right-hand side of (m) which might justify some additional investment in R but would leave previous optimal waste discharges unaltered. If, however, site $n + 1$ were chosen, a term such as

$$P_{n+1} Y_{Q_n}^{n+1} Q_{Z_i}^{n+1}$$

would have to be added to each of the equations (l) in addition to adding

$$P_{n+1} Y_{Q_n}^{n+1} Q_R^{n+1}$$

to (m).

As a result, maximizing the objective function would require each firm i for which $Q_{Z_i}^{n+1}$ is negative to reduce its level of waste discharge. This would require diverting inputs from production of Ys so that

$$(n) \qquad \sum_{i=1}^{n} (P_i Y^i - W X_i)$$

will decline from its previous level. One way of reflecting this would be to levy a tax equal to the difference on the new activity.

In ordinary English, the model developed in this section suggests the need for a basin-wide authority which will:

(1) levy a charge on waste discharge;
(2) explore the production function and implement resource improving (augmenting) investments where efficient;
(3) control land use.

These are the same results we achieved by more intuitive means in the previous chapter.

The first two tasks have been the subject of considerable research by economists and engineers and in the next chapter I will review the two river-basin studies which have come to be regarded as something of classics in this regard. In addition a very recent river-basin study in Britain will be discussed.

Land-use control as a part of environmental planning has

141

received comparatively little attention by **economists.** I will, however, also in the next chapter outline a study which is presently being conducted in Australia with the aim of helping to remedy that deficiency.

Methodology

Before proceeding to the specific case studies, though, it is necessary to review a few methodological tools which have permitted quantitative microeconomic study of real environmental problem situations. The calculus approach we have just reviewed is very useful in deriving general results and the calculus will be familiar to many readers. But models containing the general (non-linear) functions approach are usually very difficult or impossible to estimate empirically and solve mathematically. Therefore linear models are usually employed in applied analysis. *Linear programming* especially has become a basic tool in many microeconomic applied studies of environmental problems, including some of those reviewed in succeeding chapters.

The Linear Programming Model

First I briefly review the general linear programming approach by using a hypothetical example based on an industrial production problem. This type of formulation will be familiar to many readers with some background in economics. Then I indicate how an essentially ecological model (if a simple one) is embodied in a linear program to produce the 'classical' *environmental* linear programming model.

To state in the most general terms the mathematical character of the problem with which linear programming is designed to cope, one may say that it involves solving a set of linear equations subject to two side conditions: (1) that no element in the solution vector be negative, and (2) that an auxiliary linear function of the variables has a maximum (or minimum) value conferred on it. The auxiliary function is known as the *objective function*. Let us examine the following typical example of a linear programming problem.[4]

A manufacturer of ball bearings uses three types of machines – lathes, grinders and presses – in his operation, of which he has 8, 16, and 13 respectively. It is possible for him to make four types of bearings. Each bearing of the first type requires one minute on a lathe, three minutes on a grinder, and two minutes of press time.

These relationships for all the bearings are summarized in the table below.

Time (in minutes) required on	Types of bearings			
	1	2	3	4
lathe	1	3	2	2
grinder	3	2	3	1
press	2	3	3	2

The unit profits for the types of bearings are 9, 8, 11, and 6 cents for types 1, 2, 3, and 4 respectively. Thus if we let x_i represent bearing type i, we can write the objective function

$$\max z = 9x_1 + 8x_2 + 11x_3 + 6x_4$$

and the restrictions: subject to

$$1x_1 + 3x_2 + 2x_3 + 2x_4 \leq 8$$
$$3x_1 + 2x_2 + 3x_3 + x_4 \leq 16$$
$$2x_1 + 3x_2 + 3x_3 + 2x_4 \leq 13$$

and finally the non-negativity constraints

$$x_1 \geq 0, \quad x_2 \geq 0, \quad x_3 \geq 0, \quad x_4 \geq 0$$

Notice that the restrictions are in the form of inequalities rather than the equalities which characterized the constrained optimization problem of the previous section. The second line, for example, says that the number of grinder minutes used each minute must be less than or equal to sixteen. The inequality is used because we are not required to use all of the grinder time. Economic problems of this type are common.

The solution which confers maximum value on the objective function may leave some available grinder time unused.

Non-negativity restrictions give the problem economic or technological meaning. To permit a negative solution would imply running that process backward to make lathe, grinder or press time out of bearings. Mathematically they are necessary for preventing z from tending to infinite size. Any solution of the system which meets the non-negativity restrictions is called a *feasible* solution.

The linear programming problem can now be written in its general form:

$$\max z = c_1 x_1 + c_2 x_2 + \ldots + c_m x_m$$

subject to

$$a_{11} x_1 + a_{12} x_2 + \ldots + a_{1m} x_m = b_1$$

.

.

.

$$a_{n1} x_1 + a_{n2} x_2 + \ldots + a_{nm} x_m = b_n$$
$$x_1 \geq 0, x_2 \geq 0, \ldots, x_m \geq 0$$

where $m > n$. We will shortly show how the equalities in the constraint set were obtained.

In matrix notation the problem may be written compactly as follows:

$$\max z = cx$$
$$\text{subject to } Ax = b$$
$$x \geq 0$$

This is an extremely general form and many economic problems can be cast into it. To eliminate the inequalities and at the same time to help find a first trial solution, some additional variables are introduced into the problem which are called slack variables. Their real-world meaning as applied to the example above is that if a solution assigns positive values to them it means that at least part of the lathe, grinder or press time is idle. They are called slack variables because they take up the 'slack' between the time that is used in actual productive activities in the solution and the amount of time available. I now rewrite the linear programming problem with the slack variables included. You will notice that in the first constraint equation, for example, slack variables x_6 and x_7 are assigned coefficients of zero, whereas slack variable x_5, which will indicate unused lathe time in the earlier example, is assigned a coefficient of 1.

$$z = 9x_1 + 8x_2 + 11x_3 + 6x_4 + 0x_5 + 0x_6 + 0x_7$$

subject to

$$1x_1 + 3x_2 + 2x_3 + 2x_4 + 1x_5 + 0x_6 + 0x_7 = 8$$
$$3x_1 + 2x_2 + 3x_3 + 1x_4 + 0x_5 + 1x_6 + 0x_7 = 16$$
$$2x_1 + 3x_2 + 3x_3 + 2x_4 + 0x_5 + 0x_6 + 1x_7 = 13$$
$$x_1 \geq 0, x_2 \geq 0, x_3 \geq 0, x_4 \geq 0, x_5 \geq 0, x_6 \geq 0, x_7 \geq 0$$

The problem is now in what is called *standard form*. Now another term must be defined. A *basic* solution to the problem is one which uses only linearly independent vectors. The number of linearly independent vectors possible, as the reader may recall from matrix algebra, depends upon the rank of the matrix. The rank of the above A matrix and all its submatrices, containing at least three vectors, is three. The basic solution therefore uses only three activities and assigns a zero value to all others. If the solution is also feasible (in that it meets the non-negativity constraints) it is called a *basic feasible solution*. It is a basic theorem of linear programming that the optimal solution (i.e., the one that confers the highest value on the objective function) is found among the basic feasible solutions of which there is only a finite number.

It is easy to spot a basic feasible solution to the standard form linear programming problem we have written above. A basic feasible solution vector is

$$(x_1 = 0, x_2 = 0, x_3 = 0, x_4 = 0, x_5 = 8, x_6 = 16, x_7 = 13).$$

It is readily seen that this is a solution to the system, that it is feasible, and that it uses only linearly independent vectors and is therefore basic. However, it is a horrendously bad solution.

Geometrically, it is at the origin of the three-dimensional coordinate system with which we are dealing, and it confers exactly zero value on the objective function. But it is a starting-point and from here on the simplex method for proceeding toward an optimal solution takes over. The simplex method is complicated to explain in detail and I will not attempt it here. But what it does is easy to state. It provides rules for taking activities (vectors) out of the basis (the set of vectors comprising a basic solution) and for putting new vectors into the basis in such a way that three conditions are met. (1) The basic solution continues to contain a number of activities (vectors) corresponding to the rank of the A matrix, (2) feasibility is retained as vectors are replaced, (3) and for each successive replacement (iteration) the value of the objective function improves (or possibly remains unchanged). Also when set up in an appropriate tableau the method indicates when the maximum value of the objective function has been reached and iteration should stop.

What we have gone through is a highly simplified and somewhat unrealistic model of industrial production. We will see in the next chapter that with imagination the technique can be applied to a quite different kind of problem. Before proceeding to this, however, we must review briefly the (at least primitive) ecological model which is an integral part of this further application.

The Streeter–Phelps Model

As we saw in Chapter 2, roughly speaking, polluting substances discharged to watercourses can be divided into two classes – degradable and nondegradable. It was noted there that sodium chloride or ordinary table salt is a good illustration of the latter. Its behavior in water is extremely simple since all that happens to it is dilution. So, calculating the concentration that results when a given amount of it is discharged to a watercourse is a simple matter of division. Degradable substances are something quite different again since they are transformed by biological or chemical action, and the transformation process itself often works undesirable changes on the water body. The most important example is degradable organic matter which is contained in household sewage and in many industrial effluents. Bacteria feed on these effluents and convert them to plant nutrients – nitrates and phosphates – and carbon. In the process these 'aerobic' bacteria use the dissolved oxygen (DO) in the water for respiration. This results in what is termed an 'oxygen sag'. Oxygen-demanding material is, as pointed out in Chapter 2, measured in terms of pounds of biochemical oxygen demand, or BOD.

One way of visualizing the oxygen sag process is to think of a certain amount of organic waste being placed in a container of well-aerated water with an appropriate bacteria culture. As the biological reactions proceed, the unsatisfied BOD is reduced at a constant rate per unit time, and DO is depleted. At the same time some oxygen is restored to the water through the air–water interface. As time elapses, the oxygen-demanding waste is gradually consumed (that is, converted into inorganic substances) and the reaeration process continues, with the level of dissolved oxygen again reaching the saturation point for water of that temperature when the oxygen-demanding waste is completely consumed. By a well-known law of gases, saturation level varies inversely with temperature.

Alternatively, one can think of a flowing stream with uniform characteristics over a certain reach in which there is a constant input of oxygen-demanding waste at a certain point. We can now regard distances downstream as being exactly equivalent to time in the former way of looking at this situation. Thus, as we proceed downstream, we first find a decrease in the dissolved oxygen content as oxygen is consumed in the biochemical reactions on the oxygen-demanding waste, and finally a rise in the dissolved oxygen content to the saturation level still further on downstream. This process is the 'oxygen sag' in a watercourse.

While the subsequent formulas are written in terms of

time, they could just as well be written in terms of distance provided the equivalencies stipulated above are met. These formulas are commonly known as the Streeter–Phelps equations.

Biochemical oxidation is indicated as a first-order differential equation of the form

$$\frac{dL}{dt} = -k_1 L_t,$$

where L_t is the unsatisfied BOD (p.p.m.), t is time (days), and k_1 is a rate constant which is a function of the characteristics of the waste and the water temperature. If L_a is the initial first-stage BOD and is interpreted as the constant of integration, the result of integrating the above equation is

$$L_t = L_a e^{-k_1 t}.$$

Reaeration is also indicated as a first-order process. It is a function of the difference between actual DO concentration and saturation concentration, as follows:

$$\frac{dC}{dt} = k_2(C_s - C_t),$$

where C_t is the concentration (p.p.m.) of DO at time t and C_s is the saturation concentration. Once again k_2 is a rate constant which is primarily a function of temperature.

When the two reactions are combined and the resulting equation[5] written in terms of the DO deficit ($D_t = C_s - C_t$):

$$\frac{dD}{dt} = k_1 L_t - k_2 D_t.$$

After substituting $L_a e^{-k_1 t}$ for L_t, we have

$$\frac{dD}{dt} = k_1 L_a e^{-k_1 t} - k_2 D_t.$$

This is a first-order differential equation of the general form

$$\frac{dy}{dx} + Py = Q,$$

with

$$Q = k_1 L_a e^{-k_1 t}.$$

The solution of this equation is

$$D_t = \frac{k_1 L_a}{k_2 - k_1}\left(e^{-k_1 t} - e^{-k_2 t} \right) + D_a e^{-k_2 t}$$

where D_a is the deficit and L_a is the BOD concentration, both at time $t = 0$. The time at which the maximum deficit occurs, say t_c, can be found by taking the derivative of the above equation with respect to time, setting the result to zero, and solving for t_c. The resulting expression is:

$$t_c = \frac{1}{k_2 - k_1} \, ln \left[\frac{k_2}{k_1}\left(1 - \frac{(k_2 - k_1)D_a}{k_1 L_a} \right) \right].$$

At the location corresponding to this time the deficit is:

$$D_c = \frac{k_1 L_a}{k_2} \, e^{-k_1 t_c}$$

The equations just discussed transform a number of pounds of BOD discharged at a particular location into concentrations of dissolved oxygen (or, given the saturation level, dissolved oxygen deficits) at other (receptor) locations downstream. Such equations are known as transfer functions. The transfer is for 'steady state conditions', i.e., the rate of stream-flow, the rate of reaeration, and temperature are all fixed. Even if one accepts the steady state assumptions, in any even moderately developed river basin this will be too simple a model. There will be multiple points of discharge as well as multiple receptors. Before the oxygen sag will have fully recovered, another discharge will enter the system, and so on down the line. Thus the stream consists of a number of inter-connected segments. When the Streeter–Phelps oxygen balance equations are applied to these, a system of linear first-order differential equations results. But the transfer functions, which are found by solving these equations and which relate the change in DO in segment i to an input of BOD in segment *j*, fortunately simplify to a set of linear relationships if we continue to assume steady state conditions. In matrix notation we can write the system as follows:

$$Ax = r$$

where A is the matrix of transfer coefficients, x is the vector of BOD discharges in pounds, and r is a vector of DO concentration at various specified (receptor) locations. This form is extremely convenient because, as we will see in the next chapter, it lends itself easily to incorporation into linear economic models. The reader has probably already noticed in any case that this set looks very like the constraint set in a linear programming problem.

Perhaps it is unnecessary to point out that transfer functions can be derived for other substances, for example, non-degradable residuals. I have undertaken this rather extended discussion of degradable organics because they are important wastes, the transfer functions are more difficult to derive than for many other substances, and the Streeter–Phelps model is at least a primitive ecological model (since it involves behavior of organisms/bacteria in particular environments). I will have some things to say about more sophisticated ecological models and their use in economic analysis in Chapter 9.

I should also note here that transfer functions have been developed for air pollutants and are embodied in linear programming models in just the same way as for water pollution, discussed in the next chapter. Some applications of such models to air pollution situations will, as I have said, be reviewed in Chapter 8.

Chapter 7

Economic Studies of Water-Quality Management in Particular Basins

Chapter 6 has laid the methodological groundwork for a consideration of some actual case studies in this chapter. The first of them is regarded by many as the 'classic' economic water-quality management study. It was conducted in the 1960s by a Federal Government Agency in the United States and focused on the Delaware estuary region. The basic model it developed has found many other applications in both aqueous and atmospheric environments. The other case studies with different geographical setting, somewhat different methodologies, and addressing different aspects of water-quality problems are also reviewed. While all of them made significant contributions, a common deficiency of all of these studies is that they do not incorporate the possibility of land-use controls in an integral manner. In view of this an ongoing study which attempts to remedy this deficiency is reviewed at the end of the chapter.

The Delaware Study

The Delaware river basin, though small by the standards of the great American river basins and draining an area of only 12,765 square miles, holds a population of over six million. Portions of the basin, especially the Lehigh sub-basin and the Delaware estuary area, are among the most highly industrialized and densely populated regions in the world, and it is in these areas that the main water-quality problems are encountered.[1] The Delaware estuary, an eighty-six-mile reach of the Delaware river from Trenton, New Jersey, to Liston Point, Delaware (see Map 1), is most important in terms of the quantity of water impacted, the area involved, the extent of industrial activity, and the number of people affected.

Despite early industrial and municipal development in the basin, water-quality problems were neglected until the last few decades. The Interstate Commission on the Delaware River Basin (INCODEL) was formed in 1936, and under its auspices the states in the basin signed a reciprocal agreement on water-quality control. This provided the legal basis for construction of treatment plants by municipalities after the Second World War. The standards of treatment achieved were not particularly high (on the average not much more than removal of the grosser solids), and the residual waste load from the plants, together with industrial discharges, continued to place very heavy oxygen demands on the estuary. Especially during the warm summer months, DO fell, and still falls, to low levels or becomes exhausted in a few portions of the reach of the estuary from Philadelphia to the Pennsylvania–Delaware state line.

There are many water-quality characteristics which affect the value of the various services of a watercourse. As we saw in Chapter 2, and at the end of the previous chapter, one of the most central is DO, which is affected by meteorological and hydrological variables and by the discharge of organic wastes. DO is also something of a surrogate measure for other quality characteristics. The performance of waste water treatment plants is usually measured in terms of their ability to remove BOD from waste waters. Thus my discussion of the analysis of the Delaware estuary is focused primarily (but not exclusively) on oxygen conditions.

In 1957–8, at the request of the Corps of Engineers (the federal agency responsible for developing 'comprehensive' plans in the river basins of the eastern United States), the U.S. Public Health Service (which at that time was the responsible federal agency in regard to water pollution – now it is the Federal Water Quality Administration) made a preliminary study of water quality in the Delaware estuary. The data it produced regarding the quality of the estuary led state and interstate agencies, concerned with water quality, to request a comprehensive study of the estuary under the provisions of the Federal Water Pollution Control Act. The study was begun in 1961, and in the summer of 1966 a report was issued by the Federal Water Pollution Control Administration – *Delaware Estuary Comprehensive Study: Preliminary Report and Findings*.[2] The study made an effort to measure external costs as well as costs of control associated with various policy alternatives. One of its main contributions was to link the model of waste degradation and reaeration (Streeter–Phelps) for multiple points of discharge, which I described briefly at the end of the last chapter, to an economic optimization model.

The Model

Assume that a watercourse consists of n homogenous segments (thirty segments were used in the Delaware estuary study) and c_i represents the improvement in water quality required to meet a DO target in segment i. The target vector c of m elements can be obtained by changes of inputs to the watercourse from combinations of the n segments. Define another vector $x = (x_j, x_i, \ldots, x_n)$ in which the values of x refer to the volume of waste discharges in each of the segments. In a feasible solution, these values represent the waste discharges at the various points which meet the target vector c. This vector generates DO changes through the mechanism of the constant coefficients of the linear transfer function system already described at the end of the last chapter: $a_{ij} = $ DO improvement in segment i per unit reduction of x_j, $i = 1, \ldots, m; j = 1, \ldots, n$; and, of course $x_j > 0$.

If we let A be the (m by n) matrix of transfer coefficients, then Ax is the vector of DO changes corresponding to x.

Now, recalling that c is the vector of target improvements, we have two restrictions on x, namely, $Ax \geq c$ and $x \geq 0$.

The reader will have noticed that mathematically these are sets of linear constraints exactly analogous to those in the industrial production problem I used as an example in the previous chapter. All we need is an objective function to complete the problem. Let d be a row vector where $d_j =$ unit cost of x_j, $j = 1, \ldots, n$. Notice that this assumes linear cost functions.[3] We can now write the problem as a standard linear program,

$$\text{minimum value of } dx$$
$$\text{such that } Ax \geq c$$
$$\text{and } \quad x \geq 0$$

Of course, the transfer coefficients a_{ij}, as already explained, relate to a steady state of specified conditions of stream flow and temperature. Thus the model turns out to be totally deterministic, and the variability of conditions is handled in this analysis by assuming extreme conditions usually associated with substantial declines in water quality. This is a weakness in programming-type models, and an alternative mode of analysis which can handle some stochastic elements (but with unfortunately its own set of weaknesses) is discussed in connection with the Potomac case in the next section.

A linear programming model of the general type just described was constructed for the Delaware estuary. In addition to DO, it included other, nondegradable, types of material. Computation of the a_{ij}'s is, as noted in the previous chapter, easier for these. Once done, the model provided an extremely flexible tool for the analysis of alternative policies.

Analysis of Objectives

A major part of the strategy of the Delaware study was to use the model to analyze the total and incremental costs of achieving five 'objective sets', each representing a different package and spatial distribution of water-quality characteristics, with the level of quality increasing from set 5 (representing 1964 water quality) to set 1. In some runs, overall costs were minimized by the programming model. In others, additional constraints were added to represent more usual administrative approaches to the problem. The water-quality characteristics and associated levels and the areas to which they apply are shown for objective set 2 in Table 12.

Table 12. Water-Quality Goals for Objective Set 2

WATER QUALITY PARAMETER †	Trenton			Bristol		Torresdale				Camden								Chester		Wilmington		New Castle						Liston Point
	1	2	3	4	5	6	7	8	9	10	11	12	13	14	15	16	17	18	19	20	21	22	23	24	25	26	27	28	29	30
Dissolved oxygen†	5.5					5.5	4.0											4.0	5.0			5.0	6.5							
DO 4/1 - 6/15 and 9/16 - 12/31	6.5																						6.5							
Chlorides §								50	250																					
Coliforms (=/100 ml.)	5.000††					5.000††	5.000**																5.000**							
Coliforms 5/30 - 9/15	4.000††		4.000			5.000††	5.000**														5.000**		4.000††							
Turbidity (Tu)	N.L.+30																						N.L.+30							
Turbidity 5/30 - 9/15	N.L.			N.L.		N.L.+30															N.L.+30		N.L.		N.L.					
pH†† (pH units)	6.5-8.5																						6.5-8.5							
pH†† 5/30 - 9/15	7-85					6.5-8.5															6.5-8.5		7-8.5							
Alkilinity ††	20-50					20-50	20-120																20-120							
Hardness‡‡	95					95	150				150																			
Temperature††(ºF)	Present levels																						Present levels							
Phenols‡‡	0.001					0.001	0.005				0.005	0.01											0.01							
Syndets‡‡	0.5					0.5	1.0																¡1,0							
Oil and grease floating debris	Negligible																						Negligible							
Toxic substances	Negligible																						Negligible							
SECTION:	1	2	3	4	5	6	7	8	9	10	11	12	13	14	15	16	17	18	19	20	21	22	23	24	25	26	27	28	29	30

* mg/l. unless specified   ††Not less stringent than present levels   †Summer average
§ Maximum 15-day mean   ‖ Maximum level   **Monthly geometric mean   ††Desirable
range   ‡‡ Monthly mean   ‡ Average during period stated   N.L. = Natural levels

SOURCE: Allen V. Kneese and Blaire T. Bower, *Managing Water Quality: Economics Technology, Institutions*, Baltimore, Johns Hopkins Press, 1968.

The thirty sections referred to in the table are shown on Map 1. An effort was then made to measure benefits associated with the improvement in water quality indicated by the successive objective sets. Before turning to the benefit estimation, it will be useful to describe the objective sets a bit further.

Map. 1. Map of the Delaware Estuary Showing Analysis Sections

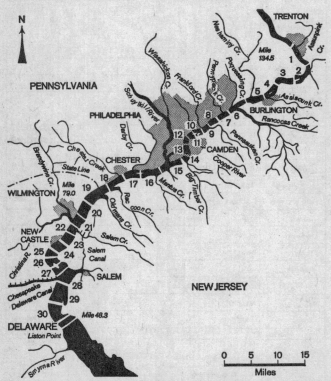

SOURCE: Federal Water Pollution Control Administration, *Delaware Estuary Comprehensive Study*, 1966.

Table 13 shows several water-quality parameters with the associated levels for the five objective sets. The general nature of the objective sets is as follows:

Objective Set 1. This is the highest set. It makes provision for large increases in water-contact recreation in the estuary. It also makes special provision for 6.6 p.p.m. levels of dissolved oxygen to provide safe passage for anadromous fish during the spring and fall migration periods. Thus this objective set should produce conditions in which water quality is basically no obstacle to the migration of shad and other anadromous (migratory) fishes.

Objective Set 2. Under this set the area available for water-contact recreation is constricted somewhat. Some reduction in sport and commercial fishing would also be expected because of the somewhat lower dissolved oxygen objective. This set, like objective set 1, makes special provision for high dissolved oxygen during periods of anadromous fish passage.

Objective Set 3. This set is similar to set 2. Although there is no specific provision for raising dissolved oxygen during periods of anadromous fish migrations, there is comparatively little difference in the survival probability under objective sets 2 and 3. Under the waste-loading conditions envisioned for objective set 3, the estimated survival 24 out of 25 years would be at least 80 percent – compared with 90 percent for set 2.

Objective Set 4. This provides for a slight increase over 1964 levels in water-contact recreation and fishing in the lower sections of the portion of the estuary studied. Generally, water quality is improved slightly over 1964 conditions and the probability of anaerobic conditions occurring is greatly reduced.

Objective Set 5. This would maintain 1964 conditions in the estuary. It would provide for no more than a prevention of further water-quality deterioration.

The costs of achieving objective sets 1 through 4 by various combinations of waste discharge reduction at particular outfalls for the waste-load conditions expected to prevail in

Table 13. Comparison of Water-Quality Goals for Objective Sets 1–5 (Set 5 represents conditions in 1964)

WATER QUALITY PARAMETER	SET	Trenton	Bristol	Torresdale	Camden (Philadelphia)	Chester	Wilmington	New Castle	Liston Point
Dissolved oxygen, mg./l. summer average	1	6.5			6.5 6.5 4.5	4.5	5.5 6.5		6.5 7.5 7.5
	2	5.5			6.5 4.0		4.0 5.0		5.0 6.5
	3	5.5			5.5 3.0		3.0 4.5	4.5 6.5	6.5
	4	4.0			4.0 2.5		2.5 3.5		5.5
	5	7.0 6.1		5.8	10		1.0	4.2	7.1
Chlorides, mg./l. max. 15-day mean	1				50 250				
	2				50 250				
	3				50 250				
	4				50 250				
	5			50	100 250 400 1,340		2,400		
Coliforms, #/100 ml. 5/30 – 9/15	1	4,000*		4,000*	5,000*	5,000*	5,000† 4,000*		4,000†
	2	4,000* 4,000*		5,000* 5,000†			5,000†		4,000*
	3	4,000*		5,000†			5,000†		4,000*
	4	5,000†					5,000†		4,000*
Monthly geometric mean	5	2,600		2,700 6,800 25,000	63,000 66,000 51,000 22,000	7,000		1,900 700	
Turbidity, turbidity units, 5/30 – 9/15	1	N.L.		N.L. N.L.+30			N.L.+30 N.L.		
	2	N.L.	N.L.	N.L.+30			N.L.+30 N.L.		
	3	N.L.		N.L.+30			N.L.+30 N.L.		
	4	N.L.+30					N.L.+30 N.L.		
Maximum level	5	23 28		29	24 22 24	27	27 37		43 43
pH. pH units, desirable range. 5/30 – 9/15	1	7-8.5		6.5-8.5			6.5-8.5	7-8.5	
	2	7-8.5	6.5-8.5				6.5-8.5	7-8.5	
	3	7-8.5	6.5-8.5				6.5-8.5	7-8.5	
	4	6.5-8.5		6.5-8.5	Present levels	Present levels	6.5-8.5	7-8.5	
Present range	5	7-8.7		6.9-7.6	6.8-7.3	6.4-7.0	5.6-7.8	6.1-7.8	
Alkilinity, mg./l. desirable range	1	20-50		20-50	20-120				20-120
	2	20-50		20-50	20-120		20-120		
	3	20-50		20-50	20-120		20-120		
	4	20-50		20-50	Present levels		Present levels		
Present range	5	25-51		33-46	34-50	13-41	4-25	10-49	
Hardness, mg./l. monthly mean	1	95		95	150	150			
	2	95		95	150 150				
	3	95		95	150 150				
	4	95		95	150 150				
	5	83		122		467			
Phenols, mg./l. monthly mean	1	0.001			0.001 0.01			0.01	
	2	0.001		0.001 0.005	0.005 0.01			0.01	
	3	0.001		0.001 0.005	0.005 0.01			0.01	
	4	0.005			0.005 0.01				
	5	0.01 0.02	0.03	0.04 0.03	0.05	0.05	0.06		

* Maximum level   † Monthly geometric mean.   N.L. = Natural levels

SOURCE: Allen V. Kneese and Blair T. Bower, *Managing Water Quality: Economic Technology, Institutions,* Baltimore, Johns Hopkins Press 1968.

1975–80 are shown in Table 14. The range in costs among the various treatment strategies is explained below.

Benefits of Improved Water Quality

The Delaware estuary comprehensive study pioneered by broadening the range of benefits considered in the water-quality planning process and by introducing quantitative estimates of recreation benefits (reduced external costs) into the process. While the benefit figures were necessarily rather rough, they appear to be sufficiently accurate to comprise a general guide to the decision-making process.

Three general categories of recreation benefits were considered: (1) swimming, (2) boating, (3) sport fishing. Analyses conducted at the University of Pennsylvania, and based on a highly simplified model of recreation participation, indicated a large latent recreation demand in the estuary region. Another study, separately sponsored, tended to confirm the order of magnitude of the estimates.[4] In computing the monetary values associated with recreation demand under each objective set, a number of factors were considered – including the recreation-bearing capacity of the estuary as influenced by improved quality. A range of benefits was calculated by the application of alternative monetary unit values to the total use projected for the estuary. The analyses indicated that the increase in the present value of direct quantifiable recreation benefits for set 1 would range between $160 million and $350 million, for set 2 between $140 million and $320 million, for set 3 between $130 million and $310 million, and for set 4 between $120 million and $280 million. Since municipal and industrial benefits were deemed to be small and to some extent canceled by negative features in regard to industrial water use (higher D O causes corrosion in cooling equipment), these ranges were taken to be rough estimates of the total benefits from improved water quality in the estuary.

A comparison of the recreation benefits with the cost estimates (Table 15) shows that objective set 4 appears to be

Table 14. Summary of Total Costs (millions, 1968 dollars) of Achieving Objective Sets 1–4 (costs include cost of maintaining present (1964) conditions and reflect waste-load conditions projected for 1975–80) Flow at Trenton = 3,000 cubic feet per second

Objective set	Uniform treatment			Zoned treatment			Cost minimization		
	Capital costs	O & M costs*	Total costs	Capital costs	O & M costs*	Total costs	Capital costs	O & M costs*	Total costs
1	180	280 (19·0)	460†	180	280 (19·0)	460†	180	280 (19·0)	460†
2	135	180 (12·0)	315†	105	145 (10·0)	250†	115	100 (7·0)	215†
3	75	80 (5·5)	155‡	50	70 (4·5)	120‡	50	35 (2·5)	85‡
4	55	57 (5·0)	130	40	40 (2·5)	80	40	25 (1·5)	65

* Operation and maintenance costs, discounted at 3 percent twenty-year time horizon; figures in parentheses are equivalent annual operation and maintenance costs in millions of dollars/year.   † High-rate secondary to tertiary (92–98 percent removal) for all waste sources for all programs. Includes in-stream aeration cost of $20 million.   ‡ Includes $1–$2 million for either sludge removal or aeration to meet goals in river sections #3 and #4.

SOURCE: Allen V. Kneese and Blaire T. Bower, Managing Water Quality: Economics, Technology, Institutions, Baltimore, Johns Hopkins Press, 1968.

Table 15. Costs and Benefits of Water-Quality Improvement in the Delaware Estuary Area* (million dollars)

Objective set	Estimated total cost	Estimated recreation benefits	Estimated incremental cost		Estimated incremental benefits	
			minimum†	maximum‡	minimum†	maximum‡
1	460	160–350				
			245	145	20	30
2	215–315	140–320				
			130	160	10	10
3	85–155	130–310				
			20	25	10	30
4	65–130	120–280				

* All costs and benefits are present values calculated with 3 percent discount rate and twenty-year time horizon.
† Difference between adjacent minima. ‡ Difference between adjacent maxima.

SOURCE: Allen V. Kneese and Blaire T. Bower, Managing Water Quality: Economics, Technology, Institutions, Baltimore, Johns Hopkins Press, 1968.

justified even when the lowest estimate of benefit is compared with the highest estimate of cost. The incremental costs of going from set 4 to set 3 suggests that the justifiability of set 3 is marginal. On the assumption that some of the more widely distributed benefits of water-quality improvement may not have been appropriately taken into account, it can probably be justified. Clearly, however, the incremental benefits of going to sets 2 and 1 are vastly outweighed by the incremental costs. The reader will have noticed in both Tables 14 and 15 that the cost estimates cover a tremendous range. I will comment further on that shortly.

Effluent Charges on the Delaware Estuary

Following the planning study just described, another important study was undertaken using the same models and data. It concerned itself with the possible use of effluent charges as an economic incentive for controlling waste discharge. The study was done in connection with the work of a special inter-departmental committee on water-quality control headed by Gardner Ackley, at the time Chairman of the President's Council of Economic Advisers. The written reports were prepared by the Federal Water Pollution Control Administration headquarters staff, primarily by Edwin Johnson.[5]

Assuming that direct controls would be effective and that waste dischargers would respond rationally to economic incentives, the study analyzed four programs for achieving alternative dissolved oxygen objectives in the estuary.

The first, and in a sense a standard of comparison for the others, is the least-cost linear programming solution (LC) – the low-cost figures in Tables 14 and 15 correspond to it. This solution uses the mathematical programming technique described earlier to obtain the minimum cost distribution of waste removals. To implement this program with the usual direct regulation as a control policy would require precise information on waste treatment costs at all outfalls and direct controls on all waste discharges. It would result in radically different levels of treatment and treatment costs at different outfalls. The reason is simply that it would concentrate treatment at those points where the critical oxygen sag can be reduced most inexpensively.

The second is the uniform treatment solution (UT). In this solution each waste discharger is required to remove a given percentage of the wastes previously discharged before discharging the remainder to the stream. The percentage is the minimum needed to achieve the DO standard in the stream and is the same at each point of discharge. This solution may be considered typical of the conventional administrative effluent standards approach to the problem of achieving a stream quality standard – the high cost estimates in Table 15 correspond to it.

The third is the single effluent charge solution (SECh). This solution involves charging each waste discharger in the estuary the same price per unit of waste discharge. The solution examines responses of individual waste dischargers and identifies the minimum single charge which will induce sufficient reduction in waste discharge to achieve the standard. Unfortunately, only treatment was permitted as a response to the charge in this study; had process changes and by-product recovery been admitted, the costs of obtaining the objective would have been reduced. Still there is no reason to think that the relative costs of the alternative strategies would be changed much.

The fourth is the zone effluent charge solution (ZECh), which used a uniform effluent charge in each zone instead of a uniform charge over all reaches of the estuary. In Map 1 the zones are designated by arabic numerals.

Table 16 indicates the economic costs (i.e. exclusive of the effluent charge paid for the remaining discharge) associated with the program for two levels of water quality. The 3–4 p.p.m. standard approximately coincides with objective set 3 in Table 12 – the highest objective set which appears to be justifiable on economic efficiency grounds.

The analysis indicates that the effluent charges system would produce the specified quality levels at about half the social cost of the uniform treatment method. Especially at the higher quality level, the cost saving is of a highly significant magnitude. The present value of the cost stream saved is in the order of $150,000,000. The result occurs because, as we saw in Chapter 5, the incentive effect of the charge is to concentrate discharge reduction where costs are lowest.

Table 16. Cost of Treatment under Alternative Programs

DO objective (p.p.m.)	Program			
	LC	UT	SECh	ZECh
	(million dollars per year)			
2	1·6	5·0	2·4	2·4
3–4	7·0	20·0	12·0	8·6

The least-cost system is capable of reducing costs somewhat further than either the uniform or the zoned charge since it programs waste discharges at each point specifically in relation to the cost of improving quality in the critical reach, but this comes at the cost of detailed information on treatment costs at each point and a distribution of costs such that some waste dischargers experience heavy costs and others virtually none. The least-cost system is closely approached by ZECh at the higher quality level. In effect, this zone charge procedure 'credits' waste dischargers at locations remote from the critical point with degradation of their wastes in the intervening reach of a stream before they arrive at the critical reach. This is a necessary condition for full efficiency when effluent charges are used to achieve a standard at a critical reach in a stream. The reason that the ZECh does not achieve quite the same efficiency as the least-cost program is that the 'credit' is not specific to the individual waste discharger but is awarded in blocks – three in this case.

Another way of putting this is that equalizing marginal

waste-water-reduction cost at all outfalls is strictly speaking a necessary condition for cost minimization only when a homogenous 'lump' of assimilative capacity is being allocated – or more formally, when all the coefficients in the transfer matrix corresponding to a binding constraint are identical. When they are not, thorough-going cost minimization requires that prices be 'tailored' for each outfall. This explains why the solution based on a single charge only approaches but does not reach the programmed cost minimization solution. How closely it will approach is an empirical question relating to the magnitude of the a_{ij}'s.

Having the tool of transfer coefficients in hand we can now treat this matter more rigorously than was done in Chapter 5. Assume two industrial dischargers with the following cost functions for reducing waste discharge:

(1) $$c_1 = f(x_1)$$

(2) $$c_2 = f(x_2)$$

where x_1 = waste discharged from plant #1,
x_2 = waste discharged from plant #2,
c_1 and c_2 are costs of reducing waste discharge.
Assuming reach #6 is the 'critical' reach and recalling the meaning of the elements in the transfer matrix,

$$R_6 = a_{61}x_1 + a_{62}x_2 \text{ (i.e., 'binding' constraint),}$$
where

(3) $$R_6 = \text{the 'standard'}.$$

Form the Lagrangian,

(4) $$L = c_1 + c_2 + \lambda(R_6 - a_{61}x_1 - a_{62}x_2).$$

At optimum,

(5) $$\frac{\partial L}{\partial x_1} = \frac{dc_1}{dx_1} + \lambda(-a_{61}) = 0$$

(6) $$\frac{\partial L}{\partial x_2} = \frac{dc_2}{ax_2} + \lambda(-a_{62}) = 0.$$

If we include the constraint $R_6 = a_{61}x_1 + a_{62}x_2$, we have 3 equations and 3 unknowns (x_1, x_2, and λ).

Solving for λ, we get:

(7)
$$\lambda = \frac{1}{a_{61}} \frac{dc_1}{dx_1}$$

and

(8)
$$\lambda = \frac{1}{a_{62}} \frac{dc_2}{dx_2}.$$

Note that:

$$\frac{1}{a_{61}} \frac{dc_1}{dx_1} = \frac{1}{a_{62}} \frac{dc_2}{dx_2}$$

or
$$\frac{dc_1}{dx_1} = \frac{a_{61}}{a_{62}} \frac{dc_2}{dx_2}.$$

Note also that $\lambda \neq 0$ unless either $\dfrac{dc_1}{dx_1}$ or $\dfrac{dc_2}{dx_2} = 0$. Because both equations (5) and (6) are equal to zero, they may be set equal to each other:

$$\frac{dc_1}{dx_1} = \frac{dc_2}{dx_2} + \lambda(a_{61} - a_{62}).$$

Thus at the cost-minimizing solution marginal costs are generally not equal.[6] But the Delaware estuary study showed that for an important real case equalizing them gets pretty close to the cost-minimizing solution.

Further Comments on the Effluent Charge Approach

At an average effluent charge of ten cents per pound of BOD, which the staff estimated would be needed for the Delaware zoned effluent charge program,[7] the funds collected by the administrative agency would amount to about $7 million per year. Nevertheless, for the 3–4 p.p.m. DO objective, the total cost to industry and municipalities as a whole – effluent charge plus cost of treatment – is about the same as the cost of treatment only under the uniform treatment program. About half of this outlay does not represent an actual resources cost but rather a rental-type payment for the use of assimilative capacity.

It should be noted that an important efficiency advantage of the effluent charges programs as contrasted with the least-cost program is their relatively smaller demand for information and analytical refinement. A study of the type already performed for the Delaware estuary could serve as the basis for an effluent charge scheme. An order-of-magnitude estimate of the required charge reveals itself. Actually, since the costs do not take account of the possibility of process change in industry, which is often cheaper than 'end of pipe' treatment, the ten cents per pound of BOD charge was probably too high and could be adjusted downward at a later point (one would need to take inflation into account). Also, the charge provides a continuing incentive for the discharger to reduce his waste load by placing him under the persistent pressure of monetary penalties. He is induced to develop new technology and as it develops to implement it. As new technology develops, the effluent charge could be gradually reduced while the stream standard is maintained, or the standard could be allowed to rise if this is deemed desirable. The process of induced technological change has particularly striking results in this field since the waste assimilative services of watercourses have heretofore been completely unpriced.

The direct control measures implicit in the least-cost program, on the other hand (as well as the effluent standard of the uniform treatment program), provide only a more limited incentive to improved technology. Moreover, the minimum cost program would require not only detailed information on current cost levels at each individual outfall, but also information on changes in cost with changing technology, in regard to industrial processes, product mix, treatment cost, etc., and would be extremely inequitable in its cost distribution.

The Delaware estuary survey was a pioneering study of water-quality management and is of continuing importance. Some of the tools it developed are in use by the Delaware River Basin Commission, and it is still frequently referred to in discussions of policy in the United States – a point I will develop a little later in the chapter. It was the first study to embody at least a rudimentary ecological model into an economic optimization framework, and it provided an illuminating analysis of several policy options including effluent charges.

The study did have some major deficiencies, however. Among them are that only a very limited range of technological alternatives for managing water quality was examined and that the stochastic aspects of water quality were not analyzed. These matters were considered, however, in the Potomac study to which I turn next. Before doing so however, I must introduce one additional piece of methodological equipment – stochastic or probabilistic generators of hydrological records.

Stochastic Hydrology

As everyone knows, the flow of rivers (one of the major determinants of their capacity to assimilate waste materials) is not constant with time. It varies seasonally in somewhat regular patterns but with a large random component. Traditionally, in designing flow regulating structures (reservoirs) an empirical device called a 'mass curve' is used to determine the yield that can be sustained from the reservoir during drought periods. Underlying this technique is the assumption that future flows (measured on a daily or monthly basis) will be an exact replication of flows observed historically (usually there are thirty years or so of good records in the more advanced countries).

An alternative, that is more defensible on statistical grounds, is to assume that the historical record is a sample from a much larger population and that what will remain invariant in the future are only certain of the moments (mean, standard deviation, skewness) of the distribution of observed flows. Based on the latter assumption, stochastic hydrology generators have been devised which can simulate long hydrologic sequences incorporating extreme values and patterns of events not in the historic record while maintaining selected moments of the frequency distribution of that record. There are difficult problems associated with such generators, but many of them have been overcome. The problems involve such things as serial correlation in the record of flows and maintaining cross and serial correlations for separate gauging stations in the same system. I will not attempt to treat these since my intent is just to acquaint the reader with the general recursive relationships used.

In these 'Markovian' models the basic recursive relation used can be represented by the following equation[8]:

$$x_{i+1} = \mu + \beta(x_i - \mu) + t_{i+1}\sigma(1 - \rho^2)^{\frac{1}{2}}$$

In this model, x_{i+1}, the flow in the $(i + 1)$st interval, is a linear function of x_i, the flow in the ith interval; of a standardized random deviate t_{i+1}; and of the population parameters μ (the population mean), σ (the population standard deviation), β (the regression coefficient of flows in the $(i + 1)$st interval on values in the ith interval), and ρ (the correlation coefficient between flows in successive time periods). The standardized random deviate t_{i+1} has zero mean and unit variance.

It can be shown that if the distribution of flows is normal and the regression functions of x_i on x_{i-1} is linear and homoscedastic (of constant variance), the conditional expectation of x_i, given x_{i-1}, is given by

$$E(x_i \mid x_{i-1}) = \mu + \beta(x_{i-1} - \mu)$$

and the expected variance of x_i, given x_{i-1}, is

$$\text{Var}(x_i \mid x_{i-1}) = \sigma^2(1 - \rho^2).$$

Thus, we can see in the recursive equation that the first two

169

terms on the right-hand side are the expected value of x_{i+1}, given x_i has occurred (February's flow, January having occurred), and the last term is the random component consisting of a randomly selected normal, deviate which, when multiplied by the expected variance of x_{i+1}, given x_i, brings the result back into the proper dimension comparable with the first two terms of the right side. It can also be shown that to treat non-normal distributions it is sufficient to alter the distribution of the random additive component and thus maintain higher moments of observed data.[9]

It is readily seen that a recursive model of this type could be used to generate indefinitely long sequences of hydrological record to be used as inputs to a simulation model. As long a generated sequence of flows as is wished (say, several thousand years) can then be used in analyzing the probabilistic performance of a reservoir, or other water quantity and quality management system elements. Stochastic hydrology is used in connection with the Potomac case study to which I now turn.

The Potomac Study

A 1961 amendment to the Federal Water Pollution Control Act of 1948, which, with minor exceptions, was the first step by the United States Federal Government into what had been an exclusive area of state sovereignty, is the starting point for discussion of the Potomac case. The feature of the 1961 Act which is most relevant to present purposes is that it provided for the inclusion of subsidized storage in federal multi-purpose reservoirs to augment low flows for the purpose of improving water quality. This opened the door to the possibility of including in federally subsidized water-quality improvement programs technological options other than treatment. Naturally this possibility drew the attention of federal agencies engaged in the planning and construction of public works related to water resources. In the eastern United States the U.S. Army Corps of Engineers is the lead agency in this respect.

In 1963, the U.S. Army Corps of Engineers submitted the *Potomac River Basin Report*. This report was the first one in which a federal water resource agency submitted a 'comprehensive' plan in which water-quality management was the major consideration. The plan took a quality objective stated in physical terms (parts per million of dissolved oxygen) as given, and recommended a program of waste treatment and low-flow regulation to meet this objective in the future. While it was a pioneering effort, the benefit evaluation techinique, based on the 'alternative cost procedure', was grossly deficient, and the range of alternatives considered for water-quality improvement was still very narrow, even though wider than that included in the Delaware study. Basically, the Corps of Engineers limited its planning to consideration of those quality improvement facilities which could clearly be implemented through existing governmental institutions. As we shall see, this restricted the range of choice greatly and led to the recommendation of a set of facilities which was far from the least costly which could have been devised to achieve the stated water-quality objective.

A later Resources for the Future study,[10] which forms the basis for my further discussion, used the Corps of Engineers data plus considerable additional information to define further the range of alternatives for water-quality management in the Potomac estuary in the neighborhood of Washington, D.C., the locus of most of the water-quality problems.

The Basin and Its Problems

The watershed of the Potomac, an area of about 14,000 square miles, lies in portions of four states and the District of Columbia. About three quarters of the population in the basin is found in the Washington metropolitan area. This area, which extends beyond the District of Columbia into Maryland and Virginia, already has a population of nearly 3 million persons and is one of the most rapidly growing metropolitan areas in the nation. The Washington area lies near the head of the Potomac estuary which is heavily used for recreation. Water supply for the area is taken from the Potomac river above the estuary. The estuary periodically experiences a low level of dissolved oxygen – a condition which could get much worse as waste loads from the metropolitan area and upstream sources mount. The Corps of Engineers as part of its planning effort projected water demands and waste loads to the year 2010. One of the central objectives of the plan was to control the effects of waste loads expected to prevail then. Among the planning assumptions was that the maximum feasible control of waste loads would result from conventional secondary sewage treatment (about 90 percent BOD removal).

The plan made public in 1963 recommended the construction by the year 2010 of sixteen major reservoirs in the Potomac basin and more than 400 headwater structures (see Map 2). These were meant to meet projected water supply, water-quality, and flood control objectives. Of the sixteen major reservoirs, ten were planned to meet projected upstream objectives for the low-flow regulation for water supply and quality control. At the same time, this group of reservoirs would provide a higher sustained flow at Washington sufficient to meet the projected municipal water diversions there. The remaining group of six reservoirs (providing 60 percent of the proposed yield – 2340 c.f.s. (cubic feet per second) out of 3931 c.f.s.) was designed to augment flows into the estuary sufficiently to maintain 4 p.p.m. of dissolved oxygen (twenty-four-hour monthly mean for the minimum month). The projected storage was based on counteracting residual 2010 waste loads and an assumed replication of the historical record of flows into the estuary (i.e., the mass curve approach was used to determine required storage to sustain flows calculated to be needed to offset residual waste loads to the extent of maintaining 4 p.p.m. DO). From a statistical point of view, the mass curve approach has great deficiencies which were discussed in connection with our earlier consideration of stochastic hydrology. I will return to this point a little later.

A benefit-cost analysis was presented which indicated that

the benefits from flow regulation would outweigh its costs. But this analysis did not do what benefit-cost analysis is intended to accomplish – assist in deciding whether a pro-

Map 2. Major Reservoirs in Recommended Plan for Potomac Basin

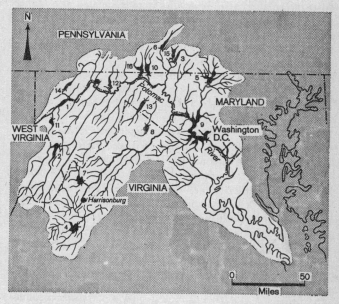

SOURCE: *PRB Report*, Vol. I, p. 30, reproduced in Robert K. Davis, *The Range of Choice in Water Management* (Baltimore, Johns Hopkins Press, 1968).

posed investment is socially worthwhile. The preset physical quality objective of 4 p.p.m. of DO was taken as given in the planning. It was assumed that treatment of the sewage from the Washington metropolitan area could not succeed in removing more than 90 percent of the waste load. This is insufficient to meet the objective. The only alternative seriously investigated was low-flow regulation to improve the waste assimilative capacity of the estuary. Benefits from low-flow regulation were taken to be the cost of a single-purpose reservoir designed to meet low-flow requirements at each point of projected need without regard to the complementary effects of meeting upstream needs. Moreover, costs of the alternative reservoirs were calculated at a higher rate of interest – presumably because it was assumed they would be implemented by state or local governments which have to pay higher rates of interest than the federal agencies use in their own calculations.

This string of planning assumptions was bound to produce positive net benefits for flow regulation. But this result was obtained without even addressing the real question – whether the 4 p.p.m. objective was justified by the willingness of beneficiaries to pay at least as much as it costs to maintain it. Clearly, the benefit-cost analysis as it was performed is not helpful in deciding whether the plan is justified.

Furthermore, for various reasons having to do with limitations on the authority of water resources agencies and their perception of problems and appropriate solutions, the planners made no concerted or systematic effort to search for and evaluate alternative ways (in addition to flow regulation) of achieving the specified water-quality objective. The measures recommended for quality control were limited to basic conventional treatment and low-flow augmentation – measures which could clearly be implemented by the federal and local government agencies which are the traditional purveyors of water services in the United States. To have implemented a program embodying the less conventional measures which the later Resources for the Future study demonstrated would have entered into a cost-minimizing solution and would have required institutional change. The possibility of such change was not contemplated in the planning process. Failure to consider institutional reform as a possible objective of the planning process is a failing frequently encountered around the world and I shall have more to say about it subsequently.

Searching for Additional Alternatives

The follow-up Resources for the Future study showed that if the plan had included certain collective measures – which no existing agency had a clear authority or incentive to finance, construct, and operate – it would have entered into a least-cost system for meeting the oxygen objective. Had such a system served as the alternative for benefit analysis, net benefits for flow regulation, at least for the larger-scale reservoir systems, would have been grossly negative. But, in general, the alternative cost-benefit estimation procedures are inappropriate in cases like this.

In going through the later analysis, the Corps assumption that wastes in the Washington metropolitan area would receive 90 percent treatment was (somewhat arbitrarily) used as a baseline. The costs of other alternatives were then weighed off against the incremental cost of flow regulation for counteracting the residual oxygen deficit.

Costs were obtained for different levels of low-flow regulation by scaling down by various amounts the Corps's proposed low-flow regulation system. The scaled-down systems were roughly optimized by using a computer simulation program which permitted the historical trace of hydrology to be regulated by the various systems.

The line between simulation models and the optimizing type of programming models, such as that used in the Delaware study, is often not very clean cut. In general, however, simulations are used to play out the implications of certain assumptions, (reservoir sizes, operating rules, etc.) either solely in terms of the behavior of the natural system upon which they have an impact or on certain economic variables – such as costs. Normally they do not contain an explicit optimizing procedure but simply enumerate a large number of alternative results. This is a problem because the number of possible alternative results can easily become unmanageably large. This was not so in the case of the Potomac study, however, because the range of variables was carefully limited and only large increments were permitted. The advantage of simulation is that it can more easily handle non-linearities and probabilistic aspects of problems than can mathematical programming.

In the first set of Resources for the Future analyses, historical hydrology was used to maintain close comparability with the Corps results. In computing costs for the successively smaller reservoir systems, account was taken of the difference in flood damage reduction and recreation services realized by any scaled-down system in comparison to the full proposed Corps of Engineers system.

Costs of several alternative ways of equivalently offsetting the waste load were also developed. These included processes for further treatment of the waste load (microstraining, step aeration, chemical polymers, powdered carbon, and granular carbon); costs for effluent distribution via pipeline along the estuary to make better use of its natural assimilative capacity; and re-oxygenation of the estuary which, like low-flow regulation, improves assimilative capacity.

Computer simulation of the effects of these processes in view of variations of river flow (using the historical hydrologic trace) into the estuary show that they need to be operated on the average only three and a half months per year in order to meet the DO objective. Because the alternative systems are high in operating cost and low in capital cost relative to low-flow regulation, they can be comparatively efficient if operated only as needed but would not be competitive if operated continuously, thereby overshooting quality goals most of the time. Accordingly, they could only enter efficiently into the quality management system if institutional means existed for carefully articulated design and operation in conjunction with other elements of the system.

Establishing combinations which would meet the standard required that if one process was reduced another had to be equivalently increased. It was possible to use computer simulation to exhaust all possible combinations of the feasible and sufficient processes given the relatively large increments defined for them. The computer program gave a complete listing and cost ranking of all systems – some 300 in all.

A sampling of alternative feasible and sufficient systems is shown in Table 17.

This analysis shows that many combinations of processes could achieve the objective at less cost than the proposed

Table 17. System Costs by General Class of Process Combinations. Three and a Half Months' Operation (present worth, fifty-year period, 4 percent discount in $ million)

Alternative systems	
1. Reoxygenation	20
2. Chemical polymers and reoxygenation	22
3. Step aeration and reoxygenation	25
4. Microstrainers and reoxygenation	28
5. Diversion and reoxygenation	33
6. Diversion, waste treatment and reoxygenation	45
7. Low-flow augmentation and reoxygenation	60
8. Low-flow augmentation, reoxygenation and waste treatment	60
9. Low-flow regulation	140

SOURCE: Adapted from various tables in Robert K. Davis, *The Range of Choice in Water Management*, Baltimore, Johns Hopkins Press, 1968.

system based upon conventional treatment and flow regulation. It is notable that all of them except the flow regulation alternative would require the construction and closely articulated operation of facilities which have not traditionally been in the purview of either the federal or local government (particularly reoxygenation and regional effluent distribution works). Another salient point is that while low-flow regulation is vastly more costly than reoxygenation or some of the other alternatives, from the point of view of the people in the basin it costs much less, because of subsidies. Low-flow regulation for water-quality improvement is a fully nonreimbursable purpose of federal water development in the United States, while no subsidy at all is available for measures like reoxygenation and waste diversion. Thus, the fact that federal water development policy is such that certain measures for development confer large subsidies on a region while others do not can also contribute to choices among alternatives which are distorted from a broader economic point of view.

Both of these factors were undoubtedly implicit considerations in the plan recommended by the Corps. It is thus possible to examine the existing institutional and policy restraints by means of economic systems analysis which is not limited by these restraints, and thus provide information on the desirability of institutional change. Such examination of institutional constraints clearly should be part of the planning process. In the case of the Potomac it appears that much could be gained by institutional arrangements permitting the design and operation of quality management systems embodying a wide range of alternatives.

Stochastic Aspects

So far, in my discussion of cases, I dealt with deterministic models. These, quite imperfectly, recognize the variability of river flow by specifying some level below which flow is unlikely to drop. The Delaware estuary study took this approach and so did the Corps study of the Potomac, as well as much of the Resources for the Future follow-on study. But the availability of the Potomac reservoir simulation model made it possible to study some aspects of the probability question in a more explicit way. It is one of the major disadvantages of optimization models such as that used on the Delaware estuary (which as already mentioned otherwise have great advantages) that it is very difficult to incorporate stochastic aspects into them.

The Corps of Engineers based its design on the specification that DO concentrations in the estuary would not fall below 4 p.p.m. based on the twenty-four-hour monthly mean for the minimum month. A standard kind of mass curve analysis was used to check that the yield of the proposed reservoirs system would be sufficient to meet the objective. As has already been noted, this analysis makes the statistically untenable assumption that future stream flow will be a replication of the past.

To help illuminate the probability aspect of the water-quality standards conventionally used in planning, a stochastic hydrology was generated for long periods of time and applied to the reservoir simulation program.

Table 18 presents some figures for the different probabilities of violating 2 and 4 p.p.m. DO levels when different

Table 18. Percentage of Time Monthly Mean DO is less than 2 p.p.m. for Five-hundred-Year Trials at Different DO Target and System Capacities

Storage capacity	DO target p.p.m.	Percentage of time < 2 p.p.m.	Percentage of time < target
82,000 acre-ft	2	0·25	0·25
140,000	2	0·03	0·03
600,000	4	0·35	.3·30
770,000	4	0·22	1·03
970,000	4	0	0·33

SOURCE: Robert K. Davis, *The Range of Choice in Water Management*, Baltimore, Johns Hopkins Press, 1968.

systems of reservoirs are operated to achieve DO targets. In this presentation it is assumed that low-flow regulation is the only means used to counteract the residual deficit after about 90 percent treatment. This is done to spell out clearly the implication for reservoir storage, even though in an optimized or least-cost system the incremental costs of achieving lower probabilities of violation would be less. It is interesting to note two main points emerging from this analysis.

(1) Reducing the probability of violating the 4 p.p.m. objective from 3·3 percent to 0·33 percent costs about 370,000 acre-feet in storage and around 50 million in dollars.

The 0·33 percent level is about equivalent to the objective used in the Corps study.

(2) If a system is operated to avoid violation of a 2 p.p.m. target, about the same low level of violation of the 2 p.p.m. level can be achieved with 82,000 acre-feet of capacity as with 770,000 acre-feet of capacity in a system operated to achieve a 4 p.p.m. target. Thus, what the level of the standard is meant to accomplish becomes a profoundly important question when reservoirs are used in a water-quality management system. We must decide whether it is more important to keep the oxygen from falling to very low levels or to keep it at higher levels more of the time. It is not necessarily true that a system operated to achieve high levels as much of the time as possible will provide greater security against extreme failure than a smaller system operated to achieve lower levels as much of the time as possible. In fact, in the Potomac instance quite the opposite was true. Water was released for the higher objective and when it was exhausted the target was missed by large margins.

What this analysis has shown is that the probability aspect of standard setting, which is usually treated by simple engineering rules of thumb, actually contains important valuation problems. The probability statement is just as important as the level of the standard in terms of its cost-benefit implications.

Conclusions from the Potomac Study

The Resources for the Future Potomac study accomplished three main things: (1) for the first time in the United States it revealed how wide a range of technical options is available for water-quality management and how restricting it is to limit consideration of alternatives to those historically included in the missions of specific agencies. (2) It showed that the alternative cost-benefit evaluation procedure, justifiable in some specific situations, can be more deceptive than helpful when applied to water-quality planning. (3) It illustrated the importance of the stochastic aspects of the problem.

As a result of this study and other objections to the Corps plan, it was abandoned and a planning process instituted in the basin which is much less limited in its consideration of alternatives.

Other Research and Experiences

I have reviewed the Delaware and Potomac studies in some detail because they were pioneering in character and of outstanding importance. There have, however, in more recent years been other studies which have tended to confirm the main results of these studies – the importance of assessing and having the capacity to implement a wide range of technological alternatives and the efficiency attributes of effluent charges. Studies of the Great Miami river in Ohio, of the Houston Galveston Bay area in Texas and of the Wisconsin river, all in the United States, may be cited. In addition to these research and planning studies the activities of several river basin authorities in West Germany have received wide attention.[11] The latter have been in operation for upwards of fifty years and have, to the satisfaction of most observers, demonstrated the efficiency of a river basin approach to water quality combined with a system of charging for effluent discharges whether to the river or to waste handling facilities.

A combination of the various economic/engineering studies and the Ruhr experience has contributed substantially to the policy-making process in a number of countries – France, Britain, West Germany, and Canada may be mentioned as leading examples. In each case river basin approaches have been developed and charging schemes have been implemented or are under development. I shall review more of this experience in the final chapter, which deals with policy.

Interestingly the studies have been much less influential in policy making in the United States than in other developed countries even though the pioneering studies were conducted in the U.S. This is not to say, however, that the studies have not received wide attention there. During the late sixties and early seventies there was much discussion of an appropriate national strategy for water-quality management and a Bill was introduced into the United States Congress based heavily on the studies and experience we have just reviewed. The Bill, introduced by Senator William Proxmire and a number of distinguished colleagues, would have revised the national strategy and based it on two main elements (1) a national system of effluent charges (2) the development of regional river basin agencies for water-quality management.[12] I will not go into the details of the Act here since it resembles the legislation which is now proposed for West Germany which is reviewed in some detail in the last chapter.

The United States Congress, however, chose to stick with the existing strategy of direct regulation and subsidies which it sought to strengthen in legislation passed in 1972. This was the result of a variety of factors: the (usually false) folklore prevalent in the government that direct regulation is a thoroughly effective device for influencing behavior, the fact that political careers have been built on this approach, and the committee structure of Congress which means that Bills have to come from the 'right' committee to have any chance of success. The water-quality legislation actually enacted has come under strong criticism from water-quality professionals and will probably receive fundamental reconsideration in a few years when its major weaknesses will have revealed themselves. When this occurs the Proxmire type of approach, which is based solidly on economic research, will no doubt get more serious consideration because it has continued to gain support. Diverse groups including the Sierra Club (one of the nation's most important conservationist organizations), the Committee for Economic Development (perhaps the most prominent business men's organization), and committees of the National Academy of Sciences have publicly favored the effluent charges regional management approach as being both more efficient and more effective than the present one.[13]

As we will see in the next section, legislation in Britain has evolved toward a thorough-going regional management approach to water-quality problems. In that section I will discuss an economic study of the River Trent which is aimed at aiding the implementation of that approach. This will also provide an opportunity to see yet a third planning methodology in operation, that of dynamic programming.

The Trent Study

As one would expect in view of its industrial history, Britain has been experiencing severe water pollution for a long time. By the middle of the nineteenth century pollution had become a serious public health problem, especially in such densely populated areas as Lancashire, Yorkshire, the Midlands and London. Epidemics, destruction of fish life, and grossly offensive river conditions prompted the appointment of Royal Commissions in 1865 and 1868 to study and report on the problem of river pollution. Since then there has been a long history of evolution of institutional arrangements for water-quality management in England. The Trent river study, which I review in this section, must be understood in the context of the later stages of this evolution.

Prior to the Water Pollution Act of 1973 the law in force was the Water Resources Act of 1963 passed just ten years earlier. The latter produced a situation in which water resource activities in any given geographical region were conducted at several levels. It left intact the existing statutory Water Undertakers of which there were about two hundred. These are enterprises with a statutory obligation to provide supplies of piped, pure, wholesome water for domestic and non-domestic consumers. The Act also continued the sewage and sewage disposal authorities, of which there were more than 1,300, which have certain statutory duties to drain houses and industrial premises. In its most important innovation, the Act extended the scope of River Authorities, which had previously developed in certain basins, to cover the entire country. Twenty-nine of these were established with responsibility for water conservation and management, land drainage, fisheries, the control of water pollution and in some cases navigation. In this context water conservation essentially meant water storage. The Act also continued certain other local institutions such as drainage boards, as well as navigation and harbour authorities.

At the national level it maintained the British Waterways Board which owned and operated the majority of the canals in the country and was also responsible for navigable rivers. The Act created the Water Resources Board at the national level. The functions of this body were mainly advisory and it had very limited executive functions.

The main reason for reviewing a few of the main characteristics of the situation prior to 1973 is to show that while institutional evolution had been going on for a long time, the 1963 Act still fell far short of creating the integrated thorough-going regional management institutions which, as we have seen, research and experience suggest could greatly improve the efficiency of water management.

In July of 1973 Parliament, being cognizant of the studies and experience elsewhere, and having made their own analyses, passed a new water Act. This Act was based on recommendations of a Central Advisory Water Committee which had been working on the question for several years.[14]

The Act completely reorganized water resources management in England and Wales: the twenty-nine River Authorities were consolidated into nine large bodies known as Regional Water Authorities, plus the Welsh National Water Development Authority. Nearly all the new water authorities preside over much larger watersheds (or in British parlance, catchment areas) than their predecessors and all of them have much more far-reaching responsibilities. In effect they have direct or indirect control over and supervision of all water-related activities from water supplies to sewage disposal. The membership of each Regional Water Authority consists of a chairman, a specified number of members appointed by the Minister of the Environment, and a specified number of members appointed by the local authorities within the water authority areas, such that these will constitute a majority. The Water Pollution Act also established a National Water Council, a consultative and advisory body set up to advise Ministers on all matters relating to national policy on water. This council is also to promote and assist the efficient performance of water authorities in their functions, including planning and research. The membership of the council consists of a chairman, not more than eight members appointed by the Secretary of State, not more than two members appointed by the Minister, and the chairmen of the various water authorities. The intent of the reorganization of water management is mainly to gain better control over water resources and to coordinate overall water uses with the limited supplies available considering both water quality and water quantity.

As regards the matter of water quality the Water Pollution Act takes initiatives in two directions. First, the water authorities have responsibilities for all sewage and sewage disposal activities, a function previously conferred on the local authorities. Secondly, new attention is given to water values, especially for recreation.

As part of the planning activity for the new Water Act and to provide methodological tools for the new authorities, the Trent research program (1969 to 1972) was carried out by the Trent River Authority, sponsored by a government grant.[15]

The River Trent is one of the more hardworking rivers in England. It flows for nearly two hundred miles through the industrial Midlands. It and its tributaries drain the great industrial complexes of Birmingham and Nottingham. Four hundred and thirty-five industrial firms discharge about seventy million gallons per day (m.g.d.) of waste water. More than 100 local authorities (prior to 1973) operated over 600 sewage treatment plants with a total dry weather flow of more than 300 m.g.d. of sewage about a quarter of which is of industrial origin. The dry-weather flow of the river (exceeded 95 percent of the time) is only 650 m.g.d.

The Trent Economic Model is based on a mathematical programming concept and computational procedure somewhat different from the linear programming model reviewed earlier. The solution procedure involves a computational device known as dynamic programming. It is an adaptation of mathematical programming designed for certain types of sequential decision problems.

The Trent Model views effluent treatment at points of discharge and intake water treatment at points of intake as interchangeable processes. In the program dischargers can choose among the limited array of effluent treatment plants with associated costs per unit of effluent treated to a level which defines the plant type. There are four types of municipal sewage plants yielding various levels of waste removal. In the case of industrial effluent control the treatment options are geared to the individual plant. The options of the intake water users (in British parlance, abstractors) are more limited because of the way in which quality states are defined. The quality state of the river is defined by the type of plant, one of ten possibilities, required to treat any amount of river water at intake point to potable standards. Industrial users have the option of taking potable water from municipal water treatment plants or installing the most elementary type of treatment plant which is assumed to yield industrially usable water irrespective of the quality of the intake water.

Thus, the program chooses that set of waste water and water treatment alternative that minimizes the cost of delivering potable and industrial reusable water in the river system. This does, of course, neglect any instream uses of the river but it is possible in the model to establish constraints on the quality of the whole river at any point in terms of sixteen different quality parameters. Thus, the model can reveal the least-cost combination of effluent treatment and water treatment plants which yield either a fixed amount of potable water at any point in the system or a certain quality for the entire river at any point in the system.

Sequential operation of the dynamic programming procedures can be illustrated by discussing in intuitive terms the way the model operates. The first upstream user of the river, say a discharger, will have the choice of, let us say, three treatment plants. Accordingly, any one of three quality states may confront the second user. If the latter is also a discharger with the choice of say three treatment plants, one of as many as nine states will confront the third user. Associated with each of these nine states is a cost composed of the costs of the particular treatment installations chosen by the upper user. The model recognizes only ten different possible states. If there are two or more combinations of installations which will give a certain state at a particular point, the model chooses the cheaper combination and throws out the more expensive alternative. Thus, as the model proceeds downstream it keeps track of the cheapest method of attaining that state.

In addition to waste water treatment and intake water treatment the model can consider such alternatives as in-river purification lakes (a technology which has received high development in the Ruhr region of West Germany), low-flow regulation, and mechanical reaeration.

The Trent Economic Model is a tool in the process of development and use. It is designed to be useful to the new British water management institutions, which themselves reflect reforms built solidly on a system conception of the water management problem. The model should assist in standard setting, planning, and the operation of works.

The Westernport Bay Land-Use Model[16]

As I have remarked previously, and as one of the models presented in the last chapter suggested, land-use questions are a necessary part of environmental planning. The matter of how to go about land-use planning for residuals management purposes has proved to be very difficult, however, and the case studies we have reviewed have hardly come to grips with the matter at all. Since they dealt with highly developed regions where the location of many activities may, for practical purposes, be regarded as fixed, perhaps this deficiency is not so serious. When new development is being planned, however, the neglect of locational factors is a fundamental difficulty.

A current economic water-quality management study in Australia is attempting to deal with the land-use question in an integral manner. Because of its uniqueness I present a brief discussion of the model they are using as the closing case in this chapter, despite the fact that the study is far from complete and appears to have some unresolved methodological problems.

The Westernport Bay region has little development at present but it contains an excellent deep-water port and large-scale future development is contemplated. At the same time the water body and surrounding land areas are of great natural beauty and important in fish and wildlife propagation. Hence there is the potential for serious conflict between development and environment. The area in question is shown in Map 3.

The purpose of the land-use model is to provide planners with rough guidelines for developing the Westernport region. It is not regarded as accurate or complete enough to be a detailed design tool. The model will be used to provide guidance on allocating limited land resources among five broad conflicting uses: (1) industrial, (2) urban, (3) farming, (4) recreation, and (5) conservation (wildlife).

The land-use model is constructed as a static economic model. Given a set of future total population projections for the Westernport region, planners would like to be able to use the model to specify the optimal geographic distribution of activities at future points in time, subject to meeting water-quality constraints (standards) at predetermined locations in the bay.

The model is structured as a linear program.[17] The program consists of four major sections: (1) land-use activities, by land zones, (2) local and regional sewage treatment and disposal activities, (3) transportation activities, based on worker trips, and (4) water-quality activities. This is shown schematically in Figure 5. Benefits (positive prices) are attached to the various land-use activities and costs (negative prices) to the sewage treatment and disposal activities and to

Map 3. Westernport Bay Environmental Study

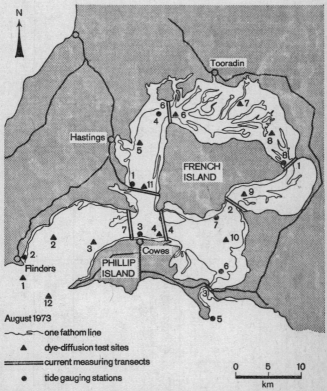

N

Tooradin

Hastings

FRENCH ISLAND

Cowes

PHILLIP ISLAND

Flinders

August 1973

〜〜 one fathom line

▲ dye-diffusion test sites

═══ current measuring transects

● tide gauging stations

0   5   10
km

Velocity (vertical and horizontal) is taken periodically at the lines to get total volume transfer for a tidal cycle. Cycle movement is done periodically.

SOURCE: Ministry for Conservation, Government of Australia, August 1973.

Figure 5. Land-Use 'Quasi' Linear Programming Model

ROWS		COLUMNS				RHS
	Land-use activities	Industrial sewage treat-ment activities (local)	Municipal sewage treat-ment activities (local and regional)	Transportation activities	Water-quality activities	
	92 land zones; up to 8 land uses per zone		Integer variables are used in this section of the model			
Objective Function	B . . . . . B	C C	C C	C C		

B – benefits (positive prices); C – costs (negative prices); RHS – right-hand side.

transportation. Water quality is constrained so as not to exceed exogeneously determined upper limits. This is done by means of incorporating a transfer coefficient matrix, of the type already discussed in the last chapter in connection with the Delaware study, into the model. Thus this is a mathematical programming model in which the objective is to maximize net benefits subject to ambient water-quality constraints.

For land-use modeling purposes, the Westernport region is divided into ninety-two land zones. Up to eight of ten possible land-use activities (see Table 19) may be employed for each

Table 19. Land-Use Categories

Category	Description
1	Urban (septic tanks)
2	Urban (sewered)
3	Agriculture
4	Agriculture (intensive)
5	Food processing
6	Intensive husbandry
7	Heavy industry
8	Light industry
9	Wilderness
10	Recreation

zone (a maximum of $92 \times 8 = 736$ activities in this section of the model). Activity levels in this part of the model are expressed in units of land area. Land use, by zone, can be constrained, either partially or totally, for a given run of the model.

Land value, net of development costs, for each land-use activity and for each zone are placed in the appropriate column of the objective function. The land prices used in the model are average zonal values rather than site specific.

Residuals generation coefficients (e.g., pounds of residual 'X' per land area per day) are specified for each land-use activity in each of the ninety-two land zones. In addition, quantities (flows) of sewage and storm water generated in each land-use activity, by zone, are provided, as are inputs to the ground-water aquifer. Residuals considered in the land-use model are:

> fresh water
> nitrates
> phosphates
> biochemical oxygen demand (BOD)
> oil and grease
> detergents
> toxicants
> heat.

The generation and discharge of industrial wastes can be incorporated in the land-activities section of the model under either light or heavy industries (see Table 19). Unfortunately, these categories are too broad for most industries. The types, and amounts, of residuals generated in industrial processes vary tremendously from industry to industry, and even from plant to plant within the same industry. Because of this, the land-use model has been structured to deal with some industrial dischargers as individual point sources. This is achieved by incorporating their industrial waste treatment activities after the land-use activities in the model. This set of activities is shown in the second section of Figure 5.

Two basic options are provided in the model for the treatment of sanitary sewage: (1) three levels of removal in 'standard' sewage treatment plants (primary, secondary, and tertiary) at local and regional facilities, and (2) oxidation ponds (lagoons). When oxidation ponds are selected to treat sewage, the land required for the ponds is subtracted from the total land available in the land zone. Land required for standard sewage treatment processes, being much less than that required for oxidation ponds, is not accounted for. Costs of sewage treatment are based on sewage flow only and not on the BOD concentration.

Sewage may be treated in each of the land zones, transported to another zone (i.e., a node in the sewage transport network) for regional treatment, discharged to the bay via one of the twenty-three discharge locations with no prior treatment, or transported out of the region directly to the ocean.

In the transportation section of the model, user costs (vehicle operating costs and value of time) for worker trips are considered explicitly. The transportation section of the model ensures some interaction within the model between where people live and where they work. A subprogram is required to distribute trips on the basis of residential zones and industrial zones. A standard gravity model is used for this purpose.[18]

The main methodological problems with the model seem to arise from the fact that certain values which are in reality simultaneously determined are taken as independent. The most important of these is the interdependency between transport costs and land values. Thus transportation activities and costs are included in a separate section of the land-use model but they are probably, at least in part, already imbedded in the land values used in the first part of the model.

Despite its remaining problems the Westernport Bay study must be regarded as a pioneering effort to fill a major gap in the existing microeconomic studies of water-quality management. Accordingly it is worth watching with interest.

Concluding Comment

As we have seen, economic studies of water-quality management have proven useful in planning, in policy making, and in the design of institutions. I will have more to say about their policy implications in the concluding chapter.

The next chapter surveys a few economic studies which have been made of the atmospheric environment. The system studies are largely analogous in methodology to those we have just reviewed with respect to water. In addition, however, the atmospheric area has seen more and larger efforts to estimate the damages associated with air-quality degradation and to evaluate national air pollution policy using benefit-cost analysis. We will take a look at these studies also.

Following this I return, in Chapter 9, to a theme introduced early in the volume – the need in principle to consider all environmental media simultaneously.

Chapter 8
Air Pollution

Introduction

Microeconomic studies of air pollution economics followed in the track of water pollution studies with a lag of several years. The economic and analytical models used were essentially identical. Since this is so we can build on the methodological discussion of the last chapter and proceed directly to a brief consideration of a few specific studies. Most of the air-quality management modeling work has been done in the United States and I will discuss U.S. cases, but it should be noted that in recent years a similar model has been built for the Rotterdam region at the Netherlands School of Economics.[1]

The Teller Study

The prototype economic study of air-quality control with respect to stationary sources was performed by Azriel Teller who used the City of Nashville, Tennessee, as a case area.[2] As in the Delaware water-quality study reviewed in the last chapter, a linear programming model was used in conjunction with environmental quality constraints, abatement costs at various locations, and an atmospheric diffusion model, to test the costs of various abatement strategies. Although atmospheric diffusion models incorporate different fundamental natural world relationships from the water-quality models based on the Street–Phelps equations reviewed in the last chapter, their mathematical form, under steady state conditions, is exactly the same. A useful addition to the type of analysis done in the Delaware case was a test of the value of forecast information in maintaining a specified maximum ambient concentration. A strategy making use of forecast information permitted techniques such as intermittent operation of control measures and short-term fuel switching when adverse meteorological conditions are forecast.

The two main strategy sets analyzed by Teller were what he called the naive approach and selective abatement.

The naive approach is the simplest method to apply in determining the degree and the cost of abatement. The approach assumes that all sources will reduce their emissions in the same proportion as the desired reduction in air-pollution concentration. As we saw in connection with the Delaware study of the last chapter many people believe that this is the most equitable procedure since a source that accounts for *x* percent of the total emissions is thus responsible for *x* percent of the reduction. In reality, however, as we have learned from our consideration of environmental diffusion models, a source that emits *x* percent of the emissions may be responsible for less than, or more than, *x* percent of the concentration. Furthermore, equiproportional abatement may imply greatly different costs per unit removal for different sources.

Selective abatement aims to find the minimum cost combination of abatement while still satisfying the air-quality standards. Selective abatement recognizes that the cost of a unit reduction of emissions is not necessarily the same for all sources, and that the effect upon a particular receptor of a unit reduction of emissions is not necessarily the same for all sources. Thus, for each source it is necessary to know the cost of abatement, the amount of emissions, and the relationship between that source and any receptor, i.e. the meteorological diffusion model. All this is familiar from our consideration of water-quality models.

A Comparison of Strategies

City-wide or industry-wide emission standards for atmospheric pollutants are examples of equiproportional abatement. They generally state that all sources of pollution of a given magnitude must reduce their emissions to a certain level. Even if a source is located on the downwind side of an air-shed, it must control its emissions to the same degree as a similar source located upwind. The consequence of emission standards is that some sources do not control their emissions enough, while others must exercise too much control. Furthermore, the level of control is specified without any consideration of cost differences. However, in those cases where the sources are small but numerous, the cost of administering selective abatement may be exorbitant, and it will then be more efficient to use emission standards to control atmospheric pollution. Examples of such small sources are private residential units, small incinerators, back-yard burning of refuse, and automobiles. Automobiles, particularly, present a special and difficult problem of regulation to which I will return later in the chapter. In general, however, Teller's research suggests that if society uses only equiproportional abatement, it has chosen an inefficient method of reducing air pollution.

In Table 20, the costs of different approaches to abatement which Teller studied in Nashville are compared. The relative cost of constant abatement and forecasting abatement differ substantially. To satisfy air-quality level 4 by constant abatement costs five and a half times as much as forecasting abatement. Within constant abatement, equiproportional abatement is relatively more expensive than selective abatement, at some levels of controls much more so.

Thus, as in the case of water pollution, implementation of the concept of uniform emission standards can come at very high cost to society.

While it is not possible to tell exactly what the effect of a flat emissions charge would be on the cost of attaining the specified environmental standard because of cost differences at various sources, it is found to be lower than the cost of equiproportion abatement. The Delaware study suggests it might be much lower.

Table 20. Estimate of the Relative Cost of Sulfur-Dioxide Abatement through Fuel Substitution. 1960 Estimate for Nashville Metropolitan Area*

	Percentage cost: air-quality level†			
	1	2	3	4
1. Constant abatement				
a. Equiproportional	48·5	66·4	86·8	100·0
b. Selective	13·0	25·8	39·4	71·5
2. Forecasting abatement				
a. Equiproportional				18·0
b. Selective				12·9

* Low-sulfur coal was substituted for high-sulfur coal.
† Sulfur-dioxide air-quality standards:

Level	Two-hour average concentration (p.p.m.)	Twenty-four-hour average concentration (p.p.m.)
1	0·50	0·30
2	0·40	0·25
3	0·30	0·20
4	0·20	0·10

SOURCE: Azriel Teller, 'Air-Pollution Abatement', *Daedalus*, Vol. 96, No. 4, Fall 1967, p. 1096.

The 'Typical City' Study

An analogous study was made by several federal agencies in the United States in preparation for the policy decisions leading to the President's proposal of the Clean Air Act of 1967. The study is interesting not only for its conclusions but as an illustration of the rough and ready economic analysis which the hectic pace of the political process often requires.[3]

The study team used an air emissions model of New York and added some industries not found in New York so as to have a more 'typical' model of the 'average' air pollution problem in the nation. They borrowed the best air diffusion model available, which was for St Louis, and proportionally shrunk the New York emission model to fit a population of two million. They assumed that the resulting model was typical of all metropolitan areas. They gathered the available data on the least costly ways for industries, space-heating plants, and households in New York to reduce sulfur oxides and particulate emissions. For example, fuel substitution (e.g., #2 oil for residual oil), processing of inputs (e.g., desulfurization of oil), process changes, and treatment of pollutants at the emission point (e.g., scrubbing and bagging). Based on this, they programmed alternative abatement strategies.

First, a strategy was developed to guarantee that sulfur oxides and particulates would not exceed a given level of human exposure. The given level was roughly the *annual* average of 60–75 percent abatement of ambient sulfur oxides and particulate levels. Abatement of the pollutants occurred only when this level would be exceeded, including abatement, when feasible, for as short as a day. When the 'typical city' was well ventilated, no abatement was required even though heavy discharges were occurring because the concentrations on people never rose to the threshold abatement level. The additional annual cost estimated for this abatement strategy was about $250–400 million.

Second, an abatement strategy was followed that would reduce sulfur oxides and particulate concentration on human beings by 60–75 percent from what would have been the level without abatement for each day of the year. Abatement was accomplished by requiring only those emitters to abate that caused an increase in pollutant concentrations on people and those emitters that could do it at the lowest cost. The results indicated an additional annual cost of about $750 million, about half to industry and half to households. Industry's costs would increase, value-added, by about a sixth of one percent. Household costs would increase by about $3 per person. Surprisingly, capital costs were only 15 percent of *direct* abatement expenditures. Operating costs, for example, from higher fuel costs associated with the substitution of low-sulfur fuels, accounted for 85 percent of the additional annual costs.

Third, a *uniform* abatement strategy was tested where all polluters within the metropolitan area were asked to reduce sulfur oxides and particulates proportionally until the goal of 60–75 percent reduction in pollution levels was achieved. The additional annual cost was estimated to be about $1·3 thousand million. Interestingly, industry's abatement share increased more than proportionally from the second strategy above. This occurred because industry discharge is often located downwind of the concentration of people as compared with discharge from space-heating plants of office buildings, apartments, and homes. This was also shown to be true in a separate study of electric power plant locations and prevailing wind patterns in the twenty largest U.S. cities.

Fourth, all emissions within and outside metropolitan areas were required to abate proportionally to reach a 60–75 percent reduction of sulfur oxides and particulate concentration on human beings. The additional annual cost was more than two thousand million dollars for this approach.

Although the team could make no claim for accuracy or scholarship, they felt the estimates to be within the range of minus 50 percent and plus 500 percent of the real cost, and this was all the accuracy that was needed to recognize the advantage of managing the common property resources of the air efficiently. While a flat emissions tax would not influence location decisions in efficient directions it would concentrate abatement where it is cheapest. The study concluded that even this would produce a result much less costly than uniform abatement.

After further study by the Council on Environmental Quality, the Treasury Department, and the Environmental Protection Agency (EPA), these considerations of efficiency, efficacy, and equity led President Nixon to propose the Pure Air Tax of 1972 in February 1972. The President had great difficulty in getting Congressional attention for the resulting

Bill, but supported it again in a later environmental message. A strong approach was particularly needed in this area because of the severe health implications of sulfur oxides discharges.

Levying a per-pound charge on the sulfur emitted by power plants and other industrial firms would elicit a variety of economic responses resulting in improved air quality.

1. The potential cost saving would lend a strong impetus to the development and installation of effective systems for sulfur removal.

2. Confronted with a charge on high-sulfur fuels, users of coal and oil with a range of fuel options would choose the low-sulfur fuels voluntarily, even though they are now more expensive.

3. By creating an economically based demand for low-sulfur fuels, the charge on sulfur oxide emissions would provide oil refiners with the strong incentive they now lack to remove sulfur in the refining process and to develop techniques for doing it less expensively. The sulfur content of coal can also be reduced by processing.

4. The emission charge would tend to divert consumers to commodities with less serious environmental effects by raising the prices of those whose production processes employ coal and oil for combustion.

The Bill proposed by President Nixon would levy a tax, beginning from the calendar year 1976, on emissions of sulfur to the atmosphere. The initial tax rate was calculated to induce curtailment in sulfur emissions sufficient to meet the 1975 air-quality standards established by the Clean Air Amendments. In years after 1976, the tax rate would depend on a region's air quality in the preceding year; it would be 15¢ and 10¢ per pound, respectively, where primary and secondary standards were violated, and zero where all standards were met.

One problem with President Nixon's proposal is that it would encourage existing firms to move operations from 'dirty' regions to 'clean' regions – and new plants to settle there in the first place – to avoid paying a charge. Therefore, in time, shifts in industrial location would degrade the quality of air in the cleaner regions and bring the entire country down to the lowest common denominator.

This problem is at least partially dealt with in identical Bills later proposed by Congressman Aspin (H.R. 10890) and Senator Proxmire (S. 3047), which would levy a flat national tax. Two main points of these Bills are particularly worth noting. First, a target level of 20¢ per pound of sulfur would be reached in 5¢ increments from 1972 to 1975. The target is greater than the estimated costs of high-level abatement but less than the estimated average cost of damages across the nation (put by EPA at about 30¢ per pound). Second, the tax would be uniform across the nation, both to ensure administrative simplicity and to avoid creating havens for polluters.

Both Bills are on the shelf while an effort is made to implement existing legislation in the United States which gives heavy emphasis to direct controls applied as uniformly as possible. Economic research and experience suggests that this approach will prove not only costly but relatively ineffective.[4] There has been considerable discussion of atmospheric emissions charges as alternatives to existing policies in other countries (Australia, Germany, Japan, Norway, and Sweden for examples). So far as I am aware, however, no such schemes have actually been implemented anywhere.

Damage Studies

While it is fair to say that economic studies of water pollution were both earlier in time and more numerous than air pollution studies, in the area of estimating damage functions work has recently been more active in the air-quality area.

One line of activity in this connection has been the effort to estimate health damages associated with various air pollutants. The most important study in this connection is by Lave and Seskin.[5] These two researchers did very extensive econometric work on a poor body of data, but the only pertinent one available. The data consisted of comparing measurements of ambient air quality in particular cities with the statistics for deaths from various types of diseases. Since ambient air quality is measured only poorly in the sense that there is no uniform standard method for locating observation points within a metropolitan area, and since mortality rates presumably reflect the influence of a great many environmental and time factors, it is difficult to infer anything from an apparent relationship between high levels of one particular environmental stress, say air pollution, and mortality rates for particular diseases. However, by using a mathematical technique known as multiple regression and subjecting their results to severe tests the authors were able to show convincingly a relationship between high levels of particulates and sulfate and extra mortality from a number of diseases including bronchitis, asthma, lung cancer, and emphysema, in addition to general mortality and morbidity rates. Their overall assessment was that the statistical relationships found were real and that rough estimates of the dollar costs of these health effects including lost wages and medical expenses suggest that over two thousand million dollars per year saving in health costs would accompany a 50 percent reduction in air pollution levels from stationary sources in major urban areas in the United States.

Many other researchers in various countries, especially in Great Britain, had established apparent simple relationships between various environmental quality, disease, and mortality. The paper by Lave and Seskin reviewed a number of these studies. The distinguishing feature of the Lave–Seskin work is its painstaking use of refined econometric techniques of estimation and careful testing of the robustness of the relationships found.

Economists have also interested themselves considerably in property damage resulting from air pollution. Sulfur and particulate pollutants cause soiling of various articles as well as blackening and corroding building facades. Some types of air pollutants, such as ozone, also corrode, crack, and weaken materials. For example, it damages automobile tires and telephone and electrical wires. Efforts to measure these increased costs caused by pollutants have not met with much success.[6]

However, economic theory suggests that the value of property is related to all the various qualitative factors. Accordingly, it is possible that econometric technique can also isolate the effect of air pollutants on property values. Indeed, statistical studies of this matter have been done and they indicate that air pollutants have a systematic and negative impact on residential property values.[7] These studies have related the sale or rental prices of residences to variables such as family income, number of rooms, age and condition of the property, distance from the center of the city, and other socioeconomic variables. Even after correcting for these variables by econometric methods, statistically significant and negative correlations were found between sale or rental prices and air pollution. Extrapolating results found in cities such as St Louis and Washington, D.C., dollar estimates of residential property losses for eighty-five United States cities due to sulfur oxide and particulate matter damages were estimated to be over six hundred million dollars. This is only the loss to residential property. It does not include commercial, industrial, or agricultural activities. Extremely crude estimates put the total annual cost of air pollutants to all types of property in the United States at a figure of thirteen thousand million dollars. It is this type of calculation which underlies the national average damage estimate by EPA noted above.

Studies of health and property damages are based on microeconomic variables – individuals, households, and firms. Therefore, if highly dependable statistical relationships could be established between air pollutants and various damages, it would be possible to estimate damage functions for particular regions in the manner, for example, of that established in the Delaware study. However, the data are poor and the conceptual structure for some modes of estimation is so weak (for example the exact relation between property values and human welfare is still controversial) that these estimates must be taken as no more than a basis for crude orders of magnitude on a highly aggregated basis. These can be of some usefulness in the assessment of broad national programs of air pollution control and, in the United States have been frequently cited by public officials as justification for the standards which have been adopted, as we have seen in the case of the Proxmire Bill, to support a proposed level of emissions charges.

A recent study which used estimates of air pollution damages in the assessment of a national program of control was done by the National Academy of Sciences in the United States for mobile source emissions. Since the costs of controlling automotive emissions may be enormous in all countries where strict emission controls are mandated and since the National Academy study can serve as an example of an unusually intensive benefit-cost study of a major piece of environmental legislation it is worth reviewing in a little detail. As the cost analysis was especially well done and sheds considerable light on some of the difficulties inherent in direct regulation approaches to environmental problems, I will focus mostly on the cost analysis. While the study made heroic efforts to quantify benefits, because of the difficulties with available estimates and techniques (a few of which were indicated in the previous section), the numbers arrived at cannot, unfortunately, be regarded as more than informed guesses.

A Benefit-Cost Analysis of Automotive Emission Controls in the United States

Photochemical smog is, as we saw in Chapter 2, a severe problem in the United States and in many other countries. That this phenomenon is related to automotive emissions (hydrocarbons, oxides of nitrogen) was first discovered at the California Institute of Technology in 1950. This institution is located in the Los Angeles basin, which has been, and continues to be, notoriously smoggy. Since the problem was, at least at first, most severe in California, that state took the lead in air pollution legislation and continues to have more rigorous automotive emission control standards than exist in the remainder of the United States, or anywhere else in the world. But by the late sixties the smog problem had become common in the United States and for a variety of reasons the automobile industry had incurred the ire of the national congress. Accordingly the most recent major piece of air pollution control legislation, the 1970 Clean Air Act, contained 'get tough' provisions on automotive emissions. The emissions standards for both the U.S. and California are shown in Table 21.

Table 21. Emissions Standard (grams per mile)

	Year	Hydro-carbon (HC)	Carbon monoxide (CO)	Oxides of nitrogen (NOX)
U.S.	1970	3·9	33·3	5·0
	1972	3·0	28·0	5·0
	1973	3·0	28·0	3·1
I.*	1975	1·5	15·0	3·1
C.†	1975	0·9	9·0	2·0
U.S.–I.	1976	0·41	3·4	2·0
U.S.	1977	0·41	3·4	0·4

* Interim – this refers to the fact that the law permitted one-year delays in certain of the standards and these have been officially granted.
† California.

Of the various automotive emissions oxides of nitrogen (NOX) are the most difficult to control. This is because they are not a component of the fuel or a result of incomplete combustion but rather synthesized from atmospheric gases by the heat and pressure present inside the engine cylinder. Since the standard internal combustion engine (ICE) depends for its thermal efficiency on high compression and associated heat the problem is a difficult one. Present plans of U.S. manufacturers call for meeting the 0·4 g/mile standard for 1977, if it is to be met at all, by the use of various add-on devices including a reducing catalyst in the exhaust system.

The National Academy of Sciences study was a broad economic consideration of the automotive emission requirements of the Clean Air Act in preparation for a scheduled congressional reconsideration of these requirements.[8] But in practice the most salient question boils down to whether the NOX standard should drop from 2·0 g/mile in 1976 to 0·4 g/mile in 1977. More generally, however, the Academy study committee set itself the following questions on costs:

1. What is the cost of meeting presently legislated emission standards as well as other possible standards?

2. How are costs affected by more or less rapid movement toward a given final emission standard?

3. How do the costs of alternative control technologies compare with those of the technologies most likely to be adopted by the industry over the next few years?

4. What are the merits of mixed control strategies, such as a two-car strategy or a small-car strategy?

The study proceeded to try to answer these questions by the use of two different methodologies. In the first, various dimensions of cost meeting emission standards were calculated for a particular intermediate size automobile. The costs thus obtained are referred to as single-car costs. The second methodology was to develop various scenarios which involved populations of specific types of cars at various points in the future. This involved simulating automobile markets and associating with these particular populations of types of automobiles on the road, costs of maintenance and fuel and the gaseous residuals that would be emitted. All of the scenarios are compared with a base scenario which supposes a continuation of the emission standard legislated through 1970 (it is assumed that with present technology this standard could be met at zero additional cost). In this way costs and emissions can be compared in each year for the period simulated, which was 1970 through 1985. In the single-car strategy all the cost comparisons are with an automobile equipped to meet the 1970 emissions standards.

It is beyond the scope of the present book to delve deeply

into all of the numerous analyses conducted. The results reported are long and complex. However, the single-car studies, which are much easier to understand and interpret in a brief discussion, shed considerable light on questions 1 and 3, and I will focus on those here. Some of the most salient results of the single-car studies are reported in Table 22.

This table shows the single-car costs of meeting standards on schedule. These reflect the lifetime cost increases over those associated with a 1970 intermediate-type automobile. The service life of the automobile is taken to be 100,000 miles and costs of fuel and maintenance are calculated on that basis. It is seen from this table that meeting the 1972 and 1973 standards involves considerable lifetime total cost increases for the standard vehicle. This is especially so of the 1973 standards. Automobiles produced to meet those standards, especially the 1973 NOX standard, sacrificed considerable fuel economy and durability for the purpose. The 1975 and 1976 standards require substantial increases in the list price of the automobiles because in these years an oxidizing catalyst will be used to control hydrocarbons and carbon monoxide emissions. But this cost is more than offset over the lifetime of the car by improved fuel economy and maintenance as compared with the 1973 standards. It thus appears that the very precise time-tables laid down in legislation produced a situation in which a huge unnecessary cost was incurred to meet the 1973 standards. This happened because there was not time to introduce the technologies for meeting the 1975 standards, which proved to be considerably less costly even though by 1975 the standards had become tighter.

One notices that meeting the 1976 standards, while less costly than meeting the 1973 standards, is still considerably more costly than meeting the 1975 standards. This is due to the general tightening of the standards but probably primarily because of the drop in permitted grams per mile of NOX from 3·1 to 2·0.

It is however the 1977 standards which produce an enormous cost increase. This cost increase is entirely due to the

Table 22. Single-car Costs of Standards on Schedule. (Lifetime Cost Increase over 1970 Intermediate – A Vehicle, 1974 dollars)

Standard	Year	List price	Life maintenance	Life fuel		Life total		Present value*
				Tax	Ex tax	Tax	Ex tax	Tax
U.S.70	1970	0	0	0	0	0	0	0
U.S.72	1972	0	275	0	0	275	275	158
U.S.73	1973	49	325	379	296	753	670	432
I.75	1975	109	100*	56	76	265†	285†	203
C.75	1975	150	113†	184	178	447	440	330
I.76	1977	176	113†	184	178	473†	466†	361
U.S.77	1978	302	75‡	467	407	844‡	778‡	649

* Lifetime maintenance and fuel costs discounted at 15 percent.   † Catalyst replacement at 50,000 miles would add $114.
‡ Catalyst replacement at 50,000 miles would add $312.

SOURCE: *Air Quality and Automobile Emissions Control*, Vol. 4: *The Costs and Benefits of Automobile Emissions Control*, Serial No. 93–24, Washington, D.C., Government Printing Office, September 1974.

drop in the NOX standards from 2 to 0·4 g/mile. In order to meet that standard with the conventional internal combustion engine the car manufacturers propose to do just about everything that can possibly be done to reduce emissions from the standard internal combustion engine. The technology involved would use exhaust gas recirculation, electronic fuel injection, and two catalysts, an oxidizing catalyst for hydrocarbons and carbon monoxide and a reducing catalyst for the oxides of nitrogen. While the study calculated that lifetime maintenance costs would drop from the 1976 level for this configuration both list and fuel costs increase dramatically both over the 1970 levels and over the 1976 levels. In addition the maintenance cost drop is probably a fake, for in order to meet the standards continuously over the lifetime of the car, it would probably be necessary to replace the catalyst after 50,000 miles or so and this is estimated to add another $312 to lifetime costs. Thus if this standard is kept and met on schedule the study concludes that $1,100 might be added to the lifetime total cost over those of a 1970 type automobile and perhaps $700 above the cost of an automobile meeting 1976 standards. The latter difference would be entirely due to the drop in NOX permitted from 2 to 0·4 g/mile. Although as we shall see when reviewing the conclusions of the study, the study committee did not take an unambiguous stand on the matter, a careful review of the evidence they present indicates that the cost of actually meeting the 1977 standards in the way Detroit proposes would be enormous and that the comparative small gain in reduced NOX emissions might be of little or no benefit.

One may reasonably ask why these specific standards were chosen in the first place? The answer has to be that the choice was essentially arbitrary. The legislation simply prescribed that emissions of all three types of residuals should be reduced from their 1970 levels by 90 percent in the new cars produced in the 1977 model year. It now appears that the 1977 oxides of nitrogen standard will be changed in new legislation to remain at the 1976 level.

There was also reason to suppose that Detroit might not choose the most cost-effective technology for meeting the standards mandated. Detroit has shown great resistance to reconsidering its commitment to the internal combustion engine and there were even some suspicions that it would try to make such a jerry-built technological response to the standards that because of cost and performance aspects of the cars produced the standards would be discredited in the public mind. Accordingly the National Academy of Sciences study considered the cost implications of some alternative engine types.

Table 23 shows the cost of meeting the 1976 standards (which, as I mentioned, it now appears will be retained longer than that) for several different engine types. The first is the conventional catalyst, the approach we have already reviewed. The second is a stratified charge engine and the third is the diesel.

Diesel engine technology is widely understood but the stratified charge concept has had much less exposure. The latter engine is very much like a standard internal combustion engine except that it has two combustion chambers. The upper, and very small one, is charged with an unusually rich fuel mixture which can easily be lighted at a low temperature. The lower chamber, which is connected to the upper chamber, is charged with an extremely lean fuel mixture which it would be impossible to light with a conventional ignition system. However, the burning rich mixture in the upper chamber ignites the lean mixture in the lower chamber and the result is a relatively low temperature combustion process which because of the lean mixture is nearly complete. The engine is thus inherently lower in all types of emissions than the standard internal combustion engine.

Both the stratified charge and the diesel engine can meet the 1976 standards and quite interestingly they can do so at costs which are much lower than even the benchmark 1970 vehicle costs. What this appears to show is that even in the absence of any emission controls it would be cheaper to build stratified

Table 23. Single-car Costs of Alternative Technologies. (Lifetime Cost Increase over 1970 Intermediate – A Vehicle, 1974 dollars)

| Standard | List price | Life mainte-nance | Life fuel | | Life total | | Present value* |
			Tax	Ex tax	Tax	Ex tax	Tax
Conventional catalyst	176	113†	184	178	473†	460†	361†
Stratified	201	13†	−465	−335	−252†	−122†	−94†
Diesel	131	−75	−955	−773	−899	−717	−533

* Lifetime cost discounted at 15 percent.   † Catalyst replacement at 50,000 miles would add $114.

SOURCE: *Air Quality and Automobile Emissions Control*, Vol. 4: *The Costs and Benefits of Automobile Emissions Control*, Serial No. 93–24, Washington, D.C., Government Printing Office, September 1974.

charge engine or diesel engine propelled automobiles. Several things must be said about this result however. In the case of the diesel there are problems of noise, performance, and smell that have limited consumer acceptance in the past and presumably would do so in the future unless they are dealt with. The stratified charge engine is free of these defects but it does share one other disadvantage with the diesel engine: it is high in initial cost and the economic gain is in future fuel and maintenance costs. This is regarded as a severe disadvantage because consumers are thought to discount future costs at a high rate. However, it is not so high in first cost compared with a conventional internal combustion engine which also meets the 1976 standards and when lifetime costs are discounted at the relatively high rate of 15 percent annually it still costs less in present value terms than the conventional engine meeting only 1970 standards. The results of the present value calculation are shown in the last column of Table 23.

Thus it certainly appears that stratified charge engines offer a much better way of meeting the 1976 standards than the technology that Detroit proposes to use. There is a fly in the ointment, however, because there is no way in which the automobile industry could tool up to produce stratified charge engines on a very large scale in time to meet the 1976 standards. Thus adhering to even those standards will force enormous costs on the owners and operators of automobiles, with the only advantage being possibly an earlier improvement in air quality. There are some doubts even about this however, since the 1976 cars equipped with oxidizing catalysts will emit much higher levels of sulfuric gases than those without catalysts. Furthermore, it is unlikely that automobile companies would introduce a technology on a massive scale and then operate it for only a comparatively few years. Thus present legislation in the United States seems to have locked the country into a technology which is costly both in economic and energy terms and in the longer run a very poor method of achieving the objectives of emissions reductions. A policy approach permitting a much more flexible response but heavily penalizing failure to act would have produced much better results. I review the elements of such a policy a little later on in this chapter.

On the basis of unfortunately extremely weak data the National Academy of Sciences study estimated that the benefits of all types to be obtained from meeting the 1977 standards could be in the range of $2\frac{1}{2}$ to 7 thousand million dollars annually. The best single point estimate was taken to be 5 thousand million dollars. The annualized cost of meeting the 1977 standards on time was estimated to be perhaps 11 thousand million dollars. Thus calculated total costs would exceed total benefits by an enormous amount.

Not going to the 1977 oxides of nitrogen standard could bring national costs down to an estimated level of approximately 5 thousand million dollars. Thus one might consider 1976 standards 'justified' by the benefits they achieve and this is certainly the interpretation favored by the proponents of the legislation. But there are two problems with this interpretation. The first is that as we have seen many times, the proper comparison is not between total benefits and total costs but between marginal benefits and marginal costs. On the assumption that cost and benefit functions behave in the manner they are normally regarded to (marginal costs rising and marginal benefits falling – the study results lend themselves support to the argument that costs behave in the usual manner in this instance) a comparison of marginal costs and marginal benefits, if that were possible, would probably suggest a lower level of control would maximize net benefits. The second difficulty with that interpretation is that it does not look at a sufficiently wide range of options. We have already seen that the study showed that if stratified charge engines could be used we could meet high standards with little if any net cost in dollars but with possibly some delay in improvement of the air quality.

The summary and concluding sections of the report are surprisingly weak in raising these broader issues bearing on needed reconsideration of the air pollution legislation. This is unfortunate in view of the powerful nature of the analysis in the report, but is perhaps accounted for by the reluctance of the National Academy of Sciences to incur the ire of a few powerful and well-known members of congress who sponsored the initial legislation.

Despite these reservations the study does develop a large amount of information which will be useful in further political debate of this public policy issue. One can be sure that politicians representing particular constituencies will dig out the things that the writers of the summary have chosen to gloss over. In view of both the conceptual and the quantitative problem with benefit-cost analysis – especially on the benefit side – this kind of informing of political processes is its most appropriate role. I put forward this point of view in connection with the Delaware study reported in the previous chapter and I will develop it much further in the next chapter when I turn to a discussion of models of integrated residuals management.

Before concluding the chapter, however, it is appropriate to consider what kind of policy device would be better than the direct emission control approach which has been adopted. How to solve the twin problems of ensuring maintenance and stimulating technology?

Fifteen years ago economists at Rand Corporation proposed the answer – a smog tax.[9] In one, possibly very powerful, version of this tax, cars would be tested periodically and assigned a smog rating, indicated by a seal or coded device attached to the car. Then, when the driver purchased gasoline, he would pay a tax, over and above the basic gasoline taxes, that would vary with his smog rating.

An individual could reduce his smog tax bill in several ways.

1. Tuning up or overhauling his engine to reduce emissions and obtain better gas mileage would be an economical alternative to paying the tax. Recently established emission standards for cars registered in New Jersey in the United States are less stringent for earlier than for more recent model years. In a pilot study, 45 percent of the cars failed the state standards. But more important, almost every car that failed

could pass after a regular 'emission tune-up' by a trained mechanic at an average cost of about $20.[10] The New Jersey work demonstrated that vehicles can be efficiently tested (it takes about 35 seconds) and that engine condition, including the recency and quality of tune-up, is extremely important to emissions.

2. A car owner has many options that would allow him to drive fewer miles per year – living closer to his job, using mass transit, or participating in car pools. Standards which simply set a permitted level of emission per vehicle-mile do nothing whatsoever to reduce the number of miles driven, but the smog tax would affect this extremely important variable, as well as emissions per mile.

3. Control devices could be installed on older cars. In 1970, in a market test, General Motors offered control kits for pre-1968 models at about $20 installed; but no one bought them. Clearly, it was nonsensical to expect anyone to make this investment since, without assurance that others would make it, any one person's effect on the situation would be negligible. Similarly no one would buy the kit if he were sure that everyone else would so do: his air would be equally clean whether he bought the kit or not – so why bother? This is an actual case of the free rider problem in the economic theory of public goods which we have previously met in a more theoretical context. A smog tax would introduce a new and persuasive element into this calculation.

4. Because consumers would demand them, manufacturers would have an incentive to design automobiles that had better smog ratings not only when they rolled off the assembly line but throughout their lifetimes. In the long run this may be the most important incentive effect of all.

Only the first of these four ways to reduce one's smog tax is relevant to the question of who should be responsible for the continued attainment of emission standards. But the New Jersey study suggests the practicability of placing the responsibility on owners and backing it up with appropriate economic incentives The tax elicits other desirable responses from drivers such as the last three alternatives, and its incentives apply to owners of pre-1968 cars that have no control systems, but whose emissions can often be cut substantially by better maintenance and certain retrofitted devices. The smog tax could be varied seasonally; and it could be raised in critical areas as a powerful spur to car pooling, reduction in frivolous driving, and use of available mass transit and demand for more.

The gasoline surcharge could also be adapted to reflect other external costs associated with the use of automobiles, such as highway and street congestion, and uncompensated social costs imposed by the manufacture of certain fuels. Size and fuel consumption variables could govern the amount of tax per gallon. The incentives to manufacturers to develop efficient low-emission technologies are obvious, and no deadline would act to freeze in a technology. For engine types that are inherently and dependably very low in emissions (such as Rankine engines), the smog tax might be canceled entirely.

I feel that a scheme of this type has many attractive features and should be tried. But, short of its full implementation, some of its incentives could be incorporated into the present law.

The first change I would like to see in the present law would be a reduction of present standards to a level which could be achieved without the use of catalytic converters. Next would be the institution of a smog tax on automobiles progressively over the remainder of the decade, until in 1981 the rate for a car still emitting at the baseline level would exceed the several hundred dollars per car associated with the catalytic system. A few urban areas with severe smog problems would be targeted for special treatment. I believe this strategy would almost certainly lead to the large-scale introduction of inherently low-emission and thermally efficient engines before the end of the decade. It would clearly be second best since it does not influence motorist behavior the way a smog tax levied on gasoline would. However it might be possible to design the tax so as to give manufacturers a special impetus to design and market low maintenance cars. For example, the charge could be based not on new car emissions but on a sample of a particular type of car population which had been on the road for (say) eight months. This proposal has deficiencies but it would be a vast improvement over the present system.

Concluding Comment

In general, economic studies of air-quality management have run several years behind water resources studies, but have been generally similar in approach and in results. Studies of air sheds using optimizing economic models incorporating atmospheric diffusion models have generally found that programmed approaches to air pollution control achieve environmental standards at much lower costs than uniform cutback programs. These studies imply the likelihood that, as in the case of water-quality management in the Delaware estuary, even a relatively simple effluent charges approach to air-quality management would distribute control efforts in such a fashion as to attain ambient standards at much lower costs than conventional administrative approaches. While these studies have been a large factor in political debate in the United States and in several other countries, the development of emission charges strategies is less well developed than are effluent charges in the realm of water-quality management. Perhaps this is just another manifestation of the fact that research and policy-making in the air-quality area has tended to lag.

Benefit-cost analysis has proved its usefulness in connection with some extremely important issues concerning mobile source emissions control. Its results also call into question the reliance which has been placed on highly specific direct regulation in that area.

I return to some general policy questions in the concluding chapter but first it is necessary to see where the frontiers of research on the economics of residuals management lie. In my view they concern the systematic treatment of the interrelationships between different kinds of residuals, and the connection between the economic analysis of residuals management and political decision making. These are the main topics of discussion in the next chapter.

Chapter 9

Research and Planning Frontiers – Integrated Residuals Management Models with Political Components[1]

Introduction

Despite its short history, the application of economic models to problems of water- or air-quality management is, as I hope the last two chapters have shown, in a relatively developed state. My earlier discussion of some of the implications of mass balance indicated, however, that pursuing the study of airborne, waterborne, and solid residuals in isolation from each other might be undesirable because of non-market linkages among them. There are at least three types of intermedia linkages which suggest the importance of integrated analysis and management of all residuals streams simultaneously. One is that a change in one or more industrial production process variables may change two, or all three forms of residuals, as, for example, when the brightness specifications on paper products are changed. A second type of linkage is the modification of one residual which also results in the modification of another, as when in-plant recirculation of heated water – in order to reduce thermal discharges – results in a reduction in fuel use, thereby reducing both gaseous and solid residuals generation. A third type of linkage is the generation of a secondary residual in the process of modifying the originally generated residual, as in the generation of sludge in the removal of BOD, or the generation of fly ash in the removal of particulates from a gaseous stream. Of course the sequence may – and often does – proceed further, as in the generation of particulates in the incineration of sludge, and the generation of a solid residual in removing these particulates from the incinerator stack.

Accordingly there have been some efforts to produce what are called 'integrated residuals management models'. The most advanced of these, although it must still be regarded as somewhat experimental and at the frontier of research, was built at Resources for the Future, Inc., over the past few years. I was at that time director of the program carrying out this work.

In addition to handling all major residuals streams simultaneously, the model also pioneered in treating the industrial sector in a more sophisticated and realistic manner than had been done before in regional economic models. In fact the linear programming submodels of industrial production processes contained within the larger overall model provide a good starting-point for discussing the regional model structure as a whole. It should also be noted that these industrial submodels, while components of the larger model, are also quite useful in their own right.

Linear programming models of industrial processes are not themselves new. For example, there exist programming models of refineries and steel mills which were designed for business operational purposes.[2] But, understandably enough, these have been built to serve the specific interest of private managers of private enterprises. They have given little or no regard to the fact that all industrial processes generate non-product outputs (both material and energy) and that the discharge of these to public environmental resources like the air mantle and watercourses is usually damaging. Since they were constructed to serve private management, these models optimize with respect to *private* costs but not in regard to any sort of concept of social costs.

They neglect the *external* costs of production which are of such central concern in connection with the efficient functioning of the whole economy. To take account of this problem, a straightforward, but important, extension of these industry models can be made by restricting the availability not only of ordinary resources but also of environmental resources, by placing limitations on the amount of residual material and energy which may be discharged to the air, watercourses, and the land.[3] By this means the private costs imposed by policies meant to diminish discharges and their associated external costs, such as effluent standards or taxes, can be quickly and inexpensively determined for alternative levels of application of these policy instruments. This is useful general information for environmental policy and management where costs are a consideration – that is to say nearly always. Quantitative industry models of this sort are now under active development.[4]

But these models, useful as they are in themselves, say nothing about the quality of the environment. To make this connection, models of the impact of different types of residuals discharge on the pertinent natural systems are needed. Taking this step is feasible since there exist reasonably acceptable 'diffusion' models for the atmosphere and watercourses which can be used to translate a quantity of residuals discharge at some point X to an ambient concentration at some point Y. We have seen the application of these taken one at a time in earlier chapters.

By means of these natural system models it is possible to widen the analysis by admitting ambient or environmental constraints rather than effluent constraints into the industrial optimization problem. Moreover, again as we have seen before, diffusion models are not limited to a single source of discharge. They can translate discharges from multiple sources to concentrations at multiple receptor points. It is therefore quite feasible to minimize the overall private cost to industry of achieving a specified ambient standard, or set of standards, pertaining simultaneously to various environmental media. This is accomplished by means of a programming model which encompasses aspects of the behavior of the actual environmental systems, i.e., watercourses and the air mantle. It may be possible to go further and develop damage functions for every level and combination of discharge and to use the model to obtain a solution in which marginal internal control costs are equated with marginal external costs for all media simultaneously. The Resources for the Future model which is structured to handle this type of problem is known as the Russell–Spofford Model.

The model is named after Clifford Russell and Walter Spofford who were primarily responsible for its detailed design. I will describe it abstractly at first and then in more detail and concreteness in connection with its trial application to an actual case.

The Russell–Spofford Model

The Russell–Spofford model is designed to deal simultaneously with the three major general types of residuals – airborne, waterborne, and solid – and reflects the physical links between them in a regional context. It 'recognizes', for example, that the decision to remove waterborne organic wastes by standard sewage treatment processes creates a sludge which, in turn, represents a solid residuals problem; the sludge must either be disposed of on the land or burned, the latter alternative creating airborne particulates and gaseous residuals.

Second, it can incorporate the non-treatment alternatives available (especially to industrial firms) for reducing the level of residuals generation. These include: input substitution (as natural gas for coal); change in basic production methods (as in the conversion of beet sugar refineries from the batch to continuous diffusion process); recirculation of residual-bearing streams (as in recirculation of condenser cooling water in thermal-electric generating plants); and materials recovery (as in the recovery and reuse of fiber, clay, and titanium from the 'white water' of paper-making machines). These alternatives are included by means of the industrial linear programming submodels already outlined.

Third, the model uses environmental diffusion models in the way already discussed but it is also capable of incorporating environmental simulation submodels. In practice the latter takes the form of an aquatic ecosystem model which translates residuals discharges into impacts upon various species of concern to man.

In addition to these features the model also incorporates a unique political (collective choice) feature. In view of the fact that this model building enterprise is at the frontier of research in environmental economics it will be accorded a somewhat fuller discussion than other models described in this book.

The model containing these features is shown schematically in Figure 6. The three main components of the overall framework may be described as follows:

1. *A linear programming model* that relates inputs and outputs of selected production processes and consumption activities at specified locations within a region, including the

Figure 6. Schematic Diagram of the Regional Residuals Management Model

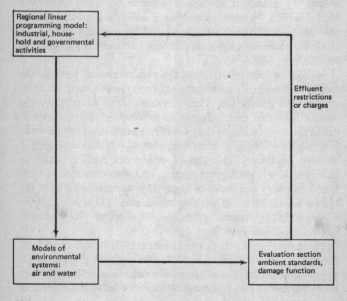

unit amounts and types of residuals generated by the production of each product; the costs of converting these residuals from one form to another (e.g., gaseous to liquid in the scrubbing of stack gases); the costs of transporting the residuals from one place to another; and the cost of any final discharge-related activity such as landfill operations.

The programming model, which actually consists of an array of submodels pertaining to individual industrial plants, landfill operations, incinerators, and sewage treatment plants, permits a wide range of choices among production processes, raw material input mixes, by-product production, materials recovery, and in-plant adjustments and improvement, all of which can reduce the total quantity of residuals to be disposed of. That is, the residuals generated are not assumed to be fixed either in form or in quantity. This model also allows for choices among treatment processes and hence among the possible forms of the residual to be disposed of in the natural environment and, to a limited extent, among the locations at which discharge is accomplished. One of the basic components of this part of the model is the extended industrial process models I discussed earlier.

2. *Environmental models – physical, chemical, and biological* – which describe the fate of various residuals after their discharge into the natural environmental systems. Essentially, these models may be thought of as transformation functions operating on the vector of residuals discharges and yielding another vector of ambient concentrations at specific locations throughout the environment (these are the by now very familiar diffusion models) and, in some instances, impacts on living things (these are aquatic eco-system models reaching beyond the Streeter–Phelps formulation). In aquatic eco-system models living creatures which participate in these processes are explicitly included in the model and the output is stated in terms of impact on living things (e.g., plankton and fish) rather than on physical parameters such as dissolved oxygen.

3. *A set of receptor-damage functions* relating the concentration of residuals in the environment and the impact on living

225

things to the resulting damages, whether these are sustained directly by humans or indirectly through impacts on material objects, or on such receptors as plants or animals in which man has a commercial, scientific, or aesthetic interest. Ideally, for the version of the model I am now discussing, the functions relating concentrations and impacts on species to damage should be in monetary terms. As I will point out a little later, whether an effort should be made to compute damage functions and include them in the model is open to some controversy.[5] But it will be convenient to assume initially that such damage functions are available and used.

The linkage between the components of the model and the method of optimum seeking may be explained in an illustrative way as follows. Solve the linear programming model initially with no restrictions or prices on the discharge of residuals. Using the resulting initial set of discharges as inputs to the models of the natural environment and the resulting ambient concentrations and impacts on living things as the arguments of the damage functions, the marginal damages can be determined as the change in damages associated with a unit change in a specific discharge. These marginal damages may then be applied as interim effluent charges on the discharge activities in the linear model, and that model solved again for a new set of production, consumption, treatment, and discharge activities. With appropriate bounds constraining consecutive solutions, the procedure is repeated until a position close to the optimum is found. This process can be looked upon as a steepest ascent technique for solving a non-linear programming problem.[6]

The Russell–Spofford model was designed for the analysis of residuals management in regions where the scale and severity of the problems justify a considerable investment in data and analysis. The model is now in the process of being applied to the Delaware valley.

I will turn to a fuller discussion of the applied model shortly but to do this it is necessary first to discuss the matter of damage functions more fully. As background for this it should be noted that, while vastly more complex than previous applications, the model as I have sketched it so far is in the format of traditional economic benefit-cost analysis which, in principle, aims at maximizing the 'efficiency' of the whole system. The model as actually applied is not an efficiency model but a 'collective choice' model. To see why this alternative was chosen it is necessary to examine the efficiency objective in benefit-cost analysis a little more closely than we have done so far.

The 'Efficiency' Objective

As I noted in slightly different terms in the first chapter, modern welfare economics concludes that if (1) preference orderings of consumers and production functions of producers (the functions defining physically efficient combinations of inputs and outputs) are independent and their shapes appropriately constrained, (2) consumers maximize utility subject to given income and price parameters, and (3) producers maximize profits subject to those price parameters, a set of prices exists such that no individual can be made better off without making some other individual worse off. For any given distribution of income, this is an efficient state. As also noted in the first chapter, given certain further assumptions concerning the structure of markets, this 'Pareto optimum' can be achieved via a market-pricing mechanism and voluntary decentralized exchange.

The fundamental conceptual basis of benefit-cost analysis is this theorem (although it is not illogical to defend such analysis on more intuitive grounds). Accordingly, it is also in principle the normative basis for the version of the Russell–Spofford model just discussed. What benefit-cost analysis does, essentially, is to attempt to simulate a market result where for one reason or another voluntary exchange does not exist and a resources allocation decision is made through the agency of government. For the most part the inputs to such a project, or system of projects, are private goods purchased by the agency implementing the program, and it is common practice to use market costs as acceptable estimates of social costs. Even this requires a long string of assumptions, such as that all markets are in competitive equilibrium and there is no unemployment of resources in the system. Methods for relaxing some of these assumptions have been developed; for present purposes I will assume that costs are acceptably measured so that the discussion can be turned to the far more serious problem of benefit measurement.[7]

In conventional benefit-cost practice, benefits are measured by making estimates of what consumers would be willing to pay in a market for alternative levels of the publicly provided goods or service. As I mentioned, this means simulating a market result where none exists in reality. For example, a function could be developed which relates incremental improvements in air quality to the 'willingness to pay' for them. Unfortunately, and especially when applied to environmental management problems, this approach presents extremely difficult practical problems of measurement and requires some very 'heroic' assumptions about distributional impacts. The practical problems are well illustrated by the air-quality benefit-cost study reported in the previous chapter. For present purposes it is appropriate to stress the conceptual problem.

For private goods bought and sold in competitive markets the matter of income distribution can be separated rather nicely from the problem of resources allocation. But, as we saw in Chapter 5 the outputs of environmental management actions are almost always 'public' goods. This means that they are provided to large groups of people simultaneously and in roughly equal physical amount. For example, a reduction in sulfur dioxide may affect major parts of an entire city and the amount I get, if I am a resident of that part of the city, is about the same as you do if you are a resident of it, and my breathing of the cleaner air does not deprive you from doing so simultaneously. This is different from a private good like an orange – if I eat it, you don't. The technical name for this phenomenon is 'jointness in supply'.

Thus the income distribution problem associated with these public goods is particularly difficult because the consumption of the goods cannot be differentiated among consumers on the basis of their voluntary choice in markets. When the supply of a public goods (like air quality in a city) changes, both efficiency (resources allocation) and distribution (of goods and services) are inevitably affected. Consequently, there is, in general, no way to be sure that equating incremental cost with the sum of incremental willingness to pay (this is the necessary condition for maximum net benefit) will be a welfare maximum. The pre-existing distribution of income cannot be maintained except through an elaborate system of side-payments tailored to each individual. Such a system of payments is a practical impossibility. This is unlike an economy consisting solely of private goods where equality of marginal cost and price (marginal willingness to pay) can be unambiguously shown to be a necessary condition for a welfare maximum, in the sense of the central theorem. In this case, allocative and distributional questions can be neatly separated.

The distributional effect associated with the provision of public goods has been a hard problem for applied public goods economics and several devices have been used to try to get around it. Thus, for example, Otto Eckstein, in his important work on benefit-cost analysis in water development,[8] explicitly assumed that the marginal utility of income (the satisfaction a person gets from his last dollar of income) is the same for all individuals. This effectively wipes out distributional considerations, because total utility (or welfare) is unaffected by how the output is distributed among recipients, but most economists regard this assumption as grossly unrealistic.

The assumption most often made implicity or explicitly by applied economists is that it is a mistake to consider individual public goods situations in isolation. Rather the whole complex of public goods should be considered. Provisions of some will affect one group adversely and another favorably and, on another occasion, vice versa. Thus, there will be a lot of cancellation of distributional effects. If one accepts this line of argument, it follows that the society that makes its decisions based on efficiency criteria (maximum net benefit disregarding distribution) will be one in which most people will finally be better off than one in which criteria are used which foreclose efficient solutions. It is further assumed that public goods are a rather small part of the economy and that private goods are allocated (through tax and subsidy policy) in an ethically sanctioned way. No economist that I know of is happy with this set of assumptions.

The scope and difficulty of empirical measurement required, as well as our inability to handle distributional questions, makes it impossible to achieve Pareto-optimal allocations of public goods by simulating markets. As I noted in Chapter 3 these considerations, and the difficulties of assigning damages individually to specific dischargers, has convinced most economists that a system of effluent charges which is a hundred percent efficient is essentially impossible. Thus they turned to the lesser objective of achieving a specified ambient quality at least cost.

Political entrepreneurs who are concerned with general taxation and the allocation of government budgets must, in a democratic society, with appropriate analytical inputs, assume general responsibility for the provision of public goods. Assessing willingness to pay in selected cases may, however, play a very useful role in helping to focus the political process, particularly when it can be shown that large overall efficiency gains are potentially possible. This is essentially the purpose for which benefit-cost analysis was used – the 'old' Delaware study reported in Chapter 7 and the auto emissions study in Chapter 8. Such evidence gives incentives to political entrepreneurs and ammunition to the public. Moreover, and most unfortunately, the economic technician and the planner or management scientist are often forced to make allocative decisions on the basis of partial evaluations because no proper political (representative government) institution *exists* to make them. In recent times, one result of this in the United States has been strong public resistance, through nongovernment means, when an effort is made to implement any project. This takes the form of milder or more aggressive forms of sabotage – often through the medium of the courts.

The evaluation of public goods is necessarily, in the final analysis, a political problem. This is true however useful our necessarily partial benefit-cost analyses may be in aiding and even guiding the political, or collective, choice process. We cannot put our final dependence on disinterested evaluations of efficiency, even if there were a practical, politically sanctioned way of doing it. This, to repeat once again, is because it is partial and because it does not resolve adequately the distributional problems inherent in public goods situations.

The general point that evaluation of public goods is in the final analysis a political problem is clearly valid. But one cannot reasonably argue, I think, that present political structures are necessarily suitable for solving environmental systems problems.[9] To try to get a handle on what government arrangements might be most suitable, we must develop at least the rudiments of a theory of collective choice. This will be a preface to my discussion of how the Russell–Spofford model was politicized in an effort to be much more systematic in introducing the interplay of technical, economical, and political forces than had been heretofore done.

Theory of Collective Choice

Kenneth Arrow, the well-known mathematical economist, pioneered the modern study of collective choice processes in his landmark book, *Social Choice and Individual Values*.[10] In it he laid down a set of properties one might feel a social choice mechanism could reasonably be expected to have. These properties are:

1. *Collective rationality.* In any given set of individual preferences the social preferences are derivable from the individual preferences.

2. *Pareto principle.* If alternative *A* is preferred to alternative

B by every single individual, then the social ordering ranks *A* above *B*.

3. *Independence of irrelevant alternatives*. The social choices made from any environment depend only on the preferences of individuals with respect to the alternatives in that environment.

4. *Non-dictatorship*. There is no individual whose preferences are automatically society's preferences, independent of the preferences of other individuals.

Arrow analyzed voting situations rigorously in view of these conditions and found that, in general, no mechanism could be devised that consistently met them all. This is his famous 'impossibility theorem'. Despite much further examination of voting systems, this theorem still stands essentially intact for the kind of choice mechanisms Arrow examined.

In an important paper providing the main conceptual basis for politicizing the Russell–Spofford model, Haefele[11] showed that representative government, with a two-party system, can provide a means of going from individual choices to social choices in a way which meets all of Arrow's conditions. The essence of his case is that the two-party system can function in such a way so as to bring out the two positions which, when voted upon in a legislature, produce the same decision as is generated if the voters can indulge in vote trading on the issue involved – a possibility not present in the once-and-for-all voting situation examined by Arrow. It must be emphasized that Haefele found that representative government *could* operate as an ideal social choice mechanism, not that it does so at present. This is analogous to saying that a competitive price structure is ideal under certain circumstances, not to saying that present market prices and outputs are at the ideal point.

Clearly, if we are to have preferences consistently aggregated over the whole range of public good issues, collective choice decisions must be made by legislative bodies encompassing the whole range of pertinent issues. Moreover, these issues must be formed within a two-party framework. Since they prominently include but reach far beyond questions of environment, the most suitable mechanism for making these legislative or policy-type decisions is a government of general jurisdiction – not a specialized government body or, even less properly, an executive-type agency.

But, unfortunately, existing governments of general jurisdiction, even if they could be reformed so as to remove some of their most obvious divergencies from the utility model of representative governments, do not suffice. The central reason is that they seldom correspond in a reasonable way to the environmental 'problem shed' boundaries. This problem appears to be more severe in the United States than in some other countries, such as Britain, where adaptation of government institutions to regional problems appears to be further advanced. I will have more to say in the next chapter about institutional arrangements relevant to environmental problems in various countries.

In order to try to discover how various different ways of structuring legislative bodies in 'problem shed' areas might influence decisions, and to help fashion an analytical tool which such bodies might use, the Russell–Spofford model was politicized.

Politicizing the Russell–Spofford Model

The political linkage with the economic-ecological model is accomplished via the distribution of benefits and costs – a consideration central to the political process but, as noted previously, usually neglected or treated very simplistically in benefit-cost analysis. Geographical distribution across local political entities is made possible by the fact that the model is location-specific in the sense that activities are assigned addresses in a grid. Accordingly, changes in environmental quality parameters, price and tax increases, and employment impacts of different solutions of the model can be associated with particular locations. These types of measures serve in lieu of damage function calculations used in the version of the model described earlier. The model is solved with no constraints on these measures to establish their *status quo* values. Then, based on an examination of socioeconomic characteristics of the area, each grid (which can be taken to be a political unit like a ward) is assigned a preference vector for these measures. Normally, these vectors would be such that meeting all preferences in all grids would not be feasible. Consequently the stage is set for a social choice process to come into play. The analytical process for aggregating preferences into social choices takes account of intensities of preferences as well as numbers for and against any issue. When preference vectors reflecting these intensities are combined, they reveal opportunities for vote trading, and vote trading, as indicated earlier, provides the key to coming to stable social choices (no Arrowian paradox).

Such a model should provide an effective instrument for analyzing the results, in terms of levels of environmental quality and distribution of benefits and costs, of various patterns of representative government. It can then be determined which patterns, in the context of the United States political system, fulfill the sets of preferences for alternative outcomes. Political patterns to be examined in metropolitan areas include, for example, a metropolitan council that could reflect the set of preferences of each political subdivision, a council of governments arrangement whereby each suburb gets one vote and the city one vote, and a pattern which breaks the city into wards and aggregates by suburb and ward. It should also be possible to examine how restrictions or boundary conditions set by higher levels of government affect the regional decision-making process.

Some preliminary runs with a simplified version of the model indicated, as one would expect from the reasoning presented in the previous section, that the metropolitan-type council would tend to fulfill individual preferences to the highest degree. It should be noted that this solution is not at all like the one that would be obtained from the sort of 'continuous referendum' which some cyberneticists have suggested could be made possible by sophisticated electronic gear. These proposals, aside from many other problems, neglect vote trading which is at the heart of the preference-aggregating function performed by representative government. Those who put them forward would seem to betray a profound misunderstanding of the functioning of democratic government.

But even if efficient and effective preference-aggregating legislative structures can be created at the metropolitan level this still leaves unresolved the question of how to approach supra-metropolitan problem sheds. The most important of these are perhaps water sheds. After the discussion of the Delaware case which follows I will have some suggestions on this in the final chapter on policy.

Discussion of the 'new' Delaware case provides an opportunity to show how the Russell–Spofford model (politicized version) might be applied in a realistic setting, and some of the problems that arise in doing so. It also affords a chance to be a little more detailed and specific about some features of this pioneering piece of work.

The 'New' Delaware Study[12]

Several specific objectives led to an illustrative application of the conceptual-mathematical model to a specific case area.

The objective was to be able to say something about the *practical* importance of including within a single model airborne, waterborne and solid residuals. As I have been at pains to point out, the regional residuals management problem cannot, in principle, be solved for air or water or solids in isolation, because of the links among forms of residuals and discharge media implied by the conservation of mass and energy in production and residuals modification processes. There was, however, prior to this case study, no hard evidence on the size of the costs implied by isolated solutions in real situations. It was hoped that the applied model would be a good enough representation of the region to yield a body of defensible evidence on this matter.

A second major aim was to generate information on the implications of various residuals management strategies within a regional context. For example: What difference does it make if there is an institution available that can construct and operate regional facilities of various types, such as regional sewage treatment plants and in-stream aeration installations? What effect is there on solid residuals management costs if the possibility of separate collection of some types of paper residuals with subsequent recycling is included? In contrast to earlier water and air studies which posed such questions independently for each medium they were here considered in the context of an integrated multi-media model.

Another objective was to consider the best method of representing and presenting the data in order to make meaningful decisions possible, in view of the complexity of the situation: the range of residuals management strategies involved, the multiple sources of residuals, the many types of residuals, and the varied distributions of impacts and costs resulting in an almost infinite number of possible combinations.

Finally, the intent was to produce an application with sufficient verisimilitude to see whether and how such models might work in an actual legislative-executive setting. Experimental work in this area was encouraging, as we have seen, but it also indicated that the inclusion of the necessary information on the distribution of costs and benefits added significantly to model size. Making the extension permitted an exploration of the degree to which the utility of a regional model, functioning in an actual geographical area, might be increased by the use of a political model which would allow potential legislative and executive users to explore distributional possibilities or aspects efficiently. A closely related objective was to explore: (a) further propositions about the effect on outcomes of structuring the legislative process in different ways; and (b) some of the questions relating to optimal jurisdiction, that is, the problem of the non-correspondence of existing units of government and the geographical reach of environmental systems. Unfortunately, at the time of writing this not all of the explorations had been completed but some preliminary results are presented at the end of this chapter.

The Region

The lower Delaware valley region, chosen for this application, is a very complex one with many individual point and non-point sources of residuals discharges. It is defined by county boundaries and is shown in Map 4. The grid superimposed on the figure is used for locating air pollution sources and receptors in the model. It is related to the Universal Mercator grid.

The region consists of Bucks, Montgomery, Chester, Delaware, and Philadelphia Counties in Pennsylvania; Mercer, Burlington, Camden, Gloucester and Salem Counties in New Jersey; and New Castle County in Delaware. The major cities in the area are Philadelphia (coterminous with Philadelphia County); Trenton in Mercer County; Camden in Camden County; and Wilmington in New Castle County. Overall, the population of the area was a little more than five and a half million in 1970. Of this, 35 percent is accounted for by Philadelphia alone, with a further 5 percent found in Trenton, Camden and Wilmington. However, other parts of the region are also heavily urbanized.

Incomes are generally high here. Using median family income as the indicator, every county except Philadelphia has higher median family income than the United States as a whole. The lowest median income outside Philadelphia is found in Salem County; the region's highest income county is Montgomery. The range between these two extremes is about $2,500 (per family per year), or about 25 percent of the lower figure. Thus, there are significant intraregional income differences, even at the highly aggregated level of counties. This is quite significant for environmental quality management,

Economics and the Environment

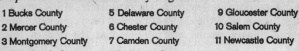

Map 4. Lower Delaware Valley Region

1 Bucks County	5 Delaware County	9 Gloucester County
2 Mercer County	6 Chester County	10 Salem County
3 Montgomery County	7 Camden County	11 Newcastle County
4 Philadelphia County	8 Burlington County	

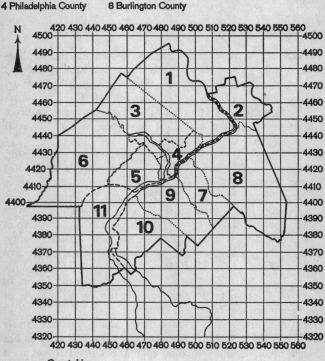

```
.............. County Line
------- State Line
——— Region Boundary
```

0   20   40
km

NOTE: The grid is in kilometers and is based on the Universal Transverse Mercator grid system.

since *a priori* one expects to find interest in a cleaner environment positively correlated with income. It also suggests that the distributional implications of environmental policy will be an important political issue in the region. This presumption is underlined by the fact that Philadelphia sits in the center of the largest industrial concentration, has the highest population density, and hence can be expected to have the greatest environmental quality problems, and which also has the lowest *per capita* income base from which to pay the bill for cleaning up.

The region as a whole contains an abundance of manufacturing plants. In fact, it is one of the most heavily industrialized areas in the United States. It has, for example, seven major oil refineries, five steel plants, sixteen major pulp and paper or paper mills, fifteen important thermal power generating facilities, numerous large and small chemical and petrochemical plants, foundaries, and large assembly plants for the auto and electronic industries. This, of course, made the task of identifying sources of residuals discharges, estimating the costs of discharge reduction for them, and including them in the regional model, an enormous one. The model used contains 125 industrial plants, forty-four municipal sewage treatment plants, and twenty-three municipal incinerators, all dealt with as point sources. In addition, there are fifty-seven home and commercial heating sources with controllable discharges, each of which is treated as an area source, i.e. not tied to a specific stack location. Other point and non-point sources distinguished in the region are incorporated as background discharges.

The large population of the region naturally produces vast quantities of residuals from consumption activities, requiring correspondingly large facilities for their handling and disposal. There are seven municipal sewage treatment plants with flows greater than ten million gallons per day (m.g.d.) and seventeen with flows greater than 1 m.g.d., counting only those discharging to the Delaware estuary which we met already in Chapter 7. On the major tributaries to the estuary and the

Schuylkill river, there are more than 120 municipal treatment plants of widely varying sizes. For the disposal of solid residuals there are seventeen incinerators currently operating with an aggregate capacity of about 6,000 tons per day, and many major and minor landfill operations. Together, on an annual basis, the heating of homes and commercial buildings is responsible for about a quarter of the total discharges of sulfur dioxide and 10–15 percent of the particulate discharges in the region.

The major recipient of waterborne residuals in this area is the Delaware estuary itself. The estuary is generally taken to be the stretch of river between the head of the tide at Trenton and the head of the Delaware Bay at Liston Point, Delaware. For analysis purposes the estuary was divided into the twenty-two reaches shown in Map 1.

The flow of the river varies widely, from month to month, and year to year. For aquatic ecosystem modeling purposes a relatively low-flow period was selected.[13]

With regard to the atmosphere, for the region as a whole, the seasonal prevailing wind pattern is roughly: winter and spring westerlies (and west-northwesterlies), summer southwesterlies, and autumn variability. The net effect of these meteorological conditions, plus the spatial pattern of discharges, is a 'mountain' of air pollution along the estuary from Wilmington to Trenton, with the highest concentrations over the Philadelphia–Camden area. The highest annual average concentration of suspended particulates measured at a station in this area was about 150 micrograms per cubic meter (μg/m^3), for the year 1967–8. (This value compares with the primary standard required by federal legislation in the United States of 75 μg/m^3.) For about the same time period, the discharges on an annual average basis were about 3,000 tons per day of sulfur dioxide, of which about seventy percent was from point sources and about thirty percent from area sources, and about 570 tons per day of particulates, about sixty-five percent from point sources and about thirty-five percent from area sources.

For the modeling of air quality, the atmospheric conditions used represent the annual joint probability distribution of wind speed, wind direction, and stability conditions for 1968, assumed to be uniform throughout the region. For neither air- nor water-quality analyses were conditions representing rare events used in the model. Ideally, explicit attention would also have been given to this aspect of the modeling but as we already saw in Chapter 7 mathematical programming models do not lend themselves well to the ideal analysis of systems in which random events occur.

Contents of the Model

The model framework used is shown again but in more detail than previously in Figure 7. It was discussed in general terms earlier in the chapter in connection with Figure 6. Here we must be a bit more detailed so as to grasp the nature of the actual application of the concepts outlined there. The model is designed to provide the minimum-cost way of simultaneously meeting three sets of exogenously determined standards:

(1) *Minimum production requirements*. This means bills of goods for the individual industrial plants, heat requirements for home and commercial space heating, and specified quantities of liquid and solid residuals requiring some disposal action by municipalities.

(2) *Levels of ambient environmental quality*. This is represented, for example, by maximum concentrations of sulfur dioxide and suspended particulates at a number of receptor locations in the region; by minimum concentrations of dissolved oxygen and fish biomass in the estuary; by maximum concentrations of algae in the estuary; and by restrictions on the types of landfill operations which can be used in the region.

(3) *The distribution of the costs among geographic areas* (*political jurisdictions*). This refers to the distribution of the costs stemming from (1) and (2) together. Specifically, it allows for constraining increases: in the cost of electricity due

241

Figure 7. Schematic Diagram of the Regional Residuals Management Model: Linear Programming Model

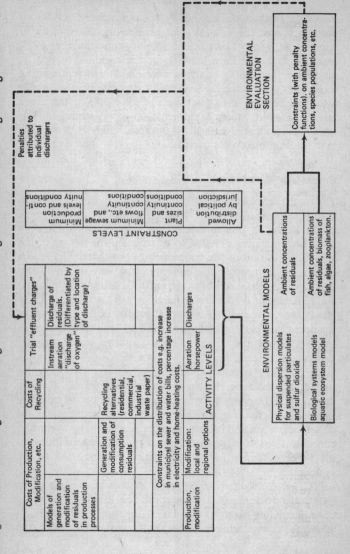

to all required discharge reduction activities (by utility service area); in the cost of home heating due to fuel switching; in municipal expenditures due to increased liquid residuals modification and more expensive solid residuals management methods.

Referring to Figure 7, and restating in more detail how the model functions – in the upper left-hand block of the diagram is found the basic driving force for the entire model – the linear programming model of residuals generation and discharge. It is in this part of the model that minimum 'production' constraints are found. A key output of this part, as mentioned in connection with Figure 6 is a vector of residuals discharges, identified by substance and location. These feed into the environmental models – the model of the aquatic ecosystem and the dispersion model for the suspended particulates and sulfur dioxide discharges. This section of the overall model, in turn, produces as output a vector of ambient environmental quality levels (for example, sulfur dioxide concentrations) at numerous designated points in the region (for example, for sulfur dioxide in the fifty-seventh political jurisdiction). These concentrations are then treated as input to the 'evaluation' submodel found in the lower right of the diagram. Here the concentrations implied by one solution of the production submodel are compared with the constraints imposed for the model run, and a procedure is used to iterate the model until all constraints are met, within some specified tolerance. I will discuss the political processes which go on in the evaluation model in a little detail shortly. But first it is necessary to expand a bit on the production and environmental submodels.

The Production Model

In point of fact, as was also indicated in connection with Figure 6, the production model consists of a number of sets of linear programs with each set arranged into a module. The modules reflect the chronological development of the model as it was expanded over time to encompass more and more of the activities in the region. A summary of this part of the model is shown in Table 24. The modules are shown in the first column. The designation MPSX derives from the particular computational routine used in the analysis. The next three columns give the dimensions of the linear program matrix for each module and the number of discharges. Residuals generated by the linear programs for these activities reflect operating conditions as of about 1970, and represent generation under steady-state conditions. Variability of residuals generation in the various activities was not considered. It will be noted that the overall program is large – over three thousand rows and nearly eight thousand columns. Three hundred and six sources of discharges, with options for reducing discharges, are included. For the number of dischargers and types of residuals being considered, there are nearly eight hundred specified residuals being discharged to the various environmental media. The next column gives the type of activities in each module. The final column shows the extra cost constraints which are the distributional linkages to the political model.

Only the enormous capacity of an electronic computer makes it feasible to solve a problem of this size. As it was, scaling the model down so that it could be dealt with by even a large computer was a difficult practical problem which I will not discuss here.

The Environmental Models

The overall model incorporates a twenty-two-reach nonlinear ecosystem model of the Delaware estuary.[14] Inputs of liquid residuals discharges to this model include: organics (BOD), nitrogen, phosphorus, toxics, suspended solids, and heat. Outputs are expressed in terms of ambient concentrations of algae, bacteria, zooplankton, fish, oxygen, BOD, nitrogen, phosphorus, toxics, suspended solids, and temperature. Three of these outputs – algae, fish, and oxygen – are constrained (all can be constrained in the model). These levels can be set

Table 24. Delaware Valley Model. Residuals Generation and Discharge Modules

Module identification	Size of linear program			Description	Extra cost constraints
	Rows	Columns	Discharges		
MPSX 1	286	1649	130	Petroleum refineries (7) Steel mills (5) Power plants (17)	57 electricity (percentage extra cost)
MPSX 2	741	1474	114	Home heat (57) Commercial heat (57)	57 fuel (percentage extra cost) 57 fuel (percentage extra cost)
MPSX 3	564	1854	157	Over-25-$\mu g/m^3$ dischargers (75)	
MPSX 4	468	570	180	Delaware estuary sewage treatment plants (36)	36 sewage disposal ($ per household per year)
MPSX 5	923	1778	86	Paper plants (10) Municipal incinerators (23) Municipal solid residuals handling and disposal activities	57 solid residuals disposal (percentage extra cost)
MPSX 6	228	394	116	Delaware estuary industrial dischargers (22)* Instream aeration (22)	57 instream aeration (absolute extra cost)
Total	3210	7719	783		

* Twelve of the Delaware estuary industrial wastewater discharges in MPSX 6 are also represented by sulfur dioxide and/or particulate discharges in MPSX 3.

either exogenously or endogenously when the vote-trading algorithm is engaged. In addition, the model includes two 57×251 (57 receptor locations and 251 dischargers) air dispersion matrices – one for sulfur dioxide and one for suspended particulates. These relate ambient ground level concentrations to residuals discharges (sulfur dioxide and particulates).

The Political Model

The political (vote-trading) part of the model is, as already indicated, based upon fifty-seven political 'districts' (hence the fifty-seven constraints found in most of the last column of Table 24). These artificial districts contain between 90,000 and 100,000 persons each. They were created because it would have been impossible to work with the very large number of existing political jurisdictions at the local level. Also, such districts might be considered prototypes of those which would be components of a political structure in a region designed for a 'one-man one-vote' regional respresentative government.

The political algorithm uses preference vectors pertaining to the way a set of constituents (or their representatives) would vote on a particular issue (environmental standard or distribution of costs), viz.

$$Y^1$$
$$N^2$$
$$Y^3$$
$$.$$
$$.$$
$$.$$

These preferences pertain to upper and lower limits on various environmental variables at specific measurement points, e.g.,

$$SO_2 \leq 25 \mu g/m^3 \text{ in jurisdiction 36,}$$
$$SP \leq 20 \mu g/m^3 \text{ in jurisdiction 36,}$$
$$DO \geq 3 \text{ mg/l in reach 4,}$$

and on associated cost variables, e.g.,

> Δ taxes, i.e., because of increased solid residuals
>   management costs ≤ 20 percent for juris-
>   diction 36,
> Δ heating bill ≤ 50 percent for jurisdiction 3,
> Δ electricity ≤ 100 percent for jurisdiction 36.

Thus, for example, if the population of jurisdiction 36 opposed any outcome which would impose a greater-than-20 percent increase in taxes on that jurisdiction, its representative would cast a 'no' vote on taxes associated with such an outcome.

The preference vectors, on the basis of which combinations of yes and no votes were assigned to various limits on environmental quality and costs, were based on field-work in the Delaware valley. Nearly every county was visited and fairly extensive interviewing of public officials, citizens groups, and individuals was done. Local papers were also analyzed to see what issues were of concern to the people of the various areas.

All of the results of the field-work were matched against 1970 Bureau of Census data (on a tract level) for such factors as population, age distribution, ethnic composition, work-force commuting patterns, education, occupation, unemployment and welfare rates, race, and home ownership. Voting data, where possible, were also used. Such analytical work as has been done, by others, on matching attitudes to socioeconomic data was also reviewed.

The results were then utilized to delineate the fifty-seven equal population districts. The purpose of the whole exercise was to construct preference vectors which would match the range and variation of the real world – the intention being to illustrate and test vote-trading operations, in conjunction with regional residuals management model, in a realistic situation.

The regional model was constructed to conform to this arrangement in several ways (some of which have already been mentioned):

(1) The area discharges from home and commercial heating

are generated by the districts defined in the political model. The level of discharges is controllable separately for each district by the use of fuel substitution (low for high sulfur oil, for example), and the added costs per average household implied by the controls may be constrained separately for each jurisdiction.

(2) Solid residuals are handled in a similar way, with generation and management options specified by district and added costs of management subject to constraint by district. Management possibilities for solid residuals include three grades of landfill (open dumps with no burning, sanitary landfills, and advanced sanitary landfills with landscaping, impervious plastic leachate (solution obtained by leaching) trap, treatment of leachate, etc.); incineration with landfill of incinerator residue; transport out of the region; and separate collection and handling of used newspapers from residences, and used corrugated containers from certain commercial and industrial sources, with recycling at paper plants in the region.

(3) The average percentage increase in household electricity bills implied by the costs of controlling residuals discharges at power plants may be constrained by jurisdiction, though the increase must be the same in each district served by a particular utility.

(4) The added costs of building bigger or better municipal sewage treatment plants for modifying discharges to the estuary are assigned to the districts served by the particular plants on the basis of population served.

The vote-trading algorithm then proceeds in the following steps:

(1) Each jurisdiction is a 'trader' and is assigned an upper or lower limits vector with entries concerning the variables just discussed, corresponding to the results of the research on preferences discussed earlier.

(2) After each run of the model, each trader's potential exchanges with all other traders are discovered and stored in the memory of the computer.

(3) All trades which are optimal (that is, no trader has any

other trade which gives him more or allows him to give up less to get a given issue) are made.

(4) Each trade means that two constraints (what each trader was trading *for*) are added to the LP model for its next iteration. Thus, if there are four trades made, eight new constraints are put on the residuals management model for its next iteration.

(5) The trades are reflected in the trading model itself by changing a previous N vote to a Y vote on the items each trader wants. This happens because the residuals management model, run with these constraints, now meets these upper or lower limits (assuming a feasible solution).

(6) The new solution of the residuals management model yields a new Y–N array by testing whether the output of environmental quality results and costs are less than or greater than each entry in the upper and lower limits vectors.

(7) New trades are made, if any are possible, and the process is repeated until all optimal trades are exhausted.

When the situation corresponding to (7) has been achieved (no further trades possible), the highest possible level of meeting vote preferences prevails that is consistent with the prices of inputs and outputs, the economic objectives of firms (profit maximization) and local governments (cost minimization), and the functioning of the technological and natural systems relationships built into the model.

Some Results

As I mentioned, unfortunately at the time of writing production runs with the large model had just gotten underway. No runs incorporating the vote-trading algorithm had been performed. A few preliminary results are of interest, however.

First the model does show that in this realistic setting of an actual case there are significant linkages among the management aspects of the different residuals types. Tighter ambient standards for the atmosphere do significantly affect the cost of maintaining water-quality standards and vice versa. This can be seen by considering the following sample results from production runs with the large Delaware integrated residuals management model.

Table 25. Additional Daily Costs of Meeting Water Standards

	Easy ambient standards – air	Tight ambient standards – air
Easy ambient standards – water	$395,640	$1,064,892
Tight ambient standards – water	$422,031	$1,309,271

High-quality landfill required for all runs

All the numbers in the table refer to total additional costs to the region for meeting environmental standards in dollars per day. The sample runs show that going from easy (relatively low) water standards to tight (relatively high) water standards costs about $26,000 per day when only easy air standards are imposed. If, however, tight air standards are required going from easy to tight water standards costs about $244,000 – almost ten times as much.

Secondly, the overall response surface seems to be relatively flat in that there appears to be a variety of strategies for meeting the environmental quality standards that do not differ very much in overall total costs to the region. This is interesting in that it suggests that distributional issues will be dominant and that there will be much grist for the vote-trading mill.

Finally, and perhaps most important, the Delaware application indicates that it is possible to develop an integrated residuals management model for a large region at a manageable cost. The cost of this model (granted that much of the basic data had been collected already) was about ten man years of effort on the part of the senior researchers, plus some research assistance, plus perhaps a hundred thousand dollars worth of computer time at commercial rates. In dollars terms the cost could be put at roundly a million dollars, or about the same as the extra cost to the region of operating with tight environmental standards for one day.

Chapter 10
Some Conclusions

In this book we have made our way through a considerable amount of economic theory, research methodology, and analysis. But from all this a few really central conclusions emerge.

Five Main Conclusions

First, developed countries should be able to reduce the amount of residuals discharge to their environment to a small fraction of what it is now without major destructive effects on their general economies as measured by the conventional macroeconomic indices. In terms of real welfare this should mark a distinct improvement. A careful study in the United States, for example, indicates that devoting to the purpose perhaps 5 percent of GNP on an annual average basis from now until the turn of the century would produce a large reduction in residuals discharge to the environmental media. Somewhat scattered benefit estimates of dubious quality suggest such an investment in environmental improvement would yield net benefits to society. A corollary is that direct attacks on pollution problems will yield much more effective and less costly results than trying to control pollution by stopping economic growth, a policy which has been frequently advocated. This is not to say that there could not be legitimate reasons for reconsidering the growth policies which have characterized most economies. These might for example involve resource conservation issues or possibly the disruptive effects on communities of the high rates of mobility which usually accompany economic growth. For example raw materials producing countries often subsidize heavily raw materials producing industries through favorable tax treatment and by other means. Eliminating these artificial inducements to basic resources exploitation would tend to induce more recovery of used materials and more conservative use of materials in general. This would serve both conservation and environmental protection. But stemming economic growth in the hopes of stopping pollution would be throwing out the baby with the bath water; there is even a strong probability that it would be throwing out the baby *without* the bath water, since pollution from existing activities would not be altered by this act alone. Measures which bear directly upon decisions to discharge residuals are to be preferred.

Second, we have much less evidence as to what economic and population development may mean in terms of environmental conditions in developing countries. One thing that does seem clear, however, is that population growth is a major factor both directly and indirectly in environmental impacts in those regions of the world and that environmental conditions there are growing worse at a fearsome rate. Unless population growth can be halted soon in those areas even the crudest analyses suggest that environmental and other catastrophies lie ahead in those countries. In one way or another such events cannot fail to involve the remainder of the world as well.

Third, economic theory and a number of substantial case studies suggest that changes in the economic incentive structure must play a large role in successful environmental management. More specifically there is strong evidence that effluent and emissions charges, if properly implemented, would have advantages in efficiency, equity, and effectiveness over the efforts to do the whole job with direct regulation which have characterized policy in most countries. Quite simple charges systems can be designed to induce responses which will cause environmental standards to be met at much lower cost than even a successfully implemented program of conventional standards. Experience in the United States and elsewhere – see for example the discussion of West Germany below – suggests that enforcement of regulation-type controls presents great difficulties and is often unsuccessful in gaining its objectives.

Fourth, once again theory, research, and in this case, experience, especially in the Ruhr area of Germany, indicate that residuals management problems are best approached on a regional 'problem shed' basis. This appears to be particularly true in the case of waterborne residuals because of the wide range of technologies, such as low-flow regulation and mechanical reaeration of watercourses, which can be applied in addition to controls at points sources. Furthermore, non-point-source waterborne residuals are of great importance and their environmental impact can be managed only through non-point technologies of the sort already indicated, and through land-use management practices. While there exists a lesser range of non-point technologies for the management of air pollution the pattern of economic activity, and therefore land-use control, can greatly affect air quality.

Fifth, reasoning about the implications of mass balance in economic systems, and at least one major case study, indicate that there are important non-market linkages among liquid, gaseous and solid residuals. Therefore tight controls placed on discharges to one medium can significantly affect the costs of achieving environmental objectives in another medium or, if discharge controls do not exist for the other medium, a transfer of environmental degradation to it. In large metropolitan complexes where pollution problems are likely to be most severe, these interrelationships may be complex and indirect but research has shown that many aspects of the situation can be modeled successfully in a quantitative manner.

Some Further Discussion of Policy Matters

Because the last three points have a direct bearing on the formation of national and provincial (or state) policy with respect to environmental management I think it worth discussing their implications in a bit more detail.

With respect to effluent charges, it must be acknowledged that most countries that have enacted environmental legislation have put almost exclusive reliance on various kinds of direct regulation and enforcement in their efforts to control pollution problems. This has certainly been true, for example, in the United States, Britain, and West Germany, and in most other countries as well.[1]

This despite the fact that there are several persuasive arguments in favor of the proposition that effluent charges would be a superior alternative to effluent standards – especially uniform effluent standards. When one reviews and gathers together what has been said earlier in the text, the following emerge as the main points: (1) A charge tends to yield a given environmental quality at least cost because a flat charge among sources automatically induces the highest levels of control at points where costs are least.[2] (2) The charge is technologically neutral so it stimulates the least-cost selection of currently available technologies and in addition induces a search for efficient new technologies. (3) The charge helps to rationalize the price structure, because if the charge is paid the private cost of production will reflect both internal cost and at least a rough approximation of external (effluent) cost. (4) The charge is more easily enforced than effluent standards since it does not come into operation at any particular level of discharge (with all the attendant information and enforcement problems) but provides an effective incentive to cut back because every unit discharged has to be paid for.[3]

Despite such notable advantages both air and water federal legislation in the United States has, as was pointed out in Chapters 7 and 8, tended over its history – essentially, the post-war period – to rely increasingly heavily on direct controls administered from the national government. The final result of this evolution was new legislation in 1972 which established a system of discharge permits to be administered at the national government level by the Environmental Protection Agency. This strategy has received strong criticism from professional economists pointed both at its inefficiency and at its likely ineffectiveness for achieving its objectives.[4] As was indicated in Chapter 7, efforts to put legislation on a different track have not borne fruit in the United States, but understanding of and support for an alternative approach based on economic incentives has grown strongly there in recent years.

In this connection it is interesting to contrast the emerging approach in West Germany where a permit enforcement system similar to that now being tried in the United States has been in effect since 1957. Legislation proposed by the West German government and deemed likely to pass would largely replace this permits system with a system of effluent charges. This legislation must be regarded as the most highly developed effluent charges scheme proposed for adoption anywhere in the world.

This being the case it is worth reviewing the main features of the proposed legislation in a little detail. The basis for this review is a document released by the German Interior Ministry in July 1973.[5] In defending this proposed new law the Interior Ministry cited the continuing decline in water quality in the Federal Republic and indicated that a major reason for considering effluent fees is that they are likely to be more effective. In addition essentially the same economic efficiency arguments reviewed just above are cited. The proposed German scheme would levy fees on dischargers in accordance with the damaging effect of their waste water and the fee would be set so that it would provide a strong stimulus for reducing waste discharges to watercourses. The choice of technologies for reducing or eliminating waste water discharges is to be left to the discharger. The system is thus designed not only to engender an efficient response at present but to motivate research and development for improved processes generating fewer residual materials. Payments are to be made by all public and private dischargers of waste water to surface waters and coastal waters without regard to the legality of the discharge or to the size or quality of the watercourses to which the discharges are made, in other words the fees are to be levied on the basis of a uniform national formula. While this is recognized to be less efficient than more precisely tailored charges the justification is that such a charge would contribute to broad progress in reducing pollution in the Federal Republic and also discourage industries from migrating from dirtier to cleaner areas where the charges would otherwise be lower. As an aside one may note an additional point that could be made in this respect: it is probably easier for a national government to make a large policy innovation of this nature than it is for provincial, state, or local governments who may be more subject to pressures from vested interests affected by the policy. The flat fee is, however, regarded as a stepping-stone to more refined management including more refined charges systems on a regional river basin basis. Regional agencies with comprehensive water-quality management responsibilities are to be created and these agencies will then implement the charges systems.

For an interim period of four years the charge will be 25 Deutschmarks per population equivalent. This is regarded as amply sufficient to spur construction of treatment plants at larger sources, although the stimulus to process change might be considerable even at smaller sources. Following this interim period the level will rise to 40 Deutschmarks per population equivalent which would stimulate the construction of high-level treatment plants for either small or otherwise high-cost discharge points and provide a strong inducement for process changes.

The charge is to be suspended for a period of time keyed to the average period needed to construct a treatment plant. If the plant is constructed by that time or the waste water discharge is otherwise reduced the charge will apply only to the remaining discharge. If it is not, the charge is to apply retroactively to the entire discharge; this provides a doubly strong incitement to action.

Charges are to be based on reports by the dischargers

themselves on their own dischargers, supplemented by random checks. The proposed formula for calculating the charges given in the Interior Ministry report generally resembles the formulas now used by the Genossenschaften to levy charges on waste dischargers in the Ruhr region. It weights suspended material of both mineral and organic types in a formula which accounts of both biochemical and chemical oxygen demand.[6] As I noted in Chapter 7 legislation resembling this proposed German law has been introduced in the United States Congress by a number of prominent senators and representatives. However, since water-quality legislation embodying a permits-enforcement approach has recently been passed it will be necessary to provide for a period of trial before any strategic reconsideration can take place.

The use of effluent charges has also been the subject of considerable discussion and debate in Britain. As we saw in Chapter 7 the new and far-reaching British Water Pollution Act, which sets up strong regional river basin management agencies, provides a broad scope for the development of charges schemes for both the intake and the discharge of water. These schemes are now under development and it remains to be seen what specific form they will take.

As I remarked in Chapter 8, research and policy development in the air pollution area has in general lagged behind similar developments in water pollution by several years; nevertheless, as we also saw in that chapter, there are several serious proposals for the institution of emission charges for atmospheric discharges in the United States and it appears that the political support, including the support of several major conservationist organizations, may be stronger for these proposals than for analogous proposals in the water area. At the present time, however, there is, so far as I am aware, no system of atmospheric charges in operation in the world. If the history of legislation in the water-quality area is any indication, however, one can expect interest in this approach to increase in the future. The economic arguments in its favor are essentially the same as for water.

In regard to the development of regional management institutions capable of implementing technologies other than point source controls, the fourth major point indicated above, there have been substantial developments in several countries. This is especially so in the water area. The British Water Pollution Act is very far-reaching in its integration of water management authority into river basin agencies. The potential for efficiency improvements in water-quality management in Britain therefore appears to be enormous. In France water-quality management is also pursued on a river-basin basis but there has not been a thorough integration of water quality and quantity functions and the approach to discharge control still appears to emphasize point-source controls very heavily. In Germany experience is mixed. The Genossenschaften of the Ruhr area have for many years combined effluent charges with unified management approaches to produce successful and efficient water-quality and quantity management under extremely stringent conditions of water supply. On the other hand, the remainder of Germany has tended to rely mostly on permit-enforcement-type approaches. The proposed new law just reviewed would of course change all that and give a powerful impetus to regional water-quality management. Czechoslovakia is also engaged in a program for developing regional management approaches and is using its effluent charges law to provide revenues for the study of optimal management systems.[7]

Once again, despite some promising starts in major river basins like the Delaware and the Ohio, U.S. national policy has worked to weaken rather than to strengthen regional approaches to the problem. One manifestation of this is the increasing centralization of direct regulation activities in the federal government. To a substantial extent this peculiarity of federal policy in the United States appears to be the result of some powerful political figures having become wedded to a particular strategic approach and not wishing to bear the political costs of admitting that it is fundamentally defective. In addition it happened that the recent environmental legislation in both the water and air areas was conceived during a

259

rather frantic period when environmentalist activity and concern was at a high level. The result is that there was much pressure to frame the legislation in such a way as to try to get as close to 'zero discharge' as possible. In such an atmosphere economics, economic research, cost-effectiveness considerations, and management concepts could play little role in the development of legislation.

The Frontiers of Research and Policy Making

I expressed my view in the last chapter that the frontiers of economic research on residuals management lie in the area of the interrelationships among various different kinds of residuals and at the interface between residuals management modeling and political decision-making processes. In these areas the state of interdisciplinary research centered on economic concepts is just at the point where it may be judged that reasonably successful experimental models have been developed. Clearly, however, both of these closely related frontier areas need further research support and additional quantitative modeling enterprises with a regional focus. Fortunately the latter are under way, if not necessarily at the appropriate level of intensity.[8] It seems that the work that has already been done is sufficiently promising to encourage the view that developed countries should support modeling enterprises of this type in all of their major regions.

But even considering only the results to date some important conclusions emerge. For example, it is clear that the various independencies resulting from the multiple residuals, and the different media involved in residuals management, present substantial difficulties for devising a coherent charges approach, taking account of all media simultaneously, and for the development of other elements of an integrated environmental management strategy. A fully integrated set of effluent charges applying to all media and to all materials simultaneously and coherently is not within the state of the art at the moment. But setting even crudely devised charges on a broad front would recognize the interdependencies among the environmental media and lead to the design of processes which use less material and less energy, and which are more conducive to recycling; it would also lead to residuals modification where appropriate. The presence of taxes for discharges to all the media, even though they were not the optimal ones, would make it impossible to simply transfer residuals from one medium to another without bearing any of the social costs of doing so.

A very promising start in the direction of a tax scheme for all routine discharges of major residuals (in terms of mass) is represented by a Bill recently introduced by Congressman Heinz of Pennsylvania in the United States Congress.[9] The Bill would amend the Internal Revenue Code to levy a tax on the discharges of taxable items by any stationary or non-stationary source of pollution into the atmosphere or into or upon the navigable waters of the United States, adjoining shore lines, or in contiguous zones or oceans. The Bill then sets the procedure for determining the tax rate which shall finally be set by Congress and reviewed at intervals. This type of approach would need considerable development but it is clearly a step in the right direction.

As for the present results on the political public choice aspects of residuals management, they suggest that, in countries where it is thought that individual preferences should govern resource use, public goods decisions should be made in a legislative setting. Since environmental improvement is only one of many public goods which can be provided in a region, if appropriate tradeoffs – given budgeting constraints – are to be made, research further suggests that the choices are best made by a government of general jurisdiction. These are questions of 'optimal jurisdiction' and are very much at the frontiers of research in environmental management.[10] But what has been done suggests that some nations at least may require fundamental restructuring of political institutions if both the technological–economic and political–collective-choice potentials of integrated residuals management are to be realized.[11] This research further suggests that it is not ridiculous to suppose that integrated quantitative residuals management models could be used in a legislative setting.

Thus, the frontier areas in research on the economics of residuals management suggest a three-step approach to coming to grips with the continuing and complex nature of this aspect of the environmental problem.

The first element of the strategy would be to develop a broad-based and coherent set of national effluent fees on all substances discharged to the environment (except those which it would be completely forbidden to discharge in this way, e.g. heavy metals and chlorinated hydrocarbons).

A second element would be to initiate integrated residuals management modeling, of the type discussed in the previous chapter or modifications of it, in all of the major metropolitan–industrial regions of a nation.[12] While, as we have seen, there are many improvements to be made in such modeling, experimental work reported in the last chapter has gone sufficiently far to indicate that this type of activity is a feasible endeavor which can provide important management information, including that needed to establish a coherent set of effluent fees for achieving regional ambient environmental quality objectives.

A third element in this grand strategy would be to develop legislative and executive institutions suitable for the thoroughly integrated management of residuals problems in environmental regions. It is ultimately only through these institutional arrangements that efficient and informed environmental management becomes possible and that value choices inherent in it can be made through the medium of representative government.

There is necessarily a certain vagueness when we try to see to the very limits of current research and study; nevertheless I feel that integrated residuals management research indicates the proper general direction for policy, at least of the more advanced economies. It is like the pointer of a compass: when used in an informed manner it can guide one in the right direction but it cannot say how fast movement should be or what obstacles will be encountered. Moving in the direction of integrated residuals management programs will necessarily be an interactive evolutionary process in which both research and policy making must play their appropriate roles.

References and Notes

Preface

1. Marshall I. Goldman, *The Spoils of Progress*, Cambridge, Mass., MIT Press, 1972.

1. Environment as an Economic Problem

1. The basic paper is K. J. Arrow and G. Debreu, 'Existence of an Equilibrium for a Competitive Economy', *Econometrica*, 22, No. 3, 1954. A summary of the literature is printed in Hukukane Nikaido, *Convex Structures in Economic Theory*, New York, Academic Press, 1968.

2. Alfred Marshall, *Principles of Economics*, 8th ed., London, Macmillan, 1930.

3. James Henderson and Richard Quandt, *Microeconomic Theory: A Mathematical Approach*, New York, McGraw-Hill, 1963.

4. Quoted in B. Lambert, *History and Survey of London*, London, 1806, Vol. I, p. 241.

5. Quoted in Laurence Reed, 'Policy Issues', in Joan Robinson, ed., *After Keynes*, Oxford, Basil Blackwell, 1973.

6. These statements are from *The Public Health as a Public Question: First Report of the Metropolitan Sanitary Association*, 'Address of Charles Dickens, Esq.', London, 1850.

2. A Brief Survey of the Substantive Nature of Environmental Problems

1. I wish to acknowledge the help of Blair T. Bower in the preparation of this chapter.

2. Ominously, the earth's temperature appears to have been declining for the past few decades.

3. We are fortunate in having available several excellent reports on possible effects of man's activities on global environment. These reports are excellent not only from the point of view of content, but also of exposition. One of these is *Man's Impact on the Global Environment: Assessment and Recommendations for Action Report of the Study of Critical Environmental Problems*, Cambridge, Mass., MIT Press, 1970, p. 47; another is William Griskin, *The Atmospheric Environment*, Washington, D.C., Resources for the Future, Inc., 1973.

4. Lester B. Lave and Eugene P. Seskin, *Air Pollution and Human Health*, Baltimore, Johns Hopkins Press, 1975.

5. ibid.

6. ibid.

7. *Synergistic* refers to an interaction between two substances in which the total effect is greater than the sum of the individual effects of the substances.

8. Reported in Horst Siebert, *Das produzierte Chaos*, Stuttgart, Kohlhammer Verlag, 1973, p. 13.

9. J. S. S. Reay, 'Air Pollution' in Joan Robinson, ed., *After Keynes*, Oxford, Basil Blackwell, 1973, pp. 160, 162.

10. See for example J. H. Kircher and D. S. Hoffman, *Nationwide Air Pollutant Emission Trends 1940–1970*, Washington, D.C., EPA Publication HP-115, 1973.

11. The passenger capacity per engine is higher for the jet than for the piston engine. However, the absolute number of jet aircraft flights now is substantially larger nearly everywhere than the number of piston engine aircraft flights three decades ago.

12. D. J. Kinnersly, 'Water Pollution', in Joan Robinson, ed., *After Keynes*, Oxford, Basil Blackwell, 1973, p. 142.

13. Siebert, op. cit., p. 18.

14. Culm represents the residual from coal cleaning. It contains substantial amounts of carbon. Often the banks of culm ignite – 495 culm banks were burning in 15 states in the United States in 1964. The problem is similar in other coal-producing countries, Britain and France for example.

15. Sewage treatment plants in the United States are currently (1974) generating sludge at the rate of about 20,000 tons per day, according to Russell E. Train, Administrator of the U.S. Environmental Protection Agency, 'Remarks of R. E. Train before the

References and Notes

Pennsylvania Environment Council', *EPA Environmental News*, Philadelphia, 16 April 1974, p. 7.

3. Impacts of Environmental Deterioration and Environmental Controls on Entire National Economics

1. I wish to acknowledge the help of Ronald G. Ridker in the preparation of this chapter.

2. Wassily Leontief, 'Environmental Repercussions of the Economic Structure: An Input-output Approach', *Review of Economic and Statistics*, Vol. III, August 1970, pp. 262–71.

3. We speak of pollution reduction activities rather than industries because in any application the pollutant reduction activities often will be a part of an ordinary industry. In some cases it may be desirable to account for these separately.

4. No account has been taken of residuals generated by the final demand sector. The procedure for doing so is, however, straightforward and I will not review it here.

5. See U.S. Commission on Population Growth and the Future, *Population Resources and the Environment* (Volume III of Commission Research Reports), edited by Ronald G. Ridker, Washington, D.C., U.S. Government Printing Office, 1972.

6. Howard C. Madsen, Kenneth J. Nicol, and Earl O. Heady made a study, 'Environmental Impacts and Costs in Agriculture in Relation to Soil Loss Restrictions and Nitrogen Fertilizer Limitations', Ames, Iowa, Iowa State University, November 1973 (xerox). They conclude that restrictions on soil erosion and modest restrictions on nitrogen fertilizer use would have little effect on farm prices by the year 2000. Strict restrictions on fertilizer use, e.g., 50 lb per acre, could, however, raise farm prices by as much as 50 percent.

7. A brief description of the project can be found in *Methods and Techniques for Evaluating the Impact of Economic and Social Activities on the Environment* ('Note by the Secretariat'), Geneva, Economic Commission for Europe, 9 October 1974.

8. The work was sponsored by Resources for the Future, Inc., Washington, D.C.

9. Henry M. Peskin, *National Accounting and the Environment*, Artikler 50, Oslo, Statistisk Sentralbyra, 1972.

10. It should be noted, however, that sulfite processes cannot pulp all species.

11. In fact, some of these transactions are virtual or imputed. For example, the value of owner-occupied housing is estimated by imputation.

12. Deflated gross national product by industry is calculated by deflating industry outputs and purchases separately and subtracting. See U.S. Department of Commerce, Office of Business Economics, *Concepts and Methods of National Income Statistics* (PB-194 900, OBE-SUP 70-02), p. 216.

13. However, at the time of writing, a substantial effort was underway to provide a conceptual, and the beginnings of a quantitative, basis for including environmental service flows in the accounts. See Henry M. Peskin, 'Environmental Assets, Residuals, and National Accounting', New York, National Bureau of Economic Research, July 1973 (xerox). Interest and activity in such an enterprise is also evident in a number of other countries.

14. See the exchanges in Milton Moss (ed.), *The Measurement of Economic and Social Performance*, New York, National Bureau of Economic Research, 1973.

4. World Perspectives

1. This of course skirts the issues surrounding the energy crisis and possible collapse of the international economic system. My view is that these can be regarded in the long term as temporary aberrations as regards the issues being discussed here, except that it appears that the price of energy will be permanently higher. Also, one should not jump to the conclusion that since growth and environmental improvement appear to be compatible that growth is therefore a good thing. This is a complex issue only partly tackled in the analysis of the last chapter.

2. For a conflicting interpretation see Roy E. Brown and Joe D. Wray, 'The Starving Roots of Population Growth', *Natural History*, January 1974, p. 46.

3. See Nicholas Wade, 'Sahelian Drought: No Victory for Western Air', *Science*, Vol. 185, 19 July 1974, pp. 234 ff.

4. Brazil has been particularly associated with this position.

5. See, for example, George Löf and Allen V. Kneese, *The Economics of Water Utilization in the Beet Sugar Industry*, Washington, D.C., Resources for the Future, 1963.

6. This publication is cited in the appendix of this chapter.

References and Notes

7. As this was being written in 1974 the picture was further clouded by several successive poor crop years in most nations of the world.

8. This means relative to completely disastrous ones. It puts one in mind of a remark once attributed to Maurice Chevalier. When asked how he felt about getting old, he said, 'It's not so great, but much better than the alternative.'

9. A fascinating account of this process is found in 'Machines and Men', Chapter XI of G. D. H. Cole's *Introduction to Economic History, 1750–1950*, London, Macmillan, 1952.

10. Sir John Hicks, *A Theory of Economic History*, Oxford University Press, 1969, p. 147.

11. For a more detailed discussion, see Robert U. Ayres, *Technological Forecasting and Long Range Planning*, New York, McGraw-Hill, 1969.

12. *Environmental Survey of Nuclear Fuel Cycle: Power Reactor Licensing and Rule Making*, Washington, D.C., U.S. Atomic Energy Commission, November 1972.

13. Sometimes different weights are assigned to different classes of recipients to reflect distributional considerations.

14. Alvin M. Weinberg, 'Social Institutions and Nuclear Energy', *Science*, 7 July 1972.

15. *Ambio*, The Royal Swedish Academy of Sciences, Vol. 1, No. 6, 1973.

Appendix to Chapter 4

1. D. H. Meadows, P. L. Meadows, J. Randers, W. W. Behrens III, *The Limits to Growth*, New York, Universe, 1972.

2. Ronald G. Ridker, 'To Grow or Not to Grow: That's Not the Relevant Question', *Science*, 28 December 1973, Vol. 182, pp. 1315–18.

5. Back to Microeconomics and the Environment

1. See Allen V. Kneese and Blair T. Bower, *Managing Water Quality: Economics, Technology, Institutions*, Baltimore, Johns Hopkins University Press, 1968.

2. There has been discussion in the economics profession as to whether the destructive use/nondestructive use (externality causing/nonexternality causing) distinction makes sense when we speak of

the use of common property resources. A 1973 Symposium Issue of the *Natural Resources Journal* is devoted to papers on this controversy. It is known as the 'Coase Controversy'. I discuss this controversy by using a simple example involving two industrial plants along a stream. Assume the upstream plant discharges a waste material which adversely affects an industrial process in a downstream plant (and, just to keep the matter simple, assume the downstream plant neither depletes the quantity of water available nor discharges anything harmful to it). One side of the argument goes that the downstream user imposes a cost on the upstream user if water is made cleaner (causes him to incur costs to improve his effluent) in just the same way as if material had been discharged and caused costs to be incurred by the downstream user. It is concluded that the activities of both parties must then be constrained either directly or by charging them a fee. However, efficient use of the resource requires that its use by only one party be restricted by means of prices. If the upstream discharge is optimally controlled by (say) levying a fee on the discharge equal to the marginal damage it does (I will elaborate on what this means later), downstream use will be appropriately controlled by the amount of deterioration which nevertheless occurs. The downstream user will still have to incur costs to treat his input water and this reflects the fact that further reduction in upstream discharge would be costly, in his own decisions. But withdrawal should not be charged for since it in no way diminishes the service flow to others from the resource. The general principle is that common property resource uses that diminish valued service flows from the resource itself should be controlled and uses that do not diminish service flows should not be. See W. J. Baumol, 'On Taxation and the Control of Externalities', *American Economic Review*, 62, June 1972, pp. 303–22.

3. Karl-Göran Mäler, *Environmental Economics – A Theoretical Inquiry*, Baltimore, Johns Hopkins University Press, 1974.

4. I will attempt to show why this is so and provide a critique of this approach (or, at least, of exclusive reliance on it, in the last chapter).

5. More technically, the total damage function is linear and goes through the origin.

6. This is formally proved in Talbot Page, 'Failure of Bribes and Standards for Pollution Abatement', Coase Theorem Symposium of the *Natural Resources Journal*, 13, No. 4 (ct. 1973), pp. 677–704.

References and Notes

7. See Baumol, op. cit.

8. A review of such studies pertaining to water can be found in Kneese and Bower, op. cit. A discussion of such models pertaining to the air is in Azriel Teller, 'Air Pollution Abatement: Economic Rationality and Reality', *Daedalus*, Vol. 96, No. 5, Fall 1967.

9. The reason why the charges approach did not produce costs fully as low as the effluent standards system has to do with the nature of transfer functions as we will see in the next chapter.

6. Some Useful Models

1. A more elaborate version of this model can be found in Allen V. Kneese and Blair T. Bower, *Managing Water Quality: Economics, Technology, Institutions*, Baltimore, Johns Hopkins Press, 1968, see especially the Appendix to Chapter 10 by Hayden Boyd. The present version is adapted from 'Analyzing "Externalities": "Direct Interaction" vs. "Asset Utilization" Models', by Herbert Mohring and J. Hayden Boyd, *Economica*, November 1971, pp. 347–61.

2. The estimation of $C(N,K)$ presents some difficult and subtle problems that are not discussed here. An especially challenging one is to place a value on the extra time required for a trip by reason of congestion.

3. For a development of this point, see Boyd, in Kneese and Bower, op. cit.

4. The numerical example is taken from Clopper Almon, *Matrix Methods in Economics*, Reading, Mass., Addison-Wesley Publishing Company, 1967, pp. 59 ff. As we will see in Chapter 9, problems with non-linear objective functions can also be solved.

5. See G. M. Fair, J. C. Geyer, and D. A. Okun, *Water and Wastewater Engineering*, Vol. 2, New York, John Wiley, 1960, for a good explanation of the derivation.

7. Economic Studies of Water-Quality Management in Particular Basins

1. A major exception is dissolved solids, particularly chlorides; aside from coastal areas problems with them are mostly found in rivers flowing through arid regions and used heavily for irrigation.

2. Federal Water Pollution Control Administration, *Delaware Estuary Comprehensive Study: Preliminary Report and Findings*,

Washington, D.C., United States Public Health Service, 1966 (mimeo).

3. Programs with linear constraints and non-linear objective functions can usually be solved if the non-linear function is not too complicated. So this condition would not necessarily have to hold. In Chapter 9, we will encounter a problem where the objective function is not linear.

4. Paul Davidson, F. Gerard Adams, and Joseph Seneca, 'The Social Value of Water Recreational Facilities Resulting from an Improvement in Water Quality: The Delaware Estuary', in Allen V. Kneese and Stephen C. Smith, eds., *Water Research*, Baltimore, Johns Hopkins Press, 1966.

5. See 'Report on the Effluent Charge Study', Federal Water Pollution Control Administration, 1966 (mimeo), and Edwin L. Johnson, 'A Study in the Economics of Water Quality Management', *Water Resources Research*, Vol. 3, No. 2, 1967, pp. 291–305. An excellent discussion of the effluent charges study is also found in Grant W. Schaumbert, jr, *Water Pollution Control in the Delaware Estuary*, Harvard Water Program, May 1967 (mimeo).

6. I am indebted to Walter Spofford of Resources for the Future, Inc., Washington, D.C., for developing this demonstration.

7. See Federal Water Pollution Control Administration mimeo, op. cit., Table 6.

8. Myron B. Fiering, *Streamflow Synthesis*, Cambridge, Mass., Harvard University Press, 1967.

9. For discussion and justification of these assertions, see Fiering, ibid., Chapter 2.

10. A full report on this study is found in Robert K. Davis, *The Range of Choice in Water Management*, Baltimore, Johns Hopkins Press, 1968.

11. A summary of the activities of these associations, called Genossenschaften, may be found in Kneese and Bower, *Managing Water Quality: Economics, Technology, Institutions*, Baltimore, Johns Hopkins Press, 1968.

12. S 3181, the Regional Water Quality Act of 1970, November 1969.

13. For a detailed discussion and critique of environmental legislation in the United States see Allen V. Kneese and Charles L. Schultze, *Pollution Prices and Public Policy*, Washington, D.C., The Brookings Institution, 1975.

14. My discussion of the 1973 Act is based on Dale C. Wheaton,

References and Notes

'Controlling River Quality Improvement: Economic Principles and British Policy Reform' (thesis), University of Nottingham, England, May 1974.

15. This discussion of the Trent research program is based on a manuscript by William A. Wright, 'Alternative Economic Approaches to Water Quality Management in the Trent River Basin', University College, Oxford, March 1972. Another good compact discussion is found in David Newscome, 'The Trent River Model – An Aid to Management', International Symposium on Mathematical Modeling Techniques in Water Resources Systems.

16. This discussion of the Westernport is based on an unpublished memordandum by Walter O. Spofford of Resources for the Future, Inc. (consultant to the project).

17. Actually it is an adaptation of linear programming called *integer programming*. This type of program restricts variables in the objective function to take on integer values only. This approach was chosen for technical reasons.

18. Gravity models are adaptations to the social sciences of the concept of gravitational potential from Newtonian physics. A detailed discussion of these models can be found in Walter Isard, *Methods of Regional Analysis*, New York, John Wiley, 1960.

8. Air Pollution

1. F. Muller 'An Operational Mathematical Programming Model for the Planning of Economic Activities in Relation to the Environment', *Socio-Economic Planning Science*, Vol. 7, 1973, pp. 123–38.

2. This discussion is based on Azriel Teller, 'Air-Pollution Abatement: Economic Rationality and Reality', *Daedalus*, Vol. 96, No. 4, Fall 1967.

3. The following exposition is based on Jack W. Carlson's 'Discussion' of Allen V. Kneese, 'The Political Economy of Environmental Quality', in *American Economic Review*, May 1971, pp. 169–72.

4. For further discussion see Allen V. Kneese and Charles V. Schultze, *Pollution, Prices, and Public Policy*, Washington, D.C., The Brookings Institution, 1975.

5. Lester B. Lave and R. Seskin, 'Air Pollution and Human Health', *Science*, August 1970.

6. R. G. Ridker, *Economic Costs of Air Pollution*, New York, Praeger, 1967.

7. R. J. Anderson and T. D. Crocker, 'Air Pollution and Residential Property Values', *Urban Studies*, No. 8, October 1971.

8. See *Air Quality and Automobile Emissions Control*, Vol. 4: *The Costs and Benefits of Automobile Emissions Control*, Serial No. 93–24, Washington, D.C., Government Printing Office, September 1974.

9. D. M. Fort and others, 'Proposal for a Smog Tax', reprinted on *Tax Recommendations of the President*, Hearings before the House Committee on Ways and Means, 91st Congress, 2nd Session, 1970, pp. 369–79.

10. New Jersey Department of Environmental Protection, Bureau of Air Pollution Control, 'Motor Vehicle Tune-up at Idle', *The New Jersey Repair Project* (The Department, no date; processed).

9. Research and Planning Frontiers

1. In preparing this chapter I have made heavy use of papers and memoranda prepared by my former associates at Resources for the Future – Blair Bower, Edwin Haefele, Clifford Russell, and Walter Spofford.

2. The example given in Chapter 6 of a production problem cast into a linear-programming format, while highly simplified, is of this nature.

3. These are analogous to the restrictions on machine time in the example of Chapter 6.

4. See C. S. Russell, 'Models for Investigation of Industrial Response to Residuals Management Actions', *The Swedish Journal of Economics*, Vol. 73, No. 1, March 1971, and Blair T. Bower, G. O. G. Löf, and W. M. Hearon, 'Residuals Generation in the Pulp and Paper Industry', *Natural Resources Journal*, Vol. 11, No. 4, 1971.

5. For technical (computational) reasons the model is structured as though it were using damage functions even though ambient standards are used instead.

6. The problem for which the model is intended to provide an approximate solution could also be stated in a completely general manner not suited to numerical solution, as the version described

in the text is, but perhaps easier to understand. The objective is to maximize, for a region, a complicated economic criterion function reflecting the costs of regional production, the benefits from regional consumption, the costs of residuals treatment, and the external damages resulting from residuals discharges, with allowance for the 'assimilative' capabilities of the regional environment. In this form, the regional residuals management problem is a general nonlinear programming problem, with both objective function and some constraints being nonlinear. For more detailed explanations of the Russell–Spofford model, see Clifford S. Russell and Walter O. Spofford, jr, 'A Quantitative Framework for Residuals Management Decisions', *Environmental Quality Analysis: Theory and Methods in the Social Sciences*, Allen V. Kneese and Blair T. Bower, eds., Baltimore, Johns Hopkins Press, 1972.

7. For further discussion of this possibility and a careful analysis of an actual situation see Edwin Haefele, 'Environmental Quality as a Problem of Social Choice', *Environmental Quality Analysis: Theory and Methods in the Social Sciences*, Allen V. Kneese and Blair T. Bower, eds., Baltimore, Johns Hopkins Press, 1972.

8. O. Eckstein, *Water Resources Development: The Economics of Project Evaluation*, Cambridge, Mass., Harvard University Press, 1961.

9. The degree to which this is true varies of course from place to place. The governing bodies of the British River Basin Authorities probably come closest of all environmental management bodies to being representative government bodies. In some areas and for some problems governments of metropolitan regions may qualify as reasonable approximations to the ideal.

10. Kenneth Arrow, *Social Choice and Individual Values*, New York, John Wiley, 1963.

11. E. T. Haefele, 'A Utility Theory of Representative Government', *American Economic Review*, Vol. 61, No. 3, June 1971, pp. 350–67.

12. I am indebted to my former associates at Resources for the Future, Inc., Clifford Russell and Walter Spofford, for extensive help in the preparation of this section.

13. The flow of September 1970 was used – about 4,000 c.f.s.

14. This is *not* the model used in the analysis reported in Chapter 7. It is an actual ecosystem model which produces outputs, by reach, in the form of plankton and fish bio-mass. It is in principle a more desirable model than the Streeter–Phelps model used there, but in

practice it presented many more complexities in its incorporation into an economic-management model framework.

10. Some Conclusions

1. Hungary and Czechoslovakia have had effluent charges systems in operation since the early 1960s and, while they have a number of defects in design, the charges systems there still appear to have been rather successful in reducing waste discharges to watercourses. See William A. Irwin, *Charges on Effluents in the United States and Europe*, for the Council on Law Related Studies, Cambridge, Mass., 1 September 1971. France enacted legislation imposing charges on waterborne effluents in the later 1960s. Again the approach adopted has some substantial problems in design but it is too early to tell how successful it will turn out to be. The Genossenschaften in the Ruhr region of Germany incorporated charges schemes in their water management activities with a high degree of success for many years. A detailed discussion of the French and Ruhr area situations can be found in Allen V. Kneese and Blair T. Bower, *Managing Water Quality*, Baltimore, Johns Hopkins Press, 1968.

2. The qualification of this point made in Chapter 7 (p. 164) should be recalled.

3. This is not to say that direct control of discharges through enforcement action is never justified. The discharge of some substances, say some of the heavy metals and chlorinated hydrocarbons, should probably be forbidden entirely. Since any discharge would be unlawful violations would be relatively easy to demonstrate and this would aid enforcement.

4. See Allen V. Kneese and Charles L. Schultze, *Pollution, Prices, and Public Policy*, Washington, D.C., The Brookings Institution, 1975.

5. 'Basis for the Establishment of a Law about Charges for the Discharge of Wastewaters into Watercourses', Proposed New Water Quality Law for the Federal Republic of Germany, by Ministry of the Interior, 1 July 1973.

6. Formulae of this type are discussed in some detail in Allen V. Kneese and Blair T. Bower, *Managing Water Quality*, op. cit.

7. Irwin, op. cit.

8. For example a team from the University of Münster is

constructing an integrated residuals management model for a region centered on Frankfurt and a study has been begun in Sweden. Work is underway on regions in the south-western U.S., primarily at the universities of Colorado and New Mexico.

9. 93rd Congress First Session, HR 635.

10. For a critique of the 'received' theory of optimal jurisdiction and a suggested approach to the optimal jurisdiction problem in an environmental setting, see Allen V. Kneese and Edwin T. Haefele, 'Environmental Quality and the Optimal Jurisdiction', in Alan A. Brown and others, eds., *Urban and Social Economics in Market and Planned Economies*, Vol. II, New York, Praeger, 1974.

11. The case for regional governments of general jurisdiction would, of course, not be argued on environmental grounds alone but in the interest of improved decision-making with respect to the whole range of public goods.

12. In some instances the concept and approach of integrated residuals management might be applicable to agricultural areas as well.

Index

Index

Index

More about Penguins and Pelicans